Merry Christmas Keith and Lily, Enjoy! Entertain with a full heart and cook with love! Best! Hope

Impress for Less!

finally . . . terrific recipes from

the finest restaurants that you

can really make at home

Hope Fox with Beth D'Addono

BICENTENNIAL
1807
WILEY
2007
BICENTENNIAL

John Wiley & Sons, Inc.

Interior photography © Big Stock Photo

Published by John Wiley & Sons, Inc., Hoboken, New Jersey
Published simultaneously in Canada

Wiley Bicentennial Logo Design by Richard J. Pacifico

For general information about our other products and services, please contact our
Customer Care Department within the United States at (800) 762-2974, outside the
United States at (317) 572-3993 or fax (317) 572-4002.

Wiley also publishes its books in a variety of electronic formats. Some content that
appears in print may not be available in electronic books. For more information
about Wiley products, visit our web site at www.wiley.com.

Library of Congress Cataloging-in-Publication Data
Fox, Hope.
  Impress for less! / Hope Fox.
     p. cm.
  Includes index.
  ISBN: 978-0-7645-9689-6 (pbk.)
  1. Cookery. 2. Restaurants—United States—Guidebooks. I. Title.
  TX714.F6887 2007
  647.957—dc22

                                                                2006030745

Interior Design by Cassandra J. Pappas

Printed in the United States of America

10 9 8 7 6 5 4 3 2

For my mother, Lois:
who taught me the love of cooking and entertaining
and who lives life with joie de vivre.
She taught me the real meaning of always
giving with a full heart.

For my father, Morris:
who left life here on earth at a very young age.
He taught me the importance of family, of making a difference
and striving for excellence and passion in life.

For my husband, David:
who's made all of my dreams come true.
For loving me and believing in me unconditionally,
you are my life partner and hero.

For my children, Maxwell and Alexandra:
for putting up with my long hours and enthusiastically sampling my food.
You always make me feel like a wonderful mother.
I will love you forever.

For my sister, Jamie:
who gives new meaning to the phrase one-in-a-million.
She's a true friend who champions me every step of the way
and doesn't let one day go by without telling me
how proud she is of me.

For each of the one hundred chefs who shared my vision:
it is their creativity and generosity that made
this book possible.

acknowledgments

A very special thank you to my editor, Justin Schwartz, who believed in me from the start and never failed to be encouraging and see the long-term potential for *Impress for Less!* I am eternally grateful.

Thank you to my agent, Linda Konner, for her loyalty, unwavering support, and true professionalism for this project.

My deepest appreciation to Beth D'Addono for her terrific writing talent. Her contribution to *Impress for Less!* was immeasurable. And thanks to Alice Thompson for her recipe editing skills.

The Wiley production and marketing team who all worked diligently to make this book a success.

The many public relations professionals who worked closely with me to bring this book to life.

A special thank you to Chef Joseph DiGironimo and his talented students at JNA Institute of Culinary Arts in Philadelphia, who worked with Beth to test the recipes in this book.

Some of the web sites that were invaluable during the research process include foodsubs.com, epicurious.com, eatdrinkdine.com, seafoodbynet.com, about.com, gourmetsleuth.com, penzeys.com, afullbelly.com, cheftalk.com, recipesource.com, ehow.com, earthy.com, whatscookingamerica.net., foodreference.com, ontherail.com, and superchefblog.com.

A heartfelt thank you to my kind and supportive friends and family. You know who you are and I will never forget your love and pride in my accomplishments. I am truly blessed.

contents

introduction

If you've ever found yourself frustrated by unclear cookbook directions or frazzled with an ingredient list that looks like it's written in a foreign tongue, you're not alone. As an avid cookbook reader, I believe there has to be a better way—and that way is found in the pages of *Impress for Less!* Finally . . . terrific recipes from the finest restaurants you can really make at home.

Like so many people, I love to dine in restaurants. But I also cook at home for my family almost every night. I have shelves of cookbooks in my kitchen, many purchased after experiencing a restaurant chef's extraordinary cuisine.

That's when the disappointment sets in. I get these books home and want to re-create a restaurant meal for a dinner party or make dinner for my family of four, and I get frustrated. I'm not a trained chef. I don't know French terms or techniques. Why can't restaurant chefs write a book that is user-friendly and that explains terms and provides a source guide for hard-to-find ingredients? Why can't they write a book for somebody like me?

That is exactly what I decided to do: write a cookbook for the many home cooks out there who share these feelings. My mission: to bring recipes from one hundred of the country's best restaurants into the home kitchen. What starts out as a complex dish you would find on a menu at a high-profile eatery—like Daniel in New York, Radius in Boston, or Commander's Palace in New Orleans—is adapted with shortcuts, easy-to-find ingredient substitutions, and helpful hints that deliver delicious results without compromising the integrity of the recipe.

This allows the reader to impress family and friends with a terrific meal—for less time, less money, and less aggravation. *Impress for Less!* offers the home cook options for unusual or regional ingredients and two different beverage pairings that give the reader another chance at re-creating that wonderful restaurant experience. I've stayed committed to the home cook on every page, because I know what it's like to be frustrated by a cookbook that's hard to understand.

I've assembled a glittering cast of culinary stars, one hundred chefs from the country's best restaurants. We mined the gastronomic scene in ten cities: Atlanta, Boston, Chicago, Los Angeles, Miami, New Orleans, New York, Philadelphia, Phoenix, and San Francisco, with chef after chef excited by the concept of making his or her food more approachable to the average home cook. Because of the nature of the business, there are instances where individual chefs have moved on to other restaurants by the time this book comes out. In a few cases, a restaurant has closed, its owner moving on to other culinary frontiers. This doesn't compromise the intent and the creativity behind the contributions each chef made to *Impress for Less!* In fact, it's just that constant state of flux that makes the national restaurant scene so dynamic.

Some of America's best-known restaurants are onboard, fine dining establishments like Le Bec-Fin in Philadelphia, Jean Georges in New York, and Mary Elaine's in Phoenix. There's also an assemblage of superstar talent from red-hot contemporary eateries like Roaring Fork in Phoenix, Blackbird in Chicago, and August in New Orleans.

The idea was to give readers the inside scoop on how restaurant chefs really work their magic. And then we give the average cook, somebody just like me, the chance to work that same magic at home.

atlanta

a dining capital of the new south

In the past decade, Atlanta has come into its own as a restaurant town to be reckoned with. Affordability, variety of restaurants, culinary diversity, and award-winning chefs are key ingredients that earn Atlanta a place at the table with other top culinary destinations. An assortment of neighborhoods offers an array of restaurants featuring cuisine that spans the globe, serving something for every taste, from African to Asian, Cajun to Caribbean, Italian to Middle Eastern. Menu selections are inspired by cultures all over the world.

"Atlanta has had an influx of high-quality, chef-owned, chef-driven restaurants, which have developed into creative concepts. That keeps dining interesting and exciting," said Pano Karatassos, founder of Buckhead Life Group, a family of twelve restaurants, three of which—Bluepointe, Kyma, and Pano's & Paul's—are featured in this chapter. "As Atlanta grows, it's attracting a very culturally diverse population, inviting new cuisines, with tapas, Thai, Brazilian steakhouses, Greek cuisine, sushi, and the list goes on. It does seem that no matter what the type of food served, it tends to be served with Atlanta's signature Southern hospitality—that's always a huge draw."

Like most cities, Atlanta's dining scene is neighborhood driven, with successful restaurants reflecting the development going on downtown. Upscale Buckhead, long a magnet for younger professionals, is home to high-rises, exclusive townhouses, and stately mansions. Buckhead is also the address for some of the city's most popular nightclubs and restaurants, including Seeger's and Aria.

Midtown is a neighborhood known for its residential diversity and energetic, young business district. Recognized as the heart of the arts in Atlanta, Midtown is also home to high-profile restaurants, including the popular Nikolai's Roof. Another hot spot with Atlanta's young professionals is Virginia-Highland, noted for its fifty-year-old shopping district made up of family-owned, one-of-a-kind retail stores and restaurants like the successful Rathbun's.

With the awarding of the James Beard Foundation's Best Chef: Southeast to Atlanta chefs three times—to Joël Antunes of Joël in 2005, Anne Quatrano and Clifford Harrison of Bacchanalia in 2003, and Guenter Seeger of Seeger's in 1996—it's clear that Atlanta's restaurant community is doing something very right.

bacchanalia

1198 HOWELL MILL ROAD   ATLANTA, GA 30318

404-365-0410   WWW.STARPROVISIONS.COM

Located in a rehabbed industrial complex in Midtown Atlanta, Bacchanalia has earned a top *Zagat* rating since 1996. Chefs and owners Anne Quatrano and Clifford Harrison, named the James Beard Foundation's Best Chefs of the Southeast in May 2003, are at the heart and soul of the operation, which is fueled largely by organic produce, meats, and wild-caught seafood. The heartland prix-fixe menu always reflects seasonal offerings, and might include a sashimi of North Carolina flounder with yuzu, fennel soup with Maine lobster, wood-grilled California squab with glazed cipollini onions, and hand-poured artisanal cheeses and desserts made from apples picked earlier that afternoon. Quatrano and Harrison, partners in life and in food, live on Summerland Farm in Cartersville, Georgia, a rejuvenated family farm that is the source for much of the restaurant's fresh, organic produce. The couple also owns Star Provisions, a gourmet specialty store, and a more casual restaurant, Floataway Café.

This satisfying seafood soup is common in Provence, and can be garnished with garlicky croutons.

mediterranean
fish soup

SERVES 6

1 tablespoon olive oil

1 onion, diced

1 bulb fennel, diced

4 cloves garlic, thinly sliced

6 cups chicken broth

6 small Yukon gold potatoes (about 1 pound), peeled and cut into ½-inch dice

One 14.5-ounce can diced tomatoes, drained

Three 2-inch-long strips orange zest (removed with a vegetable peeler)

2 bay leaves

1 sprig fresh thyme, or ¼ teaspoon dried

Pinch red pepper flakes, or to taste

1½ pounds mussels or clams, scrubbed (discard any that do not close)

1 pound cod or other firm white-fleshed fish, cut into 1-inch cubes

¾ pound medium shrimp, peeled and deveined

½ pound bay scallops, rinsed

1 cup seasoned croutons

and to drink

$ 2003 Bourgogne Chardonnay, Signature, Maison Champy, France

$$ 2002 Meursault, Domaine Matrot-Wittersheim, France

1. In a large saucepan over medium heat, heat the olive oil. Add the onion, fennel, and garlic and cook, stirring, until the vegetables soften, about 5 minutes. Add the chicken broth, potatoes, tomatoes, orange zest, bay leaves, thyme, and red pepper flakes and bring to a boil over high heat. Reduce the heat and simmer until the potatoes are fork-tender, about 10 minutes.

2. Add the mussels, cod, shrimp, and scallops and continue simmering until the mussels have opened and the other seafood is cooked through, 5 to 7 minutes. Discard any mussels that do not open.

3. Discard the bay leaves, thyme sprigs, and orange zest. Ladle the soup into bowls, top with the croutons, and serve.

chef's notes Called *bourride* (boo-REED) in France, this Mediterranean fish soup is extremely versatile and easy to make. You'll need a variety of fish and shellfish totaling 3 or 4 pounds, but the mix can change with your whim and what's on sale. At Bacchanalia, the chefs include lobster and crab, an option if you want to wow your guests.

WHERE TO BUY

Seafood:
Legal Sea Foods, 800-343-5804, www.legalseafoods.com
Star Provisions, 404-365-0410, www.starprovisions.com

aria

490 EAST PACES FERRY ROAD   ATLANTA, GEORGIA   30305

404-233-7673   WWW.ARIA-ATL.COM

This hip little restaurant in the middle of Buckhead has taken center stage since it opened in 2000, the same year it was named one of the country's best restaurants by *Esquire* magazine. Despite its crisp ambiance and animated bar scene, Aria is all about comfort food. Chef and partner Gerry Klaskala's seasons-driven menu delivers home-style cooking for serious foodies. Klaskala's signature talent is his love of "slow foods"—braises, stews, steaks, and chops cooked over a rolltop French grill. A few examples of this satisfying, thoughtful cuisine include creamless celery root soup with black truffles and Parmigiano-Reggiano, oak-grilled lamb tenderloin with grilled red onions, arugula and warm pecan-crusted goat cheese, and an excellent porcini mushroom ravioli with baby spinach, walnuts, and sage brown butter.

Klaskala and his partners, George McKerrow, Jr., and Ron San Martin, also own another favorite Atlanta restaurant, Canoe.

At Aria, this dish is served with celery whipped potatoes, sugar snap peas, and French baby carrots.

short ribs

braised in wine

SERVES 4

One 750-milliliter bottle
Zinfandel

1 tablespoon olive oil

8 beef short ribs
(about 3½ pounds)

1 teaspoon coarse salt

½ teaspoon freshly ground
black pepper

1 medium onion,
cut into large dice

1 carrot, peeled and
cut into large dice

1 stalk celery,
cut into large dice

1 leek (white part only),
cut into large dice

6 cloves garlic, peeled

3 sprigs fresh thyme,
or ½ teaspoon dried

4 cups chicken broth

1. In a 1½-quart saucepan over high heat, bring the wine to a boil. Reduce the heat and simmer until the wine is reduced by half, 15 to 20 minutes. Remove from the heat and set aside.

2. Preheat the oven to 350°F.

3. In a large heavy Dutch oven or roasting pan, heat the oil over high heat. Season the ribs with the salt and pepper and add them to the pan. Cook, turning frequently, until the ribs are browned well on all sides, 5 to 7 minutes.

4. Remove the ribs from the pan and set aside. Discard all but 1 tablespoon of oil from the pan and return it to medium-high heat. Add the onion, carrot, celery, leek, garlic, and thyme and cook, stirring and scraping up any brown bits from the bottom of the pan, until the vegetables are lightly browned, about 5 minutes.

5. Return the ribs to the pan and add the reduced wine and the chicken broth. Over high heat, bring to a boil, then cover the pan with a lid or seal tightly with aluminum foil. Transfer the pan to the oven and cook until the ribs are very tender, about 2½ hours.

6. Remove the pan from the oven. Remove the lid or foil and allow the meat and juices to cool for about 1 hour. Spoon off and discard the fat that rises to the surface of the stew.

7. To serve, remove the ribs from the pan and set aside. Bring the sauce to a boil over high heat. Reduce the heat to medium and simmer until the liquid is reduced by about a third and makes a light-bodied sauce, about 15 minutes. Return the ribs to the pan, heat through, and serve.

WHERE TO BUY

Organic beef: Whole Foods, multiple locations, www.wholefoods.com

Short Ribs (*continued*)

and to drink
$ 2001 Edmeades Vineyard
Zinfandel, California
$$ 2002 Chiarello Vineyards,
Giana Zinfandel, California

chef's notes This recipe uses braising to deliver melt-in-your-mouth-tender beef and great depth of flavor. Braising isn't so much about individual components as integrated flavors. The technique turns tougher, cheaper cuts of meat into tender dishes by breaking down the tendons and sinews in the meat with liquid, usually wine or stock, or, as in this dish, a combination of both. Braised foods can be prepared ahead of time and reheated without losing a hint of flavor. In fact, they often taste better the next day. If desired, for a smoother finish to your sauce, after removing the fat from the juices, strain the liquid through cheesecloth or a fine-mesh sieve.

If you'd like to substitute brisket for the short ribs in this recipe, shorten the oven cooking time by 30 to 45 minutes.

canoe

4199 PACES FERRY ROAD   ATLANTA, GA 30039

770-432-2663   WWW.CANOEATL.COM

From its gorgeous view of the Chattahoochee River to its progressive menu of New American fare, Canoe is a favorite dining destination in the historic Vinings area of Atlanta. Selected as one of the best new restaurants in the country by the James Beard Foundation after it opened in 1995, Canoe's kitchen is now in the capable hands of executive chef Carvel Gould, a Buckhead native known for her unfailing attention to detail and creative use of regional ingredients. Dishes like house-smoked salmon with crispy Yukon gold potato pancakes and slow-roasted Carolina rabbit and porcini mushroom with Swiss chard and country bacon add a creative twist to traditional Southern cuisine. A thoughtful wine list and a wide selection of wines by the glass earned the restaurant a *Wine Spectator* award. A few photos on the walls hark back to the restaurant's early days. Before its incarnation as Canoe, the place was Robinson's Tropical Gardens, a segregated dance club that attracted the white teenagers of nearby Buckhead to the sounds of Little Richard, Otis Redding, Big Joe Turner, and Big Mama Thornton.

You can save time by using just red beets for this delicious salad, although the combination of red and yellow beets is downright stunning. Remember not to combine the two beets until you're ready to serve. Use a good-quality store-bought vinaigrette, unless you have time to make your own.

marinated beets
with goat cheese

SERVES 4

8 cups water

6 cups chicken broth

1 cup sugar

4 tablespoons coarse salt, plus more for the salad

3 red beets, peeled (a scant pound)

2/3 cup balsamic vinegar

3 yellow beets, peeled (a scant pound)

2/3 cup champagne or white-wine vinegar

2 cups goat cheese, at room temperature

3/4 cup walnuts, chopped

4 shallots, minced

4 tablespoons extra-virgin olive oil

2 cups mixed salad greens, torn into bite-size pieces

Freshly ground black pepper, to taste

1. Have two medium nonreactive pots ready and evenly divide the water, broth, sugar, and salt between them. To one pot, add the red beets and balsamic vinegar. To the other, add the yellow beets and champagne vinegar. Bring both mixtures to a boil over high heat. Reduce the heat to medium and simmer until the beets are fork-tender, about 30 minutes. Remove from the heat and let the beets cool in their liquid. When cool to the touch, drain the beets, discarding the liquid, and dice into 1/4-inch cubes.

2. Cream the goat cheese with an electric mixer until very light and fluffy, about 5 minutes. Set aside.

3. In a small, dry frying pan over medium-high heat, toast the walnuts until they just start to brown, about 1 minute. Remove from the heat and set aside.

4. To serve, in a bowl, toss together the yellow and red beets, 1/2 cup of the walnuts, the shallots, olive oil, salad greens, and salt and pepper to taste. Divide the beet mixture among serving plates and top with a spoonful of whipped goat cheese and some of the remaining 1/4 cup walnuts.

WHERE TO BUY

Goat cheese: Di Bruno Brothers, 888-322-4337, www.dibruno.com
Piping bag: Fante's, 800-44-FANTE (443-2683), www.fantes.com

chef's notes Canoe's version of this recipe is assembled a bit differently. A line of goat cheese is piped onto the plate, topped with the beet mixture and garnished with the lettuce. The end result and flavor is pretty much the same, but the *Impress for Less!* version is easier to put together.

Even if you've never used a piping or pastry bag, it's not difficult (although it does take a bit of practice to get the hang of it) and the effect is really professional. A pastry bag is typically fitted with a decorative tip on the small end and can be filled with everything from whipped cream to whipped goat cheese. Fill the bag three quarters full, twist the top, and apply pressure with one hand as you squeeze the filling out, using your other hand to guide the tip. Small, disposable bags work best for detail work. Large bags are great for piping textured foods like mashed potatoes and, as in this case, whipped goat cheese.

Alternatively, you can put your mixture into a resealable plastic bag and cut one corner to make a small opening. Pipe the mixture through the opening you've created.

and to drink
$ 2004 Forefathers
Marlborough Sauvignon Blanc,
New Zealand
$$ 2004 Crocker Starr Napa
Sauvignon Blanc, California

joël

3290 NORTHSIDE PARKWAY NW   ATLANTA, GA 30327

404-233-3500   WWW.JOELRESTAURANT.COM

Joël Antunes, chef and owner of Atlanta's high-profile Joël, has enjoyed a meteoric rise to culinary success. From humble beginnings, cooking side by side with his grandmother in her Provençal kitchen, to earning five diamonds in the kitchen at the Ritz-Carlton Buckhead and the coveted James Beard Foundation's Best Chef: Southeast award in 2005, Antunes's star continues to ascend. At Joël, he blends classic French dishes with Asian and Mediterranean accents, as in his baked John Dory (a mild white fish also called St. Peter's fish) with butternut curry gnocchi in a Thai mushroom broth and roast squab with apple confit and polenta in a Madeira sauce. The restaurant's stylish indoor-outdoor setting, *très chic* lounge, and award-winning wine list makes Joël a highlight of the Atlanta dining scene.

In this recipe, turbot or cod can stand up to the bracing Asian flavors of lemongrass and cilantro. The baked turbot can stand alone, or garnish it with the optional sweet-and-sour daikon. Daikon, also known as Japanese radish, is a larger, milder cousin to the common red radish and looks like a fat white carrot. Although readily available in most produce departments, you can substitute turnips or parsnips in this recipe. The daikon must be prepared the day before you make the fish.

baked turbot

with sweet-and-sour daikon

SERVES 4

1 daikon (or turnip, or 2 parsnips), peeled

2 cups water

1 tablespoon honey

1 tablespoon rice wine vinegar

½ teaspoon soy sauce

2 tablespoons plus 1 teaspoon unsalted butter

Four 6-ounce turbot or cod fillets

1 tablespoon olive oil

1 stalk lemongrass, tough outer leaves removed and discarded, stalk finely chopped (or 1 teaspoon freshly grated lemon zest)

1 tablespoon freshly grated lime zest

Coarse salt and freshly ground black pepper, to taste

1 tablespoon chopped fresh cilantro

1. Slice the daikon into silver dollar–size wafers. Bring a small saucepan of salted water to a boil, add the daikon wafers, and cook 5 seconds. Drain the wafers and place in a plastic container with a cover. In the same saucepan, bring the 2 cups water, the honey, vinegar, and soy sauce to a boil and boil for 2 minutes. Remove from the heat and pour over the daikon. Refrigerate at least overnight and up to 2 days.

2. Preheat the oven to 350°F.

3. Grease a shallow baking dish with 1 tablespoon of the butter and arrange the fish inside. Drizzle the fish with the olive oil and sprinkle the lemongrass, lime zest, salt, and pepper over the fish. Bake until the fish is just opaque all the way through, about 10 minutes. Garnish with cilantro.

4. While the fish is baking, finish the daikon by melting the remaining 1 tablespoon plus 1 teaspoon butter in a small sauté pan over medium heat. Drain the daikon and cook in the pan, tossing, until heated through.

5. To serve, place a circle of daikon pieces on each serving plate and top with the fish.

and to drink

$ 2004 Morande Sauvignon Blanc, Chile

$$ 2003 Gruet Chardonnay, New Mexico

chef's notes Lemongrass, which looks like a woody scallion, is used in Southeast Asian cooking to infuse dishes with a bright lemon flavor. It's important to remove the stringy outer leaves from the stalk, then use about 6 inches of the base, discarding the top and the very bottom. Available in Asian markets and some specialty produce markets, lemongrass has a flavor uniquely its own, although you can approximate it by substituting lemon zest—the zest from half a lemon equals 1 stalk lemongrass.

WHERE TO BUY

Lemongrass and daikon: Hong Kong Supermarket, 404-325-3999

pano's & paul's

1232 WEST PACES FERRY ROAD   ATLANTA, GA 30327

404-261-3662   WWW.BUCKHEADRESTAURANTS.COM

The flagship of Pano Karatassos's burgeoning restaurant empire, Pano's & Paul's is a sumptuous romantic restaurant that conjures up fine dining's gilded age. Chef Gary Donlick's updated continental and American menu is never fussy, concentrating instead on dishes that are intensely flavored without being contrived. This is the place to splurge on something special like foie gras, lobster, or caviar. Try the signature dish of fried lobster tails with honey mustard and drawn butter, or the classic Dover sole, deboned tableside and sautéed with brown butter and crispy fried capers. Beef lovers won't do better than the filet pepper steak or the retro mixed grill of beef and veal tenderloin. For dessert—what else?—vanilla bean crème brûlée is a timeless favorite.

Chef Donlick serves this dish with pheasant instead of chicken. Pheasant is a flavorful game bird that can be pricey, so chicken or Cornish hen halves make a fine substitution.

roasted chicken breasts
with mushroom and andouille stuffing

SERVES 6

3 tablespoons olive oil

1 medium shallot, minced

½ pound assorted mushrooms, rinsed and patted dry just before use

1 large clove garlic, minced

Coarse salt and freshly ground black pepper, to taste

4 links andouille sausage (about 1 pound), or equivalent amount of kielbasa, cut into ½-inch dice

6 boneless, skinless chicken breast halves

1½ cups chicken broth

6 cloves garlic, sliced

2 teaspoons chopped fresh rosemary, or ½ teaspoon dried

½ cup heavy cream

1 tablespoon chopped fresh parsley

1. Preheat the oven to 350°F.

2. Heat 2 tablespoons of the olive oil in a large sauté pan over medium heat. Add the shallot and cook, stirring, until just softened, about 2 minutes. Add the mushrooms and minced garlic and cook until soft, about 5 minutes more. Season with salt and pepper to taste. Add the sausage and cook until lightly browned, 5 to 7 minutes. Remove the pan from the heat and cool to room temperature.

3. Lightly flatten each chicken breast by placing it between layers of plastic wrap and pounding gently with a meat mallet or the back of a small heavy skillet. Place a spoon of the mushroom-sausage mixture in the center of each breast. Roll the breast around the mixture and secure with wooden skewers or toothpicks. (If you have any leftover stuffing, just heat it in a nonstick pan and serve it on the side.)

4. Season the breasts lightly with salt and pepper. Place a large oven-proof nonstick sauté pan over high heat and heat the remaining tablespoon olive oil. Add the chicken and cook until just browned, 7 to 8 minutes. Transfer the pan to the oven and cook until the chicken is firm to the touch and the juices run clear when the thick part of the breast is pierced with the tip of a sharp knife, about 10 minutes.

5. Transfer the chicken to a plate and cover to keep warm. Return the same pan to high heat and add the broth. Using a wooden spoon, stir, scraping up any browned bits from the bottom of the pan. Add the sliced garlic and rosemary, lower the heat, and simmer until the liquid is reduced to about ½ cup, about 6 minutes. Stir in the cream and remove from the heat. Season with salt and pepper.

6. Spoon the sauce over the chicken breasts and garnish with parsley.

and to drink
$ 2002 Qupe Central Coast
Syrah, California
$$ 2000 Arcadian "Gary's
Vineyard" Pinot Noir, California

chef's notes Andouille sausage, made with pork or turkey, can usually be found with other smoked meats and sausages at the supermarket. Andouille is a spicy smoked Cajun sausage that's used in jambalaya and gumbo. Polish kielbasa is a good stand-in.

The sauce for this recipe is made by reducing the chicken broth from 1½ cups to ½ cup of liquid. Reducing is simply boiling or simmering a liquid until its volume decreases through evaporation. This does two things: thickens the consistency of the liquid and intensifies the flavor of the ingredients.

For a smoother sauce, you may strain the liquid after adding the cream.

WHERE TO BUY

Andouille sausage and pheasant: D'Artagnan, 800-327-8246, www.dartagnan.com

kyma

3085 PIEDMONT ROAD   ATLANTA, GA 30305

404-262-0702   WWW.BUCKHEADRESTAURANTS.COM

There's nothing staid about Kyma, Buckhead's elegant and upscale homage to all foods Greek. From its dramatic interior to its right-now interpretation of Greek classics, Kyma is the crown jewel in the Buckhead Life Restaurant Group crown (BLRG). Opened in 2002 by BLRG president Pano Karatassos, Kyma (pronounced KEY-ma) is run by his son, chef Pano I. Karatassos. A CIA graduate, the young Karatassos has worked with some of the industry's finest chefs, including Thomas Keller at French Laundry, Jean-Georges Vongerichten at Jean Georges, and Eric Ripert at Le Bernardin. Involved in the family business since age 16, Karatassos mines his Greek heritage with a menu full of char-grilled, whole fresh fish flown in daily from Mediterranean waters, braised cumin-flavored boneless lamb shank with Greek macaroni and caramelized eggplant, and tender wood-grilled octopus with red onions and red wine vinegar. Kyma, which means "wave" in Greek, boasts an invigorating wine list heavy on wines from Karatassos's homeland.

This tasty eggplant stew can be served hot or cold. If you can't find the long, light-colored Japanese eggplants, regular eggplants will work. And if sweet Vidalias aren't in season, any mild sweet onion can substitute (see Chef's Notes, page 19).

eggplant and sweet onion
casserole

SERVES 4 TO 6

¼ cup olive oil

6 medium Vidalia onions, sliced (about 6 cups)

10 Japanese eggplants (about 3 pounds), cut on the bias into 1-inch-thick slices

4 cloves garlic, halved

1 tablespoon chopped fresh thyme, or 1 teaspoon dried

Coarse salt and freshly ground black pepper, to taste

1¼ cups prepared tomato sauce

⅓ cup chopped fresh parsley

1. Preheat the oven to 300°F.

2. In a large sauté pan, heat 2 tablespoons of the oil over medium heat. Add the onions and cook, stirring frequently, until they are reduced in volume by about half and golden in color, about 20 minutes. Remove from the pan and set aside.

3. Wipe out the sauté pan with paper towels. Return to medium heat and add the remaining 2 tablespoons oil. Add the eggplants, garlic, thyme, and salt and pepper to taste and cook until the vegetables soften, about 15 minutes. Drain on a paper towel and cool.

4. In a 3-quart decorative casserole, pour in enough of the tomato sauce just to cover the bottom. Top with a layer of the caramelized onions, then a layer of the eggplant slices and tomato sauce and sprinkle with pepper. Continue layering in that order, until all the ingredients are in the pan, finishing with the tomato sauce and onions.

5. Cover with a lid or seal tightly with aluminum foil and bake until hot and bubbly, about 20 minutes.

6. To serve, garnish with parsley.

and to drink
$2003 Fresco Averoff, Greece
$$ 2002 Mercouri Estate, Greece

WHERE TO BUY
Divina Renieris Estate Extra-Virgin Olive Oil:
Eurogrocer, 201-490-8781, www.eurogrocer.com
Olive Oil Shopper, 888-490-8781, www.oliveoilshopper.com

chef's notes   Using prepared tomato sauce makes this dish come together quickly, or try chef Pano's recipe. For extra flavor, use Divina Renieris Estate Extra-Virgin Olive Oil, the olive oil of choice at Kyma. The Renieris family grows and crushes the olives, and bottles this exceptional oil on their family estate.

Vidalia onions are a large, sweet onion usually available from March through August. Ideal for slicing and serving with burgers or in salads, Vidalias also caramelize well in cooked dishes. Or you can cook with Bermuda or Spanish onions, as long as you add 1 teaspoon of sugar per onion to the recipe. You may also substitute Italian eggplant for Japanese eggplant, but because Italian eggplant can be bitter, first soak the slices in cold salted water for 30 minutes to remove the bitter juices. Drain and pat dry.

• • •

Tomato Sauce

2 tablespoons mild olive oil

1 medium onion, sliced

2 cloves garlic, sliced

4 cups fresh tomatoes or canned tomatoes in juice, halved

1 tablespoon fresh chopped oregano, or 1 teaspoon dried

2 teaspoons sugar

1 bay leaf

1 tablespoon coarse salt

1 teaspoon freshly ground black pepper

$1/4$ cup extra-virgin olive oil, or to taste

1. Heat the mild olive oil in a medium saucepan over high heat. Add the onion and garlic and cook, stirring constantly, until browned, about 5 minutes.

2. Add the tomatoes, oregano, sugar, and bay leaf. Bring to a boil and reduce the heat to medium. Continue simmering for 45 minutes, stirring occasionally.

3. Remove from the heat and allow the sauce to cool. If desired, press through a food mill for a smoother sauce. Stir in the salt, pepper, and extra-virgin olive oil.

nikolai's roof

255 COURTLAND STREET NE   ATLANTA, GA 30303

404-221-6362   WWW.NIKOLAISROOF.COM

You are literally on top of the world at Nikolai's Roof, the fabulous dream of a restaurant on the thirtieth floor of the downtown Hilton hotel. Take in the romantic panoramic skyline view, then tuck into chef Olivier de Busschere's inventive Russian-accented French cuisine. A date-night tradition since 1976 (gentlemen are still asked to don jackets), Nikolai's Roof was the first restaurant in town to earn a coveted Michelin four-star rating. The chef flawlessly executes dishes like carpaccio of Kobe beef with fresh shaved petit Basque cheese and apple–pine nut chutney, foie gras–stuffed morel mushrooms, or seasonal borscht topped with roasted muscovy duck breast and chervil-infused crème fraîche. The menu helpfully pairs each dish with the perfect wine from the restaurant's comprehensive list.

We've omitted the truffles from this recipe. See the Chef's Notes and Where to Buy if you'd like to incorporate them into chef de Busschere's satisfying version of this northern Italian comfort food. Serve it as a side dish or as a vegetarian main course.

wild mushroom
risotto

SERVES 4

2 tablespoons extra-virgin olive oil

3 tablespoons unsalted butter

½ cup finely chopped shallots

1 pound mixed wild mushrooms or a combination of button, cremini, or shiitake mushrooms, rinsed and patted dry just before use

Coarse salt and freshly ground black pepper, to taste

8 cups chicken broth, or as needed

2 cups arborio rice

1. In a medium sauté pan over high heat, heat the olive oil and 2 tablespoons of the butter. When the butter has melted, lower the heat to medium and stir in the shallots. Cook, stirring, for 1 minute. Add the mushrooms and salt and pepper to taste. Cook, stirring occasionally, until the mushrooms just begin to brown, about 15 minutes. Remove from the heat and set aside.

2. Pour the broth into a small saucepan and place at the back of the stove. Bring the broth just to a simmer. Lower the heat so that the broth stays just below a simmer.

3. In a large, heavy saucepan, heat the remaining tablespoon butter over medium heat. Add the rice and stir until all the grains are just coated with butter. Add the heated broth to the rice, 1 cup at a time, stirring constantly and letting the pan become almost dry between additions of broth. Continue cooking, adding broth, until the rice is tender with just a little crunch, 20 to 25 minutes. Stir in the mushrooms and serve.

chef's notes The Nikolai's Roof version of this dish includes truffles, prized for their musky flavor and adored by chefs the world over. You can cut the cost—fresh truffles can run between $45 and $450 for 3 ounces—by buying canned or jarred truffles, typically in the $15 to $20 range for a 1-ounce container. Chef de Busschere also recommends using Oregon black truffles instead of the more expensive Black Perigord truffles. Oregon truffles, available at market from November to March, are just as aromatic at a fraction of the price. Another option is a drizzle of truffle-flavored oil, available in most supermarkets.

and to drink
$2002 Cuvee Alexandre Casa Lapostolle Merlot, Chile
$$ 2002 Terrunyo Carmenere, Chile

WHERE TO BUY
Truffles: Earthy Delights, 800-367-4709, www.earthy.com

rathbun's

112 KROG STREET (STOVE WORKS BUILDING)   ATLANTA, GA 30307

404-524-8280   WWW.RATHBUNSRESTAURANT.COM

Chef Kevin Rathbun has a real talent for fashioning distinctive modern American cuisine from fresh, simple ingredients using local products and organics as much as possible. His talents earned him a place on *Bon Appetit*'s Hot 50 Restaurants list in March 2005. Rathbun, a Kansas native who honed his skills in his home state, as well as in Dallas and New Orleans, opened Rathbun's in May 2004 in the Stove Works, an old factory complex that produced potbelly stoves in its heyday.

Rathbun partnered with pastry chef Kirk Parks and general manager Cliff Bramble to deliver a wow of a menu, organized into Small Plates, Raw Plates, Soup Bowls, Side Plates, Big Plates, and Second Mortgage Plates. You might be tempted to stay busy with a handful of small plates like Blue Point oysters two ways (cornmeal-fried and lemongrass-stewed), short smoked salmon tostadas with habanero and tiny greens, and panfried kefalotiri cheese with Greek olive oil and lemon. But then you'd be missing home runs like the 20-ounce bone-in rib eye anointed with warm Point Reyes blue cheese vinaigrette or the Maine lobster and roasted green chile soft taco, with Cascabel cream and tomato pico. Thankfully, Parks's dessert list includes small-portion samplers of winners like banana peanut butter cream pie, banana bread ice cream sandwich, and orange and chili brûlée.

This shrimp and okra dish, which has been featured on the Small Plates section of Rathbun's menu, is a delicious summer appetizer. Either fresh or frozen okra will work.

garlic shrimp
and okra with basil

SERVES 4

20 fresh okra or one 16-ounce package frozen, sliced

1 tablespoon olive oil

1½ pounds extra-large shrimp, peeled and deveined

2 cloves garlic, thinly sliced

1 shallot, thinly sliced

1¾ cups diced ripe tomatoes, or one 14.5-ounce can chopped tomatoes

4 tablespoons (½ stick) unsalted butter

¼ cup chopped fresh basil leaves

2 teaspoons coarse salt

½ teaspoon freshly ground black pepper

1. If using fresh okra, bring a medium pot filled two thirds full of salted water to a boil. Add the okra and cook just until the pods turn bright green, about 1 minute. Drain and rinse in under cold running water. Quarter each pod lengthwise.

2. In a large sauté pan over medium heat, heat the olive oil. Add the shrimp, garlic, and shallot and cook, stirring constantly, until the shrimp just begin to turn pink, about 3 minutes. Add the fresh or frozen okra, tomatoes, butter, basil, salt, and pepper. Bring to a boil, lower the heat, and simmer until the shrimp are firm and just cooked through, about 3 minutes more.

and to drink

$ 2004 Geyser Peak Sauvignon Blanc, California
$$ 2002 Gregory Graham Knights Valley Viognier, California

chef's notes If you like spice, add minced fresh chiles along with the tomatoes, or a teaspoon or two of chili powder. Better yet, add a seeded, minced habanero, the spiciest of peppers, for an impressive heat that will work well with both suggested wines.

Okra is especially popular in Southern cooking, where it often turns up in stews and gumbos, deep fried in cornmeal, or pickled. Okra should have a pleasant, mild flavor and a pleasing crunch, but it can become mushy (and even slimy) if overcooked. Blanching the fresh okra pods quickly in boiling water before adding them to dishes is a good way to ensure that they come out crisp.

WHERE TO BUY

Organic okra:

Diamond Organics, 888-ORGANIC (888-674-2642), www.diamondorganics.com

Morningside Farmers' Market, 404-313-5784, www.morningsidemarket.com

Whole Foods, multiple locations, www.wholefoods.com

bluepointe

3455 PEACHTREE ROAD   ATLANTA, GA 30326

404-237-9070   WWW.BUCKHEADRESTAURANTS.COM

This star in the Buckhead Life Restaurants constellation offers a dramatic setting for chef Doug Turbush's bold cuisine. At home in one of the city's most stunning modern buildings, Bluepointe is a soaring multilevel space that offers plush seating, a sushi bar, and plenty of Asian design accents. The menu is a marriage of East and West, with seafood being its specialty. Start with wok-fried calamari pasta with pencil-thin asparagus and chili, a house signature. Standout dishes include peanut-crusted grouper in Masaman curry and scallops with sushi rice cakes and passion fruit butter. Carnivores should try a salt-crusted prime rib for two, which could easily feed four. The wine list and martini list are both excellent.

Chef Turbush uses tangerine juice to poach this pork loin at the restaurant, but orange juice is a fine substitute. Wild rice, couscous, or quinoa are other good choices for a side dish.

curried orange pork
with soy-glazed sweet potatoes

SERVES 4 TO 6

8 cups chicken broth

1 teaspoon freshly grated
lemon zest

6 cups orange juice

2 tablespoons Thai red
curry paste

1 tablespoon sugar

1 teaspoon flat-leaf
parsley, chopped

1 teaspoon chives, chopped

1 teaspoon fresh
thyme, chopped

Coarse salt and freshly
ground black pepper,
to taste

2 pounds boneless
center-cut pork loin roast

2 tablespoons
unsalted butter

1 teaspoon cilantro, chopped

**Soy-Glazed Sweet
Potatoes**

1 tablespoon unsalted butter

One 1-inch piece
fresh ginger, peeled
and finely minced

2 large sweet potatoes,
peeled and cut into
$1/2$-inch cubes

2 cups water or low-sodium
chicken broth

$1/2$ cup light brown sugar

$1/4$ cup soy sauce

1. Preheat the oven to 350°F.

2. In a large saucepan over medium-high heat, combine the chicken broth and zest. Boil until the liquid is reduced by half, about 15 minutes. Add the orange juice, curry paste, sugar, parsley, chives, thyme, and salt and pepper. Simmer for another 10 minutes over medium heat.

3. Add the pork loin, bring back to a boil, then reduce the heat and simmer gently until an instant-read thermometer inserted into the center of the pork reads 140°F, about 30 minutes. (If the center of the roast is submerged in liquid, remove the roast from the pan to accurately check the temperature.)

4. To make the soy-glazed sweet potatoes, melt the butter in a medium saucepan over medium-low heat. Add the ginger and gently cook for 1 minute; add the cubed sweet potato and stir to coat with the butter. Add the water or chicken broth to just cover the potatoes, then stir in the brown sugar and soy sauce. Cook until the potatoes are just tender, about 15 minutes. Transfer the cooking liquid to a separate pot and reserve the potatoes. Simmer the cooking liquid until it is reduced to a syrupy consistency, about $1/4$ cup. Pour over the sweet potatoes and toss gently.

5. Remove the pork from the pan, cover, and keep warm. Strain the liquid the pork cooked in through a fine-mesh strainer and return it to the pan. Simmer again until the liquid becomes thick enough to coat the back of a spoon, about 15 minutes. Whisk in the butter and cilantro and season again with salt and pepper to taste.

6. To serve, slice the pork and top with the sauce. Serve with the sweet potatoes on the side.

Curried Orange Pork (*continued*)

and to drink
$ 2001 Gundlach Bundschu
Pinot Noir, California
$$ 2002 Pisoni Santa Lucia
Highlands Pinot Noir, California

chef's notes High-quality pork is the secret to this recipe. Look for a bright pink color when selecting your pork. Chef Doug Turbush recommends Niman Ranch pork for its depth of flavor. To keep the meat moist, make sure not to bring the pork over 140°F.

Poaching is a moist-heat cooking method that is particularly healthy, as no fat is added during the cooking process. Poaching retains food's flavor, tenderness, and moisture through a gentle simmering process.

WHERE TO BUY
Pork:
Lobel's, 877-783-4512, www.lobels.com
Niman Ranch, 866-808-0340, www.nimanranch.com

seeger's

111 WEST PACES FERRY ROAD   ATLANTA, GA 30305

404-846-9779   WWW.SEEGERS.COM

Chef Guenter Seeger spent the first twenty years of his career sharpening his culinary skills and developing an abiding respect for fresh and local ingredients, first in the Black Forest region of his native Germany, then in hotels and restaurants in Switzerland and France. He crossed the pond in 1984, first working in D.C., then taking on the Atlanta Ritz-Carlton's Dining Room in 1985. An Atlanta legend ever since, Seeger garnered a James Beard Foundation award for best chef in the Southeast and put the Dining Room on the map, earning it Mobil five-star and Triple A five-diamond awards. He opened Seeger's on a quiet Buckhead side street in 1997. Everything, from its European-style bungalow setting and minimalist decor to its dazzling cuisine and excellent service, sets this restaurant apart. The wine list is also superb, with more than a thousand selections from which to choose. Chef Seeger's bold flavor pairings and artful presentations include modern dishes like Icelandic halibut with garden vegetables and olive oil sauce and crispy tempura smelts with black truffle mayonnaise. Choose from a daily changing menu, offered in several multicourse tasting options as well as special seasonal prix-fixe menus, such as a black truffle menu in warm weather, that should not be missed. Seeger's is truly a mecca for foodies interested in the art of fine dining.

This crowd-pleasing appetizer is bumped up a notch with the addition of horseradish cappuccino (see Chef's Notes, page 29). You can skip this step and just serve with a little horseradish mixed with sour cream on the side. But the cappuccino is a dazzler.

smoked salmon
with potato pancakes

1 pound russet potatoes, peeled and quartered

2 teaspoons coarse salt, plus more to taste

1 cup heavy cream

3 large eggs, separated

¾ cup cornstarch

½ teaspoon freshly ground black pepper, plus more to taste

2 tablespoons unsalted butter

½ cup sour cream

1 tablespoon prepared horseradish

6 slices smoked salmon

1. In a large pot, cover the potatoes with cold water and add 1 teaspoon of the salt. Bring to a boil over high heat; lower the heat and simmer until the potatoes are fork-tender, about 10 minutes. Drain, mash with a potato masher or large fork, and set aside.

2. Preheat the oven to 200°F.

3. In a large mixing bowl, combine the cream, egg yolks, cornstarch, the remaining 1 teaspoon salt, and ½ teaspoon pepper. Add the potatoes and stir until smooth.

4. In a bowl using an electric mixer, whip the egg whites and a pinch of salt until soft peaks form. Carefully fold the whites into the potato mixture, folding just until the egg whites are incorporated (a few white streaks are fine).

5. In a large sauté pan over medium heat, melt the butter. Working in batches, spoon the potato batter by tablespoons into the pan. Cook until the batter begins to set and brown around the edges, about 1 minute. Turn and continue cooking until the tops of the pancakes spring back when touched lightly with your finger, another 30 seconds to 1 minute. Transfer the cooked pancakes to a sheet pan and place in the oven. You should have about twenty 3-inch pancakes.

6. In a small bowl, stir together the sour cream and horseradish.

7. On individual serving plates, serve a slice of smoked salmon, 3 or 4 potato pancakes, and a tablespoon of the horseradish sauce.

chef's notes At Seeger's, this dish is served with horseradish cappuccino, which makes for a wonderful presentation and isn't really hard to make. The easiest way to seed a cucumber is to cut it lengthwise and scrape the seeds out with a spoon.

• • •

Horseradish Cappuccino

1 cucumber, peeled, seeded, and chopped

$1/3$ cup prepared horseradish (or 2 tablespoons freshly grated horseradish)

2 cups whole milk

Coarse salt and freshly ground black pepper, to taste

1. In a large saucepan over high heat, combine the cucumber and horseradish. Add the milk and bring to a boil.

2. As soon as the milk comes to a boil, stir to blend and then strain out the solids using a fine-mesh sieve. Discard the solids and season the liquid to taste with salt and pepper. To serve, place 1 cup of liquid in a medium saucepan and whisk vigorously over medium-high heat until frothy. Serve in a shot glass or cappuccino cup along with the salmon and potato pancakes.

and to drink
$ 2002 Charles Baur Pinot Blanc, California
$$ 2003 Chalone Pinot Blanc, California

WHERE TO BUY

Smoked salmon: Browne Trading Company, 800-944-7848, www.brownetrading.com

boston

dining, beantown style

Long considered a bedrock of culinary conservatism, Boston has shed its traditional skin to become a vibrant and respectable restaurant town.

Beantown's own brand of celebrity chefs spices up a dynamic dining landscape, garnering accolades in industry bibles like the *Zagat Survey* and *Food & Wine* magazine. Todd English, one of the first to get national acclaim, has expanded his hometown domain (Figs, Olives) to include outposts in Las Vegas, Tokyo, Aspen, and New York City. Ming Tsai (Blue Ginger) commands one of the hottest shows on the Food Network, *East Meets West*. And Michael Schlow, who first made his name in Boston at Café Louis, is the creative force behind one of the hottest restaurants on the East Coast, Radius, which is featured in this chapter.

Of course, the new crop of top toques doesn't take away from Boston's longstanding tradition of straightforward cuisine: The freshest seafood, thickest clam chowder, tangiest baked beans, and sweetest Boston cream pie all helped put Boston on the culinary map.

Then there are the city's walkable neighborhoods, replete with ethnic eateries and bustling markets like Haymarket and Faneuil Hall. You'll find Italian in the North End, Asian in Chinatown, fusion flair along Newbury Street, with its high-end shops and restaurants, an eclectic mix of gay-owned and ethnic restaurants in the South End, and of course traditional Beacon Hill is home to some of Boston's best, including Pigalle, which is included in our restaurant lineup.

Boston, like many top towns, has an annual restaurant week showcasing the city's best restaurants at a discounted rate. Head to town during the third week of August, when dozens of terrific spots offer a three-course prix-fixe lunch for the decimal equivalent of the year (in 2007, $20.07) and many offer dinner for just $10 more. Popular places book up quickly, so make your plans early to enjoy a dining city that marries cutting-edge cuisine with the kind of traditional food that never goes out of style.

the blue room

1 KENDALL SQUARE   CAMBRIDGE, MA 02139

617-494-9034   WWW.THEBLUEROOM.NET

A visit to Cambridge isn't complete without a meal at the Blue Room, a nationally acclaimed restaurant housed in a renovated factory that is anything but blue. Stylish without a hint of pretense, the Blue Room is decked out in bare wood beams, brick and granite walls hung with local art, cozy chenille banquettes, soft lighting, and zinc-topped tables. Chef Jorge Lopes, a native of Aveiro, Portugal, and a graduate of the Johnson and Wales Culinary Program, uses seasonal and locally sourced ingredients to create wood-grilled fare with influences ranging from New England to the Mediterranean and Latin America to Southeast Asia. The menu changes at least eight times a year, taking advantage of the microseasonal changes that come with living in New England. A few of chef Lopes's featured dishes might include roasted Vermont quail with warm raisin, pistachio, and prune couscous and pepper caramel sauce; grilled Bell & Evans chicken livers with mustard greens and balsamic vinaigrette; and whole branzino, grilled with braised fennel, arugula, and lemon beurre blanc.

When you go, ask about the restaurant's back-room wine list, a collection of rare, older vintages and award-winning wines that are part of the Blue Room's impressive cellar.

This simple side dish looks gorgeous and adds an exotic touch to a meal of grilled steak or chicken. Many supermarkets now carry precut squash-in-a-bag in the produce section, which eliminates the only time-consuming part of this recipe: peeling and cutting the squash.

curried winter
squash puree

SERVES 4

4 tablespoons (½ stick)
unsalted butter

One 1½- to 2-pound festival
or butternut squash, peeled,
seeded, and cut into 1-inch
cubes, or 1 pound
precut squash

1 russet potato, peeled and
cut into 1-inch chunks

½ cup chopped onion

1 teaspoon peeled,
minced fresh ginger

Pinch ground ginger,
or to taste

¼ teaspoon ground
coriander

¼ teaspoon curry powder

Coarse salt and freshly
ground black pepper,
to taste

1. Melt 1 tablespoon of the butter in a large heavy sauté pan over medium heat. Add the squash, potato, onion, and fresh ginger and cook, stirring, until the vegetables soften, about 8 minutes. Add the ground ginger, coriander, and curry powder and cook, stirring, just until the spices are fragrant, about 1 minute.

2. Transfer the vegetables to a medium saucepan, cover with water, and simmer, uncovered, until they are very soft, about 10 minutes. Drain. Puree the vegetables with a handheld mixer or in a food processor.

3. Return the puree to the pan and stir in the remaining 3 tablespoons butter. Season to taste with salt and pepper, reheat over medium heat if necessary, and serve.

chef's notes For this recipe, chef Lopes uses festival squash, an aromatic specialty squash that looks like a green-and-orange-striped pumpkin. Butternut squash is a good substitute. If you do peel the squash yourself, cut it lengthwise and place it cut side down, then cut it into smaller pieces. Peel the pieces with a sharp paring knife or sturdy vegetable peeler.

Curry isn't a spice at all. Or more specifically, it isn't one spice, but a mixture of spices, and many chefs blend their own top-secret combinations. You can do this at home by using equal parts ground coriander, ground cumin, ground pepper, turmeric, and ground ginger and toasting in a dry, hot pan over medium heat for about 1 minute.

and to drink
$ 2002 Yalumba Bush Vine
Grenache, Australia
$$ 2002 Turkey Flat Grenache,
Australia

WHERE TO BUY

Festival squash: Verrill Farm, 978-369-4494, www.verrillfarm.com
Organic produce: Diamond Organics, 888-ORGANIC (888-674-2642),
  www.diamondorganics.com
Spices: Penzey's Spices, 800-741-7787, www.penzeys.com

clio

370 COMMONWEALTH AVENUE   BOSTON, MA 02215

617-536-7200   WWW.CLIORESTAURANT.COM

Recognized in 2004 as one of the top fifty restaurants in America by *Gourmet* magazine, Clio is the elegant setting for chef/owner Kenneth Oringer's world-class cuisine. Located in the hipster boutique Eliot Hotel, Clio features French-inspired cooking with strong Asian influences. Specialties include chilled lobster and Nantucket bay scallops teased with a hot and sour broth spiked with Thai herbs, or wild Alaskan salmon slow cooked with red ginger vinaigrette and Jerusalem artichokes. Reconciling Asian flavors seamlessly with French technique is just one of chef Oringer's talents. He creates plates that are downright gorgeous, each a picture-perfect balance of color, texture, and substance. The James Beard Award–winning chef also owns the adjacent sushi bar, Uni. No wonder most Bostonians mention Clio as their favorite place for a memorable evening of upscale fare.

In this recipe, chef Oringer pairs fresh scallops with three kinds of citrus and fruit to create a showstopping appetizer. Save time and buy cut-up watermelon from your supermarket salad bar.

scallop ceviche
with watermelon, mint, and grapefruit

SERVES 4

½ pound sea scallops, each sliced horizontally into thirds

1 tablespoon fresh lemon juice

1 tablespoon fresh lime juice

½ tablespoon fresh grapefruit juice

2 teaspoons grated fresh lime zest

2 teaspoons grated fresh lemon zest

2 tablespoons grapeseed or light olive oil

Pinch red pepper flakes, or to taste

1 teaspoon coarse salt

1 teaspoon freshly ground black pepper

½ small seedless watermelon, cut into 1-inch cubes (about 2 cups)

1 tomato (preferably heirloom), cut into thin wedges

¼ cup fresh mint leaves, or 1 tablespoon dried

1 grapefruit, peeled and cut into segments, pits removed

¼ cup fresh tarragon leaves, or 1 tablespoon dried

and to drink

$ 2003 Firstland Sauvignon Blanc, Marlborough, New Zealand

$$ Crocker & Starr Sauvignon Blanc, Napa

1. In a nonreactive bowl, combine the scallops, lemon juice, lime juice, grapefruit juice, 1 teaspoon each of the lime and lemon zest, the oil, red pepper, salt, and pepper. Let stand for 3 minutes.

2. To serve, divide the watermelon among 4 plates. Top the watermelon with the tomato wedges, mint, a quarter of the scallops, the grapefruit segments, the remaining teaspoon each of lemon and lime zest, and the tarragon.

chef's notes   You can use any kind of ripe tomatoes in the recipe, but if you can get heirloom tomatoes, they're something special. Compared to the commercial hybrids found at most supermarkets, heirloom tomatoes are prized for their colorful varieties, texture, flavor, aroma, and tenderness. Look for them in season at farmers' markets and at specialty greengrocers.

Ceviche is a popular Latin American appetizer made of raw seafood that has been marinated in citrus juice, usually lime juice. The acidity of the lime juice "cooks" the seafood.

WHERE TO BUY

Sea scallops: Browne Trading Company, 800-944-7848, www. brownetrading.com

Seafood and produce: Super 88 Market, 877-281-1688, www.super88market.com

il capriccio restaurant

888 MAIN STREET   WALTHAM, MA 02153

781-894-2234

One of the best Italian restaurants in Boston isn't in the city's famed Italian North End. Il Capriccio is about twenty minutes west of the city in Waltham, a northern Italian destination restaurant that lures suburbanites and city folk alike with its promise of outstanding cuisine and free parking. Owned by chef Rich Barron and sommelier Jeannie Rogers, Il Capriccio takes diners on a trip through the Piedmont and Tuscan regions of Italy, with dishes like porcini mushroom soufflé and homemade lobster and scallop lasagna with baby spinach. Rogers is responsible for the restaurant's numerous *Wine Spectator* awards, delivering a wine list ripe with little-known wines from Italy that you won't find anywhere else.

For this dish, chef Barron marries the earthy flavors of fungi with poached eggs for a memorable starter or a sophisticated brunch item. He uses chanterelles, oyster mushrooms, and cèpes, but a half pound of whatever mushrooms you can find in the market works just fine. Barron, like most chefs, is in love with truffles. You can capture a hint of truffle essence by using a drizzle of truffle oil, sold in most supermarkets.

sautéed wild mushrooms
with poached egg and truffle

SERVES 4

½ pound mixed mushrooms (chanterelle, oyster, shiitake, white mushrooms)

2 tablespoons olive oil

1 tablespoon unsalted butter

¼ cup dry white wine

Leaves from 1 sprig fresh rosemary, or 1 teaspoon dried

Leaves from 2 sprigs fresh thyme, or 1 teaspoon dried

Coarse salt and freshly ground black pepper, to taste

4 large eggs

Truffle oil, for drizzling

1. Trim and chop the mushrooms, leaving the pieces fairly large.

2. In a medium sauté pan over medium heat, heat the olive oil and butter until the butter melts. Add the mushrooms and cook, stirring, until they soften but still hold their shape, about 2 minutes. Add the wine, rosemary, and thyme and cook, stirring, until the wine has almost evaporated.

3. Season the mushrooms to taste with salt and pepper and transfer them and any juice left in the pan to a platter. Keep warm.

4. Meanwhile, in a large sauté pan, bring 2 inches of water to a boil. Lower the heat so the water barely simmers. Crack each egg into a small cup and gently slip the eggs into the water. Cook until the eggs are just set, 2 to 3 minutes.

5. Remove the eggs from the water with a slotted spoon and place them on the mushrooms. Drizzle with truffle oil and serve immediately.

chef's notes Before you cook with fresh mushrooms, trim off the bottom of the stem (discard very tough stems like those on shiitakes) and use a soft brush to remove any dirt or grit from the caps. You don't want to rinse them, because mushrooms will absorb water and get mushy when you cook them.

Truffle oil is made by soaking slices of white or black truffles in oil, usually olive oil, to imbue it with rich, earthy flavor. Truffle oil is an ideal substitute for (or an addition to) fresh truffles. It's best used to enhance the flavor of raw meats, pasta dishes, soups, eggs, salads, grilled meats, and cheeses.

and to drink
$ 1998 Icardi Barbera Suri di Mu, Italy
$$ 1998 Pertimali Brunello di Montalcino, Italy

WHERE TO BUY
Truffle oil:
Eurogrocer, 201-476-1747, www.eurogrocer.com
Trader Joe's, multiple locations, 800-SHOP-TJS, www.traderjoes.com

tryst

689 MASS AVENUE   ARLINGTON, MA 02476

781-641-2227   WWW.TRYSTRESTAURANT.COM.

Paul Turano opened the much-anticipated Tryst, a 100-plus-seat restaurant in Arlington, Massachusetts, featuring alluring, eclectic American style, with dishes ranging from grilled meats and fish to pasta and creative vegetable combinations. The atmosphere is warm yet lively, perfect for an intimate dinner for two as well as a stimulating evening with friends.

A few weeks after opening, Tryst received glowing reviews from the *Boston Globe, Boston Magazine*, and the *Boston Herald*, among others. It was voted one of the area's best new restaurants by *Boston Magazine*, and was hailed as one of the most romantic restaurants by *Zagat*. Since then, Tryst has also been featured on *TV Diner with Billy Costa* and *The Phantom Gourmet*.

This recipe is a variation of a trout dish often featured on Tryst's menu. Chef Turano uses lobster in the stuffing, but you can use cleaned shrimp to save time. And any whole fish will work, although trout is readily available at most supermarket seafood counters. Wrap the trout with high-quality, thick-cut bacon for the best flavor.

bacon-wrapped trout
with shrimp-cornbread stuffing

SERVES 4

Stuffing

8 tablespoons (1 stick) unsalted butter

2 stalks celery, finely chopped

1 carrot, peeled and finely chopped

1/2 cup finely chopped fennel

2 tablespoons finely chopped Spanish onion

1 bay leaf

2 store-bought corn muffins, cut into 1/2-inch cubes

1/2 cup heavy cream

1 pound peeled, cooked medium shrimp, chopped

1 tablespoon minced scallion

1 tablespoon chopped fresh basil

Trout

4 small trout (3/4–1 pound each), heads and pinbones removed by your fish seller

Coarse salt and freshly ground black pepper, to taste

16 slices bacon

2 tablespoons canola oil

1 tablespoon olive oil

4 cups mixed baby lettuces

1 cup cherry tomatoes

1/4 cup thinly sliced red onion

2 tablespoons balsamic vinegar

1. To make the stuffing, melt the butter in a large sauté pan over medium heat. Add the celery, carrot, fennel, onion, and bay leaf and cook, stirring, until the vegetables are soft, about 4 minutes. Fold in the corn muffins and cream and cook until the cream just simmers. Remove from the heat and cool completely.

2. When cool, remove and discard the bay leaf and fold in the shrimp, scallion, and basil. Set aside.

3. To make the trout, preheat the oven to 400°F.

4. Season the inside of the trout with salt and pepper and then fill each with a quarter of the stuffing mixture. Using 4 slices of bacon for each trout, wrap the bacon around the trout in a crisscross pattern.

5. In a large ovenproof sauté pan, heat the canola oil over medium-high heat. Add the trout to the pan and cook until the bacon is lightly browned, 1 to 2 minutes per side.

6. Place the pan in the oven and cook until the trout is opaque all the way through, 6 to 10 minutes.

7. While the trout is cooking, in another large sauté pan, heat the olive oil over medium heat. Add the greens, tomatoes, and red onion to the pan and cook, stirring, until the greens start to wilt, about 1 minute. Add the vinegar, remove the pan from the heat, and keep warm.

8. To serve, divide the greens among 4 serving plates, creating a bed for the trout. Remove the trout from the oven, slice each in half at an angle widthwise, and place the halves on top of the greens.

WHERE TO BUY

Balsamic vinegar: Eurogrocer, 201-476-1747, www.eurogrocer.com

Organic bacon: Diamond Organics, 888-ORGANIC (888-674-2642), www.diamondorganics.com

Bacon-Wrapped Trout (*continued*)

and to drink
$ 2002 Concha Y Toro
Terrunyo Sauvignon Blanc,
Chile
$$ 1999 Trimbach Riesling
Frederic Emile, Alsace, France

chef's notes   Pinbones are the small bones found in most fish fillets, sticking directly out of the thickest part of the fillet. There's nothing tricky about removing these bones, and it sure beats getting a mouthful of needle-sharp bones when you take a bite. Take a few minutes and pull them out, using a needle-nose pliers or specialized fish tweezers. Most restaurants remove them before cooking the fish.

l'espalier

30 GLOUCESTER STREET   BOSTON, MA 02115

617-262-3023   WWW.LESPALIER.COM

When Frank McClelland was growing up on his grandparents' gentleman's farm in New Hampshire, he developed an abiding love for the fruits of the land. He learned to appreciate the smells and tastes of fresh produce, and master time-honored traditions like pickling, canning, bread baking, and preparing sorbets from fresh fruit purees. Chef McClelland's love for cooking with seasonal ingredients, combined with his classical French training, is the life force behind his five-diamond restaurant L'Espalier, which he opened in 1978. Located in an 1880 townhouse in the heart of fashionable Back Bay, on the corner of Newbury and Gloucester Streets, L'Espalier offers romantic dining in a gracious, stylish setting. Working closely with local farmers, he offers locally foraged wild mushrooms, heirloom vegetables, and artisanal cheeses from places like Lazy Lady Farm and Hope Farm in Vermont. Three- and five-course degustation menus are available, including a degustation of seasonal vegetables that is absolutely gorgeous.

This recipe showcases asparagus enhanced by the flavors of Provence. The flavored butter can be made two to three days ahead and refrigerated. Wrap any extra butter tightly in plastic and store in the freezer for use as a sauce on pasta, fish or grilled meats, and vegetables.

asparagus salad
with provençal butter

SERVES 6

Provençal Butter

½ pound goat cheese

2 tablespoons unsalted butter, at room temperature

2 teaspoons coarsely ground black pepper

2 teaspoons coarse salt

1 teaspoon curry powder

3 tablespoons capers, drained and rinsed

1 tablespoon chopped fresh tarragon, or 1 teaspoon dried

1 tablespoon chopped fresh chervil or flat-leaf parsley

½ red onion, finely diced

Asparagus

24 stalks jumbo asparagus

1 tablespoon extra-virgin olive oil

12 cherry tomatoes

1 tablespoon balsamic vinegar

1 teaspoon sugar

Leaves from 2 bunches arugula (about 1 pound), rinsed and dried

2 cups croutons, store-bought or homemade (see Chef's Notes)

Salt and freshly ground black pepper, to taste

1. To make the Provençal butter, in a bowl, mix together the goat cheese and butter with a large wooden spoon or handheld mixer. When soft and fluffy, add the remaining Provençal butter ingredients except the onion and mix until well blended.

2. Stir in the onion. Place the butter in the center of a piece of plastic wrap and roll into a log shape. Refrigerate until firm.

3. Meanwhile, to make the asparagus, use a potato peeler to strip off the tough outer skin from the bottom two thirds of each asparagus stalk. Bring an inch of water to a boil in the bottom of a large pot fitted with a steamer basket. Add the asparagus and steam just until it turns bright green and is crisp-tender, about 4 minutes.

4. Immediately transfer the asparagus to a large bowl of ice water. Let stand until cold. Drain the asparagus and pat dry with paper towels.

5. In a large sauté pan, heat the olive oil over medium heat. Add the cherry tomatoes and cook, stirring, until the skins just begin to blister. Remove the pan from the heat and add the balsamic vinegar and sugar and stir. Add the arugula, croutons, and 6 tablespoons of the Provençal butter to the pan. Toss to coat and season with salt and pepper.

6. Divide the arugula and tomato mixture among 6 plates. Crisscross asparagus stalks over the top of each and serve.

WHERE TO BUY

Capers: Gourmet Pasta Cheese, 800-386-9198, www.pastacheese.com

Goat cheese: South End Formaggio, 888-212-3224, www. formaggiokitchen.com

and to drink
$ 2002 Pierre Boniface,
"Les Rocailles," France
$$ 1996 Egly-Ouriet Brut
Grand Cru, France

chef's notes Store-bought croutons are just fine, but home-made are better. All you need is day-old bread (baguettes work well), extra-virgin olive oil, coarse salt, and freshly ground black pepper.

• • •

1. Preheat the oven to 375° F.

2. Cut bread into ½-inch cubes and toss in a bowl with enough extra-virgin olive oil to coat the bread. Toss again with generous amounts of salt and pepper. For an extra kick, add a bit of paprika, chili powder, or curry powder. Place in a single layer on a baking sheet and bake until just crisped, 4 to 5 minutes. Store on paper towels in an airtight container.

lumière restaurant

1293 WASHINGTON STREET   WEST NEWTON, MA 02465

617-244-9199   WWW.LUMIERERESTAURANT.COM

Lumière means "light" in French, an appropriate moniker for Michael and Jill Leviton's enlightened restaurant in Newton, just five miles west of Boston. Powered by chef Michael Leviton's classic bistro cuisine and modern cooking techniques, Lumière also incorporates the bold, clean flavors of the Mediterranean and the Pacific Rim. Opened in 1999 to accolades from *Gourmet, Saveur, Food & Wine*, and the *New York Times*, Lumière is also known for its award-winning wine list of eighty-plus bottles, with twenty wines being served by the glass. The restaurant, which literally glows with candlelight and the luminous shadows cast by copper mesh lampshades, is a soothing, intimate setting for a truly remarkable dining experience. Try the house-made duck liver mousse terrine with dried apricots, golden raisins, and candied ginger marmalade, or the amazing roasted duck risotto with butternut squash, Swiss chard, hazelnuts, Parmesan, and sage oil. Reserve a table for a Sunday through Thursday night, and order the three-course prix fixe menu, including wine pairings, for $50, the best deal in the house.

The secret to the winning flavor of this simple grilled steak recipe is in the olives—Cerignola, Lucques, or Picholine are three great choices, but any imported green olive will work fine.

sirloin steak with grilled asparagus and green olive vinaigrette

SERVES 4

¼ cup pitted, coarsely chopped green olives

2 tablespoons finely chopped shallot

2 tablespoons chopped fresh flat-leaf parsley

1 tablespoon grated fresh lemon zest

1 tablespoon fresh lemon juice

1 tablespoon red-wine vinegar

6 tablespoons extra-virgin olive oil, plus more for brushing the asparagus

Coarse salt and freshly ground black pepper, to taste

Four 8-ounce sirloin steaks, preferably from Niman Ranch

20 spears jumbo asparagus, cut into 5-inch pieces, tough outer skin removed with a vegetable peeler

1. In a small bowl, whisk together the olives, shallot, parsley, lemon zest, lemon juice, vinegar, and 6 tablespoons of the olive oil. Season with salt and pepper to taste and set aside.

2. Prepare an outdoor grill or a grill pan for high-heat cooking. Season the steaks generously with salt and pepper and grill, turning once, until they reach the desired doneness, 6 to 10 minutes. Transfer the steaks to a platter and let rest 5 minutes.

3. Meanwhile, brush the asparagus with olive oil and season with salt and pepper. Grill over low heat until just heated through, about 5 minutes.

4. Place 5 asparagus spears and 1 steak on each of 4 plates. Combine any meat juices that collected on the platter with the vinaigrette, spoon the vinaigrette over the steaks, and serve.

chef's notes Why do so many grilled steaks come out dry and lifeless? They're cooked to death. Remember that meat will continue to cook after it's been removed from the heat source, so err on the side of caution and take it off before you think it's done. Another common mistake is to poke and prod the meat while it's cooking. Put it on the grill and let it cook, turning it once. You can judge the doneness of steak by pressing the meat with your finger. Very rare meat offers little resistance, medium rare is slightly springy, medium is firm and springy, while well done is quite firm.

After you've removed your steaks from the grill, let them rest about five minutes so the juices have a chance to redistribute themselves. If you poke at it before resting, the juices will flow out onto the plate and your steak will turn into grade-A shoe leather.

and to drink

$ 2002 Artazuri Artazu Navarra, Spain

$$ Domaine Tempier Bandol Rouge, France

WHERE TO BUY

Beef: Niman Ranch, 866-808-0340, www.nimanranch.com

oleana

134 HAMPSHIRE STREET   CAMBRIDGE, MA 02139

617-661-0505   WWW.OLEANARESTAURANT.COM

Chef and owner Ana Sortun is one of the city's culinary treasures— and so is Oleana. Here, flavors from all over the Middle Eastern Mediterranean sing loud and clear, as they do in the hot, crispy fried mussels starter, and in the tuna and black olive–laden deviled eggs. Fish gets jacked up with Turkish spices, then grilled until it just barely caramelizes. In warm weather, the back patio is a hidden utopia—a homey garden that hits the perfect note of casual refinement. The seasonal menu at Oleana includes many Ottoman-influenced Turkish specialties. The ambiance is warm and comfortable, with details such as interesting spice blends, pressed coffees, and homemade ice creams. Sortun, a 2004 James Beard Foundation nominee for best chef in the Northeast, holds a degree from La Varenne Ecole de Cuisine in Paris. Originally from Seattle, she has been a part of Boston's culinary scene since 1990, working at such kitchens as Aigo Bistro in Concord, 8 Holyoke in Harvard Square, and Casablanca in Cambridge. She opened Oleana in January 2001.

This appetizer recipe was inspired by chef Sortun's friend Armen Mehrabyan, who grows, harvests, and dries teas and cooking herbs in Armenia.

armenian bean and walnut
pâté

One 16-ounce can red kidney beans, rinsed and drained

½ white onion, finely chopped

1 bay leaf

½ cup water

½ cup pomegranate molasses or pomegranate juice

¼ cup walnut halves, lightly toasted

4 tablespoons (½ stick) unsalted butter, at room temperature

½ teaspoon chopped garlic

1 tablespoon chopped fresh dill

1 tablespoon chopped fresh mint or basil

1 tablespoon chopped fresh flat-leaf parsley

Coarse salt and freshly ground black pepper, to taste

2 tablespoons toasted chopped walnuts

Pita wedges, carrot sticks, or other vegetables, for serving

SERVES 8

1. In a small saucepan, combine the beans, onion, bay leaf, and water. Simmer until the onion is tender, about 10 minutes. Drain well and discard the bay leaf.

2. In a food processor, puree the bean mixture with the pomegranate molasses or juice, walnut halves, butter, and garlic until smooth. Transfer to a medium bowl.

3. Stir the dill, mint, and parsley into the beans. Season with salt and pepper and spoon the mixture into a crock or serving bowl. Garnish with the chopped walnuts and serve with toasted pita wedges or carrot sticks and other veggies.

chef's notes Pomegranate molasses is not molasses at all, but a highly concentrated syrup made from cooked-down pomegranate juice. It is used in many Middle Eastern and East Asian dishes, and adds a wonderful sweet-and-sour taste to braised meats, fish dishes, and dressings. It is commonly sold in Middle Eastern and Asian food stores. You can substitute pomegranate juice, found in the produce section of most supermarkets, although it won't add the same depth of flavor.

and to drink

$ 2002 Solex Chardonnay, California

$$ 2000 Domaine Marcel Deiss et Fils Engelgarten, Alsace, France

WHERE TO BUY

Pomegranate molasses: Kalustyan's Specialty Foods, 212-685-3451, www.kalustyans.com

radius

8 HIGH STREET   BOSTON, MA 02110

617-426-1234   WWW.RADIUSRESTAURANT.COM

In 1985, Brooklyn-born Michael Schlow traded a baseball scholarship and a ninety-two-mile-an-hour fastball for a set of Wusthof knives and a place at the Academy of Culinary Arts in New Jersey. It marked the beginning of a journey that led to the opening of Radius in January of 1999, garnering accolades including Best New Restaurant 2000 by *Food & Wine* magazine, the James Beard Foundation Award for best chef in the Northeast in May 2000, and a place in *Gourmet's* 50 Best American Restaurants list, September 2001. Schlow's modern French menu puts emphasis on seasonal ingredients, classical technique, and stellar presentation. Schlow's deft flavor combinations are legendary; crispy sweetbreads with apples, lentils, smoked bacon, and horseradish and homemade potato gnocchi with escargots, smoked bacon, vegetable pearls, and Parmigiano are two cases in point.

Thin-cut pork chops cook in no time, making for a quick and tasty supper. If you happen to dread cauliflower, this recipe will change your mind. The cauliflower comes out slightly crunchy and spicy, caramelized for sweetness.

pork chops with hot cherry peppers, seared cauliflower, and onions

¼ cup extra-virgin olive oil

1 head cauliflower, cut into small florets

1 red onion, thinly sliced

¼ cup canola oil

Eight ¾-inch-thick loin pork chops

Coarse salt and freshly ground black pepper, to taste

¼ cup sliced hot cherry peppers

⅓ cup seasoned bread crumbs

2 tablespoons unsalted butter

⅓ cup grated Parmigiano-Reggiano cheese

⅓ cup coarsely chopped fresh flat-leaf parsley

2 lemons, halved

SERVES 4

1. Preheat the oven to 350°F.

2. In a large sauté pan, heat the olive oil over high heat for 1 minute. Add the cauliflower and cook without stirring until it begins to brown, 1 to 2 minutes. Then cook and stir until the florets brown on all sides, about 4 minutes. When the cauliflower starts to become tender (but still has a bit of crunch), add the red onion and cook for 2 more minutes.

3. While the cauliflower is cooking, place 2 large, ovenproof sauté pans over high heat. Add 2 tablespoons of the canola oil to each and heat for 30 seconds. Season the pork chops with salt and pepper and add 4 to each pan. Cook, turning once, until browned, 1 to 2 minutes per side.

4. Transfer the pans with the pork to the oven and roast, turning the chops once, until the meat is firm to the touch, 8 to 10 minutes.

5. When the pork chops are done, remove them from the oven and let them rest 2 to 3 minutes in the pans.

6. Meanwhile, add the hot peppers, bread crumbs, butter, salt, and pepper to the pan with the cauliflower and cook until the cauliflower is very tender, about 2 minutes more. Lower the heat to medium and stir in the cheese and parsley; cook until just heated through, about 1 minute.

7. Place 2 pork chops on each of 4 plates and top with the cauliflower mixture. Squeeze the lemons over the top and serve.

WHERE TO BUY

Pork:

Lobel's, 877-783-4512, www.lobels.com

Niman Ranch, 866-808-0340, www.nimanranch.com

and to drink

$ 2003 Frey Organic Pinot Noir, California

$$ 2000 Belle Pente Murto Reserve Pinot Noir, Oregon

chef's notes All pork chops are not created equal. This recipe calls for loin chops, which have a T-shaped bone running through the meat. They are particularly well marbled, making them ideal for grilling or the high-heat searing called for in this recipe. And don't overcook your pork; it should be medium (still slightly pink inside). Let it rest before cutting into it.

Niman Ranch out of Oakland, California, is one of the most respected pork producers, treating their animals humanely, feeding them all-natural feeds, and allowing them to mature naturally. Niman Ranch pork is carried in such markets as Dean & Deluca, Whole Foods, and Wegmans, or you can order directly from the company.

pigalle

75 CHARLES STREET SOUTH   BOSTON, MA 02116

617-423-4944   WWW.PIGALLEBOSTON.COM

Named for the famed red light district in Paris, Pigalle showcases the talents of chef Marc Orfaly, who owns the restaurant with his wife, Kerri Foley. Orfaly has worked with some of the nation's most respected cooks, including Mark Peel and Nancy Silverton at Campanile in L.A., Rocco DiSpirito at Union Pacific in New York, and Todd English at Olives in Boston. His vision for the cozy, fifty-seat Pigalle is realized in adventurous, rustic French fare and dishes that bridge the gap between a master chef like Escoffier and a brazen Turk like Anthony Bourdain. A typical Pigalle experience might begin with steak tartare served with potato chips and toasted brioche, a silky vichyssoise, and seared foie gras with papaya. Entrées include classics like bouillabaisse and cassoulet, every Francophile's fave. A creative cocktail list and a mostly French wine list complete the *ooh-la-la* Left Bank experience.

Orfaly serves this colorful appetizer with Cape Cod lobster, but shrimp is a good stand-in. If you can't find chorizo, kielbasa is just fine. Frozen vegetables are a time-saver, but fresh always tastes better.

shrimp succotash
with chorizo and corn grits

Grits

1 cup milk

½ cup instant grits

3 tablespoons unsalted butter

½ cup frozen corn kernels, thawed

Coarse salt and freshly ground black pepper, to taste

Succotash

½ pound spicy Spanish chorizo or kielbasa

1 cup peas, fresh or frozen

1 cup edamame, fresh or frozen

½ cup frozen corn kernels, thawed

1 cup lima beans, fresh or frozen

2 tablespoons unsalted butter

1 tablespoon chopped shallot

½ pound medium shrimp, peeled and deveined

2 tablespoons water

Coarse salt, to taste

1 tablespoon minced fresh chives

SERVES 4

1. To make the grits, in a small saucepan over medium-high heat, bring the milk to a boil. Lower the heat to medium-low and whisk in the grits. Switch to a wooden spoon and cook, stirring, until very thick, about 10 minutes. Stir in the butter and corn and season to taste with salt and pepper. Keep warm.

2. To make the succotash, remove the sausage from its casing, crumble, and fry in a medium nonstick sauté pan over medium heat until browned, about 10 minutes. Set aside.

3. If using any fresh vegetables, fill a pot with salted water and bring to a boil over high heat. Add the vegetables and cook 3 minutes. Strain and place in a bowl of ice water until cool. Drain and pat dry with paper towels. Thaw any frozen vegetables and set all aside.

4. Melt the butter in a large sauté pan over medium heat. Add the shallot and cook, stirring, 1 minute. Add the sausage, peas, edamame, corn, limas, and shrimp. Add the water and cook, stirring, until the shrimp are just cooked through, about 4 minutes. Season to taste with salt.

5. Place ½ cup grits in the center of each of 4 plates. Spoon the succotash around the grits, garnish with the chives, and serve.

WHERE TO BUY

Spanish chorizo: La Tienda, 888-472-1022, www.tienda.com

and to drink
$ 2003 Paul Zinck Pinot Blanc,
Alsace, France
$$ 1999 Trimbach Pinot Gris
Reserve Personelle, Alsace,
France

chef's notes There are two kinds of chorizo sausage: Mexican chorizo, which needs to be cooked, and Spanish chorizo, which is dry-cured. Both are made of pork and zesty spices.

Edamame are green soybeans, usually sold fresh in the pod or parboiled and quick-frozen. A terrific source of protein, edamame are popular as a snack in Japanese restaurants, where they are served parboiled, salted, and eaten directly from the pods.

upstairs on the square

91 WINTHROP STREET   CAMBRIDGE, MA 02138

617-864-1933   WWW.UPSTAIRSONTHESQUARE.COM

UpStairs on the Square is the 2003 incarnation of UpStairs at the Pudding, a much-loved fixture above the Hasty Pudding Club for more than twenty years. When partners Mary Catherine Deibel and Deborah Hughes lost their lease, they found the perfect digs, coincidentally occupying space that also housed a Harvard theatrical club dating back to 1906. UpStairs on the Square is actually two restaurants in one; the second floor is home to the more casual Monday Club Bar, and the third floor features the formal pink fantasy land that is the Soiree Room. Decorated by the artsy Hughes in a riotous vision of magenta, zebra stripes, gold leaf, and mirrors, the restaurant is quite beautiful. And the food, overseen by Hughes and chef de cuisine Amanda Lydon, a graduate of Le Cordon Bleu, is as brightly drawn as the memorable decor. A typical meal might start with steak tartare spiked with cognac aïoli and shoestring potato frites, then move on to olive oil–poached fluke with Woodbury littlenecks, fingerling potatoes, and leeks. The artisanal cheese plate is not to be missed.

This recipe was designed for day boat lobster, but shrimp makes a fine substitution. You can use cleaned, cooked frozen shrimp and frozen peas, fava beans, and corn, but fresh green beans are a must. Aïoli is a garlic-infused homemade mayonnaise, but in this version, we just dress up store-bought to save time.

shrimp salad
with orange aïoli and green beans

SERVES 6

Shrimp Salad

1 cup mayonnaise

1 teaspoon grated fresh orange zest

2 tablespoons fresh orange juice

2 pounds cooked, peeled shrimp, cut into ¾-inch pieces

Juice of 1 lemon

Juice of 1 lime

Coarse salt, to taste

Green Bean Salad

2 cups fresh green beans, trimmed

1 head frisée lettuce, torn into bite-size pieces

1 cup frozen corn, thawed

1 cup frozen baby peas, thawed

1 cup frozen fava beans, thawed

2 seedless oranges, peeled and chopped (or one 11-ounce can mandarin orange segments, drained)

1. To make the shrimp salad, in a large bowl, whisk together the mayonnaise, orange zest, and orange juice. In another large bowl, toss the shrimp with the lemon juice, lime juice, and salt. Fold the shrimp into the mayonnaise, cover, and refrigerate.

2. To make the green bean salad, bring a pot of salted water to a boil. Add the green beans, bring the water back to a boil, and cook 1 minute. Drain the beans and immediately transfer them to a bowl of ice water. Let cool, drain again, and pat the beans dry with paper towels.

3. Place the beans in a crisscross pattern around the perimeters of 6 serving plates. Place the frisée in the center of the plates and cover with shrimp salad. Scatter the corn, peas, and fava beans around the plates. Arrange the orange segments around the perimeter of the plates and serve.

chef's notes At UpStairs on the Square, the chef decorates this dish with edible flowers. It makes for a beautiful garnish, and you'd be surprised at how many flowers from your garden are fit to eat. A few include carnations (peppery), chive flowers (oniony), dianthus (a hint of cloves), impatiens (pretty but little flavor), nasturtiums (citrusy), and rose petals (perfumed with rose). Guests may be unsure about munching on a whole flower, so separate the blossom into petals, scattering to add color and eye appeal to your plate. (Do remember, however, that any flower that has been sprayed with pesticides is unsuitable for eating, so never use flowers that come from a florist or nursery that may have used pesticides. If in doubt, buy edible flowers from a specialty grocer.)

and to drink

$ 2002 Devevy Bourgogne Blanc, France

$$ 2002 Vincent and François Jouard Chassagne-Montrachet, France

WHERE TO BUY

Organic produce:

Boston Organics, 617-242-1700, www.bostonorganics.com

Diamond Organics, 888-ORGANIC (888-674-2642),
  www.diamondorganics.com

chicago

the deep dish on chicago dining

When it comes to food, Chicagoans have more to relish than the city's famous aged beef, bratwurst, and deep-dish pizza.

In fact, dining in America's third largest city has never been better. Top local chefs take home buckets of national cooking awards and appear regularly on the Food Network. New restaurants seem to open their doors daily, offering a dizzying variety of every imaginable cuisine. The Windy City has it all: chic hot spots crowded with beautiful people, an endless array of steakhouses, most of which are prime, contemporary chef-owned shrines to haute cuisine, and every kind of ethnic food you could possibly crave.

Despite the fact that many restaurants deliver sticker shock along with their menus (this is no longer the bargain food town it once was), Chicago is still blessed with some of the best restaurant service of any big city. There's a distinct lack of attitude in Chi-town, a simple fact that transforms just about every eating foray, from fancy to mom-and-pop, into a friendly experience. The city's ethnic neighborhoods, including Greektown, Little Italy, and Chinatown, still deliver the best bang for the buck. There are also plenty of Chicago restaurants where you can bring your own beer or wine with no corkage fee.

Several highly regarded chefs, including Jean Joho at Everest and Arun Sampanthavi-vat at Arun's, preside at restaurants that have been longtime favorites of local epicures. But relative newcomers, most notably Chef Rick Tramonto at Tru and Graham Elliot Bowles at Avenues in the Peninsula Hotel, have raised the bar to lofty heights. All of these restaurants are featured in this chapter, which highlights ten of the city's very best restaurants with ten recipes you really can make at home.

ambria

2300 N LINCOLN PARK W   CHICAGO, IL 60614

773-472-5959   WWW.LEYE.COM

Polished dark woods, ultrasuede banquettes, and etched glass are combined with Art Nouveau architectural touches at this romantic special-occasion restaurant owned by executive chef Gabino Sotelino. A landmark on the Chicago dining scene since 1980, Ambria combines haute—but never haughty—French cuisine with influences from Sotelino's native Spain. Interpreted by chef de cuisine Christian Eckmann, the seasonal menu might offer crispy veal sweetbreads with fava beans and chorizo; foie gras with roasted apples, pistachios, and Sauterne sauce; and juniper-scented venison loin with butternut squash, jamón serrano, and a cocoa balsamic reduction. The encyclopedic wine list and impressive cellar earned an Award of Excellence from *Wine Spectator*.

This version of an Ambria menu favorite combines Spanish rice with fish, clams, peas, and salsa verde, which means "green sauce" in Spanish. Cod, sole, or halibut can be substituted for the hake.

hake with bomba rice,
clams, peas, and salsa verde

SERVES 4

Clams

½ pound littleneck clams

¼ cup olive oil

1 clove garlic, chopped

2 shallots, chopped

1 cup white wine

2 tablespoons apple-cider vinegar

Rice and Peas

2 tablespoons olive oil

1 clove garlic, chopped

1 tablespoon finely chopped fresh flat-leaf parsley

1 cup Spanish Bomba rice (arborio can substituted)

1 teaspoon coarse salt

1 cup cold water

½ teaspoon freshly ground white pepper

½ pound fresh or thawed frozen peas

Salsa Verde and Hake

4 tablespoons extra-virgin olive oil

3 cloves garlic, minced

1 tablespoon chopped fresh flat-leaf parsley

1 teaspoon all-purpose flour

1 cup cold water

Coarse salt and freshly ground white pepper, to taste

Four 6-ounce hake fillets

1 tablespoon unsalted butter

1. To make the clams, scrub the littlenecks under cold running water and discard any that are open. In a deep saucepan over medium-high heat, heat the olive oil. Add the garlic and shallots and cook, stirring, until softened, about 2 minutes. Add the clams, white wine, and vinegar and bring to a boil. Cover the pot and cook until the clams open, about 5 minutes. (Discard any clams that do not open.)

2. Use a slotted spoon to transfer the clams to a bowl. When cool enough to handle, remove and reserve the clam meats and discard the shells. Strain the liquid the clams cooked in through a fine-mesh sieve and reserve separately.

3. To make the rice and peas, set a medium saucepan with a tightly fitting lid over medium-high heat. Add the oil. Add the garlic and cook, stirring, 1 minute. Add the parsley and rice to the pan and cook 1 more minute. Pour in 1 cup of the liquid the clams cooked in and 1 cup water. Bring to a simmer, stir in the salt and pepper, cover the pot, and cook over low heat until the rice is tender, about 15 minutes.

4. Meanwhile, if using fresh peas, bring a medium pot of salted water to a boil. (If using frozen peas, just thaw them and don't precook.) Add the peas and cook until tender, 3 to 4 minutes. Drain the peas and cool them in a bowl of ice water. Drain again and pat dry.

5. To make the salsa verde and hake, in a small saucepan set over medium heat, warm 2 tablespoons of the olive oil. Add the garlic and cook, stirring, until the garlic starts to sizzle, about 1 minute. Add the parsley and flour and cook for 1 minute more. Add the cold water, season with salt, and bring just to a boil. Set aside.

6. Heat a large sauté pan over medium heat. Season the hake with salt and white pepper. Add the remaining 2 tablespoons oil to the pan and cook the fish, skin side up, until golden brown on the bottom, about 3 minutes. Remove the fish and set aside.

7. Measure the remaining liquid the clams cooked in and add cold water to make 2 cups total. Pour the liquid into the pan the fish cooked in and bring to a simmer over medium heat. Put the fish back into the pan and poach the fish for 3 minutes. Flip the fish over and continue to poach until just heated through, about 3 more minutes.

8. Take the saucepan off the heat; remove the fish to a platter and cover with foil to keep warm.

9. Reheat the salsa verde, whisking to blend. Add the clam meats to the sauce, season with salt and pepper, and keep warm.

10. Melt the butter in a small sauté pan over medium heat and add the peas. Cook until just warmed through.

11. To serve, divide the rice among 4 plates and place a fish fillet on top of the rice, skin side down. Spoon the peas around the fish. Spoon the clams and salsa verde over the fish and serve.

and to drink
$ 2004 Basa Rueda Blanco, Spain
$$ 2003 Val de Sil Bodegas Senorio, Ribeiro, Spain

chef's notes Bomba rice is a classic short-grain rice grown in Calasparra in southeastern Spain. What makes this rice unique is that it expands in width like an accordion rather than in length, as do other rice varieties. Bomba absorbs three times its volume in water (rather than the normal two), yet the grains remain distinct, making it the best choice for paella and many other Spanish dishes. If you must use a substitute, choose Italian arborio rice.

WHERE TO BUY

Bomba rice and other Spanish ingredients: La Tienda, 888-472-1022, www.tienda.com

Spanish olive oil: Di Bruno Brothers, 888-322-4337, www.dibruno.com

avenues

THE PENINSULA CHICAGO   108 E. SUPERIOR STREET, CHICAGO, IL 60611

312-573-6754   WWW.CHICAGO.PENINSULA.COM

Expect the unexpected at Avenues in the tony Peninsula Hotel. In the hands of talented chef de cuisine Graham Elliot Bowles, contemporary American cuisine is revved up and ready for action. Bowles, one of *Food & Wine* magazine's Best New Chefs for 2004, was called "one of the most adventurous chefs working today" by *Chicago* magazine. And no wonder. He deftly combines texture, flavor, and substance throughout his seafood-dominated menu with pairings that are wonderful without going over the top.

Whether feasting on his line-caught black cod served with stewed Boston lettuce, candied pancetta, and lovage-clam vinaigrette or tucking into chorizo-crusted Atlantic halibut with petite vegetable ratatouille, it's clear that this chef is doing great things. His twelve-course tasting menu is the ultimate high for the committed foodie. Sommelier Aaron Elliott will gently lead you through the restaurant's vast wine list.

Although chef Bowles usually makes this savory dish with lobster, it works just as well with grade A tuna, salmon, or scallops.

cardamom tuna
with potatoes, baby bok choy, and ginger-scallion vinaigrette

SERVES 4

1 tablespoon cardamom seeds, toasted and crushed

2 tablespoons unsalted butter, softened

Coarse salt and freshly ground black pepper, to taste

¾ pound red bliss or purple potatoes, peeled and halved

1 tablespoon sesame oil

1 teaspoon lime juice

1 teaspoon soy sauce

4 scallions, thinly sliced on the bias

1½ teaspoons finely chopped peeled fresh ginger

1 teaspoon seeded, finely chopped jalapeño

1 teaspoon toasted sesame seeds

8 baby bok choy, halved lengthwise

2 teaspoons vegetable oil

Four 6-ounce tuna steaks

1 tablespoon chopped fresh cilantro

1. In a small bowl, stir together the cardamom seeds and butter. Season with salt and pepper and refrigerate.

2. Bring a medium pot of salted water to a boil. Add the potatoes and cook until tender when pierced with the tip of a knife, 15 to 20 minutes. Drain the potatoes and keep warm.

3. In a small bowl, whisk together the sesame oil, lime juice, and soy sauce. Stir in the scallions, ginger, jalapeño, and sesame seeds. Set aside.

4. Bring a large pot of salted water to a boil. Add the bok choy and cook until the stalks soften and the leaves wilt, about 1 minute. Drain the bok choy and cool in a large bowl of ice water.

5. Heat the vegetable oil in a large sauté pan over high heat. Drain the bok choy and cook for 30 seconds on each side to sear. Keep warm.

6. In another large sauté pan over medium-high heat, melt the cardamom butter. Sear the tuna steaks, turning once, until they reach the desired doneness, 2 to 3 minutes per side for medium rare.

7. Place a quarter of the potatoes in the center of each of 4 plates. Toss the bok choy in half of the ginger-sesame vinaigrette, and place 4 bok choy halves on top of the potatoes on each plate. Place the tuna on top of the bok choy. Drizzle the remaining vinaigrette on top of the tuna and around the plate. Garnish with the cilantro and serve.

WHERE TO BUY

Specialty vegetables and sushi-grade tuna: Fox & Obel Food Market, 312-410-7301, www.fox-obel.com

chef's notes Aromatic cardamom is used to flavor dishes common to India, the Middle East, North Africa, and Scandinavia. It is available in the spice section of the supermarket, usually in pods from which you'll have to extract the seeds.

Toasting is the best way to bring out the essence of whole spices and seeds like cardamom. Simply heat a nonstick sauté pan over medium heat, add the spices, and cook, shaking the pan frequently, until you start to smell a fragrant aroma. Remove the seeds immediately from the pan to prevent them from burning.

arun's

4156 N. KEDZIE AVENUE   CHICAGO, IL 60618

773-539-1909   WWW.ARUNSTHAI.COM

You've never been to a Thai restaurant like this one, guaranteed. Possibly the finest Thai dining in the country, Arun's is chef and owner Arun Sampanthavivat's valentine to the complex cookery of his homeland—he was born and reared in Trang, a southern province in Thailand. Arun's serves an upscale twelve-course feast (priced at $85 at the time of this writing), which the chef customizes for each patron. Thai food, with its bold flavors of garlic, cilantro, chiles, and fish sauce, is served in six appetizers, four entrées, and two desserts, family-style. The attentive waitstaff gets a bead on every customer's adventurousness, tolerance for spice, allergies, and dislikes, and then the chef gets busy. Dishes might include lotus-shaped dumplings stuffed with shrimp and shallots, delicate fresh crab spring rolls, and tender, chilled pork satay salad perfumed with Thai basil and cilantro. Lobster tail may arrive with jumbo shrimp in garlic-ginger sauce, beef tenderloin in a red curry and peanut sauce flavored with star anise, and green curry chicken with Thai baby eggplant. Sticky rice topped with egg custard is a typical dessert. The wine list includes a number of Alsatian whites that pair perfectly with Thai food.

This recipe for pad thai is a simplified version of Thailand's most popular noodle dish. While all ingredients are available in Asian grocery stores, and sometimes the Asian section of the supermarket, a few simple substitutions make this dish easy to prepare. Use white vinegar instead of tamarind juice, omit the daikon and dried shrimp, and substitute scallions for garlic chives.

pad thai

4 cups thin rice noodles

½ cup fish sauce

¼ cup tamarind juice or white vinegar

¼ cup palm sugar or granulated sugar

5 teaspoons corn oil

1 teaspoon minced garlic

1 teaspoon minced shallot

¼ cup cooked shredded pork or chicken (leftovers are perfect)

¼ cup firm tofu, diced

¼ cup chopped cooked shrimp

3 large eggs, beaten

1 cup chicken broth

½ teaspoon paprika

6 scallions, cut into 1-inch pieces

1 cup fresh mung bean sprouts

1 lime

2 tablespoons finely chopped peanuts (optional)

Crushed red pepper flakes, to taste

SERVES 4

1. Soak the rice noodles in warm water to cover for 20 minutes. Drain well and set aside.

2. In a small saucepan, combine the fish sauce, tamarind juice, and sugar. Set over medium heat and cook, stirring occasionally, until the sauce thickens to a syrup, 6 to 8 minutes. Set aside.

3. In a wok or large sauté pan set over high heat, heat the oil. Add the garlic and shallot and cook, stirring, until fragrant, about 30 seconds. Add the pork, tofu, and shrimp. Cook, stirring, until heated through, about 2 minutes. Add the eggs and continue to stir until they begin to set.

4. Stir in the rice noodles. Stir in the broth and bring to a boil. Stir in the tamarind mixture and the paprika. Continue cooking until all ingredients are well mixed and heated through.

5. Stir in the scallions and bean sprouts and remove the wok from the heat. Transfer the pad thai to a platter, squeeze the lime over the top, garnish with the peanuts and red pepper flakes, and serve.

chef's notes Pad thai is a wildly popular dish, and if you can make it with authentic ingredients like tamarind juice and palm sugar (a dark, unrefined sugar), the flavor will be more authentically Thai. Tamarind juice, for example, has a mellower, sweeter flavor than white vinegar, which is distinctively sour.

Stir-frying is all about speed, and takes a little practice to get used to. But you can't beat it for putting a meal on the table in 15 minutes or less. One of the secrets to stir-frying is to have all your ingredients measured and on hand before you put your wok or pan on the fire.

and to drink

$ AV Trimbach Riesling, Alsace

$$ 2004 Pikes Riesling, The Merle Reserve, Australia

WHERE TO BUY

Tamarind, palm sugar, and other Thai ingredients:

Import Food, 888-618-8424, www.importfood.com

Temple of Thai, 877-811-8773, www.templeofthai.com

carlos'

429 TEMPLE AVENUE   HIGHLAND PARK, IL 60035

847-432-0770   WWW.CARLOS-RESTAURANT.COM

Located in an unassuming storefront in suburban Highland Park, Carlos', the intimate French restaurant owned by Debbie and Carlos Nieto, has been wooing and wowing North Shore diners since 1981. In truth, fans will drive for miles for a taste of chef Ramiro Velasquez's inventive contemporary French menu. And no wonder. He certainly has a way with foie gras, serving it ingeniously both hot and cold, either pan-seared with grenadine-infused caramelized onion or as a cold medallion perched atop banana bread with vanilla syrup. Then there's the John Dory with "scales" of crispy potatoes and sun-dried tomato risotto. Both the degustation and à la carte menus are well complemented by the 17,000-bottle wine cellar. Jackets are required for gentlemen, adding to the special-occasion aura that surrounds this inviting dining experience.

Chef Velasquez uses a pastry bag to stuff these rigatonis with goat cheese. To save time, simply dot a layer of rigatoni with the cheese mix, then repeat, much as you would put together a baked ziti. He also shaves black truffle into the goat cheese stuffing. We've omitted this pricey ingredient but offer a source for truffles if you'd like to make the dish to the chef's exact recipe.

rigatoni stuffed with goat cheese
and sauce espagnole (brown sauce)

SERVES 6

Sauce Espagnole

1 tablespoon vegetable oil

½ pound beef chuck, cut into ½-inch cubes

2 carrots, chopped

½ yellow onion, chopped

2 stalks celery, chopped

2 tablespoons tomato paste

2 plum tomatoes, chopped

¾ cup dry red wine

1 bay leaf

1 teaspoon dried thyme

1 teaspoon black peppercorns

4 cups beef broth

Coarse salt and freshly ground black pepper, to taste

Rigatoni

1 pound rigatoni pasta

1 cup (4 ounces) crumbled goat cheese

½ cup (4 ounces) cream cheese, softened

2 tablespoons chopped leaves from fresh herbs of your choice (chives, tarragon, thyme)

Coarse salt and freshly ground black pepper, to taste

1 tablespoon olive oil

1. To make the sauce espagnole, in a large saucepan, heat the oil over medium heat. Add the beef and cook, stirring frequently, until it is browned on all sides, about 5 minutes. Remove from the pan with a slotted spoon and set aside.

2. Add the carrots, onion, and celery to the pan the beef cooked in. Cook, stirring, until browned, about 6 minutes. Stir in the tomato paste and chopped tomatoes and continue cooking until the tomatoes release their juices.

3. Stir in the red wine, scraping the bottom of the pan to release any browned bits. Return the beef to the pan and add the bay leaf, thyme, and peppercorns. Bring to a boil, lower the heat, and simmer, uncovered, until the wine is reduced by half.

4. Stir in the beef broth and bring to a boil. Reduce the heat and cook at a bare simmer, uncovered, stirring occasionally, until the liquid is reduced to about 3 cups, about 45 minutes.

5. Pour the sauce through a fine-mesh sieve into a bowl. Discard the solids. Season the sauce to taste with salt and pepper and set aside.

6. To make the rigatoni, cook the pasta according to package directions. Drain well and place in a large bowl of cold water until cool.

7. In a small bowl, beat the goat cheese and cream cheese together until smooth. Fold in 1 tablespoon of the herbs. Season to taste with salt and pepper.

8. Preheat the oven to 400°F.

9. Drain the rigatoni well. In a large sauté pan over medium heat, heat the olive oil and sauté the rigatoni until it starts to brown. Put a layer of rigatoni in a 13 x 9-inch pan, followed by spoons of the cheese and a layer of sauce, then repeat until you have 2 layers, or until all ingredients are used.

10. Bake until heated through and bubbling, about 20 minutes. Garnish the pasta with the remaining fresh herbs and serve.

and to drink

$ 2001 Bricco Mondalino
Barbera Monferrato, Piedmont,
Italy
$$ 2000 Ferrando Carema
"Etichetto" Nebbiolo,
Piedmont, Italy

chef's notes Sauce espagnole, also known simply as brown sauce, is one of the five "mother sauces" that make up the foundation of French cookery. In the early 1800s, Antonin Carême, one of the founding fathers of French "grande cuisine," created the methodology by which hundreds of sauces would be categorized, with infinite variations. Learn the basics and you'll be able to prepare hundreds of recipes like a pro. The five mother sauces are béchamel sauce (white), velouté sauce (blond), brown (demi-glace) or espagnole sauce, hollandaise sauce (butter), and tomato sauce (red).

WHERE TO BUY

Truffles: Earthy Delights, 800-637-4709, www.earthy.com

blackbird

619 W RANDOLPH STREET   CHICAGO, IL 60661

312-715-0708   WWW.BLACKBIRDRESTAURANT.COM

Blackbird, an eatery in the West Loop section of the city named for the French slang term for a Merlot grape, is leading a growing cadre of independent restaurants that have turned Chicago into more than just a steakhouse town. Delivering a peerless approach to market fresh New America cuisine, chef Paul Kahan delivers contrasting flavors and the vibrant tastes of fresh seasonal ingredients from local farms in a handsome, minimalist setting. Winner of the James Beard Foundation's award for best chef of the Midwest in 2004, Chef Kahan offers cooking rooted in both French and American classics. A few sample menu items include a Carr Valley Marisa cheese salad with black Mission figs, fennel, favas, spring radishes, honey, and lavender, or the seared loin of Wilderness Lodge elk with favas, kohlrabi, sour cherries, and vanilla. Avec, a wine bar located next door to Blackbird, serves wines and accompaniments from southern France, northern Italy, and the Mediterranean coast of Spain.

Bouillabaisse (BOOL-yuh-BAYZE) is a traditional fish stew from Provence.

bouillabaisse

with edamame and tomatoes

SERVES 4

1 tablespoon extra-virgin olive oil

5 cloves garlic, thinly sliced

1 medium onion, halved and thinly sliced

1 bulb fennel, halved and thinly sliced

2 pounds small red new potatoes, cut into ¼-inch-thick slices

1 bay leaf

Pinch saffron

One 14½-ounce can diced tomatoes

2 cups frozen or fresh edamame

4 cups clam juice

4 cups water

2 tablespoons Pernod

2 teaspoons sriracha (Thai chili sauce)

¼ cup chopped fresh flat-leaf parsley

Leaves from 1 sprig fresh thyme, chopped, or 1 teaspoon dried thyme

Coarse salt and freshly ground black pepper, to taste

1½ pounds white-fleshed fish fillets (such as whitefish, pike, bass, or cod), cut into bite-size chunks

16 mussels, scrubbed (discard any that are open)

16 littleneck clams, scrubbed (discard any that are open)

1 pound medium shrimp, peeled and deveined

1. In a large stockpot, heat the oil over medium heat. Add the garlic, onion, fennel, potatoes, and bay leaf and stir until all are coated with the oil. Turn the heat to low, cover the pot, and cook, stirring every 5 minutes, until the vegetables are soft, about 10 minutes.

2. Uncover the pot, raise the heat to medium-high, and stir in the saffron, tomatoes, and edamame. Cook, uncovered, stirring frequently, until the edamame are tender, about 5 minutes. Add the clam juice, water, Pernod, sriracha, parsley, and thyme. Season lightly with salt and pepper.

3. When ready to serve, bring the soup to a boil and add the fish, mussels, clams, and shrimp. Simmer until the clams and mussels open and the shrimp and mussels are cooked through, about 5 minutes. Discard any mussels or clams that don't open, season the soup with salt and pepper to taste, and serve.

chef's notes Both edamame (fresh soybeans) and sriracha (Thai chili sauce) are available in most supermarkets. Look for fresh edamame packaged in the produce section (you'll need to shell them if they're in the pods), or find shelled, frozen edamame in the freezer case. Sriracha chili sauce—an addictive blend of red chiles, garlic, and sugar—can be found in the Asian foods aisle of most supermarkets.

At Blackbird, Chef Kahan makes a fish fumet (foo-MAY), or concentrated stock, for the foundation of this bouillabaisse. This gives the dish a greater depth of flavor than just using clam juice and water, but the abbreviated recipe still yields delicious results. Try making this stock at home when you have a little extra time. The rich and wonderful flavor it lends to soups and sauces will be ample reward for your extra trouble. Ask at your local fish store for fish bones; if they have some you'll often get them for free.

Chef Paul Kahan's Fish Fumet

• • •

2 tablespoons unsalted butter

3 pounds fish bones from white-fleshed fish (do not use heads), rinsed

1 cup white wine

1 small bulb fennel, with fronds, coarsely chopped

1 onion, coarsely chopped

1 stalk celery, coarsely chopped

1 carrot, coarsely chopped

2 cloves garlic, smashed

1 orange, halved

$\frac{1}{2}$ teaspoon fennel seeds

5 black peppercorns

1 bay leaf

$2\frac{1}{2}$ quarts (10 cups) cold water

1. Melt the butter over high heat in a 5-quart saucepan. Add the bones and cook, stirring, until they are opaque. Add the wine, bring to a boil, reduce the heat, and simmer for 5 minutes.

2. Add the remaining ingredients, bring to a boil, reduce the heat, and simmer 5 minutes more. Turn off the heat and let the mixture sit for 5 minutes.

3. Line a colander with cheesecloth and set it over a large bowl. Ladle the stock away from the bones and pour it through the cheesecloth. (This prevents clouding the broth.) Discard the solids left in the pan. Use the fumet immediately, or keep refrigerated for up to 2 days or frozen for up to 3 months.

and to drink

$ 2003 Brick House Gamay Noir, Oregon

$$ 2000 Chateau Montelena Estate Zinfandel, California

WHERE TO BUY

Sriracha:

Temple of Thai, 877-811-8773, www.templeofthai.com

Thai Grocery, 773-561-5345

everest

440 SOUTH LASALLE STREET   CHICAGO, IL 60605

312-663-8920   WWW.LEYE.COM

Everest is truly a towering achievement in fine French cuisine. Located on the fortieth floor of the Chicago Stock Exchange building, the seventy-five-seat Everest is known for both its spectacular view and its superb cuisine, directed by chef-owner Jean Joho. "Though the restaurant has a spectacular, unobstructed cityscape as a backdrop, the food is what commands attention," said *Chicago* magazine, which has voted Everest four stars every year since it opened in 1984. Joho has earned consistent accolades for his approachable French food, which is perfectly prepared but never stuffy. His signature touch is to set aristocratic and working-class ingredients side by side. "I like to blend noble ingredients like caviar and foie gras with simple ingredients like potatoes and turnips," he says. "The union of simple and noble makes for unique flavor combinations." The à la carte menu offers several Everest favorites, including creamy carnaroli risotto topped with 24-karat gold leaf and poached tenderloin of beef. For dessert, the over-the-top "fantasy of chocolate" lives up to its name, with five different cocoa pairings keeping company together on one beautiful plate.

This easy version of ratatouille substitutes chicken breasts for the guinea hen breasts used at Everest. Ratatouille (ra-tuh-TOO-ee) is a popular dish in the Provence region of France made with eggplant, tomatoes, garlic, herbs, onions, zucchini, and peppers, all simmered in fragrant olive oil.

72 IMPRESS FOR LESS!

sautéed chicken breast
ratatouille

SERVES 6

10 tablespoons extra-virgin
olive oil

2 bay leaves

1 sprig fresh thyme, or
$\frac{1}{2}$ teaspoon dried

3 cloves garlic, minced

6 boneless, skinless
chicken breast halves
(about 4 ounces each)

6 tablespoons ($\frac{3}{4}$ stick)
unsalted butter, softened

1 tablespoon chopped fresh
basil, or 1 teaspoon dried

1 small ($\frac{1}{2}$ pound) zucchini,
cut into $\frac{1}{2}$-inch dice

1 large ($\frac{1}{2}$ pound) yellow
squash, cut into $\frac{1}{2}$-inch dice

1 green bell pepper,
cut into $\frac{1}{2}$-inch dice

1 red bell pepper,
cut into $\frac{1}{2}$-inch dice

$\frac{1}{2}$ small eggplant,
cut into $\frac{1}{2}$-inch dice

$\frac{1}{2}$ onion, finely diced

One 14$\frac{1}{2}$-ounce can diced
tomatoes, drained

Coarse salt and freshly
ground black pepper,
to taste

1 teaspoon chopped fresh
flat-leaf parsley,
or $\frac{1}{2}$ teaspoon dried

1 teaspoon chopped
fresh thyme,
or $\frac{1}{2}$ teaspoon dried

1 cup Riesling or other
white wine

(continued)

1. In a large nonreactive bowl, combine 4 tablespoons of the olive oil, the bay leaves, thyme sprig, and 1 clove of the minced garlic. Add the chicken, turn to coat, and refrigerate for at least an hour and overnight if possible.

2. Remove the chicken breasts from the oil, discard the oil, and pat the breasts dry with paper towels. Using a small sharp knife, make an incision in the thickest part of the side of each breast, creating a small pocket. In a small bowl, stir together the butter and basil. Set aside a tablespoon of the butter mixture, and divide the rest among the chicken breasts, spooning it into each pocket. Set the chicken aside.

3. Preheat the oven to 375°F.

4. In a large, heavy sauté pan over medium heat, heat 2 tablespoons of the remaining oil. Add the zucchini, squash, bell peppers, eggplant, and onion and cook until softened, about 5 minutes. Remove the vegetables from the pan and drain on paper towels to remove excess oil.

5. Wipe out the pan, add 2 more tablespoons of the olive oil to it, and place over medium heat. Add the tomatoes and remaining 2 cloves minced garlic and cook, stirring, 5 minutes. Return the cooked vegetables to the pan. Season to taste with salt and pepper, stir in the parsley and thyme, and simmer gently for 5 minutes more.

6. Heat the remaining 2 tablespoons olive oil in a heavy skillet over medium-high heat. Season the chicken with salt and pepper and cook on both sides until golden brown, about 8 minutes. Transfer the pan to the oven and bake until the chicken is cooked through, about 5 minutes.

7. Transfer the chicken to a plate and cover with foil to keep warm. Return the pan to the stove top, place over high heat, and add the wine. Use a wooden spoon to stir, scraping up any brown bits from the bot-

2 cups chicken broth

6 sprigs fresh chervil or thyme

tom of the pan, and simmer until the wine is reduced by half. Add the broth and simmer until reduced by half again, about 15 minutes.

8. Strain the sauce through a fine-mesh sieve. Whisk in the reserved tablespoon basil butter, season to taste with salt and pepper, and keep warm.

9. To serve, spoon the ratatouille onto 6 warmed plates. Slice each chicken breast into 4 pieces, slicing on the bias, and arrange the chicken over the ratatouille. Spoon the sauce on top and garnish with a sprig of fresh chervil.

and to drink

$ 2002 Broadley Vineyards Willamette Valley Pinot Noir, Oregon

$$ 2001 Morgan Pinot Noir, Monterey, California

chef's notes   The guinea hen, used by chef Joho for this recipe, is a cousin to the pheasant. The best guinea hens are farm raised on a whole-grain diet without the addition of any hormones or steroids. They have 50 percent less fat than chicken. A whole bird is typically $2\frac{1}{2}$ to 3 pounds.

WHERE TO BUY

Guinea hens: D'Artagnan, 800-327-8246, www.dartagnan.com

naha

500 NORTH CLARK STREET   CHICAGO, IL 60610

312-321-6242   WWW.NAHA-CHICAGO.COM

Chef Carrie Nahabedian returned to her native Chicago in 2000 from Four Seasons Beverly Hills to open Naha—Nahabedian's family nickname—with cousin and managing partner Michael Nahabedian. With the help of another family member, architect Tom Nahabedian of Collaboration, a Beverly Hills design firm, Naha was transformed into a clean, contemporary space adorned with locally commissioned artwork. Chef Nahabedian's cooking style combines her Armenian roots and the California lifestyle she enjoyed while working on the left coast. That influence is clear both in her use of seasonal ingredients and in Naha's wine list, which includes many selections from Sonoma, Napa, and Central Coast and some thirty wines by the glass. Start with dishes like tartare of ahi tuna topped with caviar and duck liver with roasted preserved quince, and for the main event, roasted squab and foie gras with black Mission figs and Thompson grapes or Barnegat Light sea scallops scented with vanilla bean, citrus, and spices. The restaurant's cozy front lounge offers a special menu of meze, Mediterranean small dishes, including flat bread with tomatoes, goat cheese, and artichokes; lamb kebabs; and feta cheese–phyllo triangles made from the chef's mother's recipe.

marinated roast leg of lamb
with beans, tomatoes, garlic, and olives

20 cloves garlic, peeled, plus 10 cloves garlic, peeled and chopped

1 cup plus 4 tablespoons olive oil

1/4 pound thick-sliced bacon, cut into 1-inch pieces

1 medium onion, finely diced

Two 15-ounce cans great Northern beans, drained and rinsed

4 sprigs fresh thyme

1 bunch fresh parsley, leaves and stems

1 bay leaf

4 cups chicken broth

One 6- to 8-pound semi-boneless leg of lamb

Coarse salt and freshly ground black pepper, to taste

Leaves from 2 bunches mint, torn

1 lemon

1 cup oil-packed sun-dried tomatoes, drained

1 cup pitted kalamata olives, rinsed and halved lengthwise

1. Place 20 garlic cloves in a small, heavy saucepan and add 1 cup of the olive oil. Cook over medium-low heat until the oil begins to simmer and the garlic is softened but still firm enough to keep its shape, about 15 minutes. Remove the pan from the heat and let the garlic cool in the oil. (The garlic can be cooked and refrigerated up to a week.)

2. Place the bacon in a large, heavy saucepan and cook over high heat until it just begins to crisp. Add the onion and cook, stirring, until the onion softens, about 5 minutes. Add 4 garlic cloves, the beans, sprigs of thyme, parsley, and bay leaf. Stir until well mixed. Add 2 tablespoons of the remaining olive oil and the chicken broth and bring to a boil. Cook until the beans are very tender and the flavors blended, about 10 minutes. (Do not overcook or the beans will be mushy.) Remove from the heat and let cool.

3. Meanwhile, preheat the oven to 375°F.

4. With a sharp knife, remove any thick excess fat from the lamb. Season the lamb with salt and pepper and then rub it with the remaining 2 tablespoons olive oil. Place the lamb in a heavy roasting pan and rub with half of the mint and half of the chopped garlic. With the tip of a paring knife, gently jab the lamb in various spots, making little slits, and divide the remaining chopped garlic into the slits throughout the meat.

5. Roll the lemon on your countertop, pressing down firmly with the palm of your hand (this produces the maximum juice). Slice the lemon in half and squeeze the juice over the top of the lamb.

6. Place the lamb in the oven and roast until it reaches the desired doneness, or until an instant-read thermometer inserted in the thickest part of the leg but not touching the bone registers 130°F for medium rare, 140°F for medium. This will take about 1 hour and 30 minutes. Baste the lamb frequently with the juices that accumulate in the pan.

7. Remove the lamb from the roasting pan and let rest for 10 minutes on a cutting board. Slice the lamb and transfer to a serving platter or individual plates. Place the sun-dried tomatoes around the lamb and sprinkle with the olives. With a slotted spoon, spoon the beans over the meat. Bring the juice the beans cooked in to a boil, add the remaining mint, and infuse for a couple of minutes. Spoon the cooked garlic on top of the beans and drizzle with the mint sauce.

chef's notes Naha's version of this recipe uses dried flageolet (flah-joh-LAY) beans, truly the caviar of beans. Flageolets are small, tender kidney beans that are very popular in French cooking. They range from creamy white to light green in color. We substituted great Northern beans in this recipe. Flageolets, like all dried beans, must be rinsed under running water and picked through for any debris or blemished beans. Dried beans should soak in water for several hours or overnight to soften before cooking. To soak beans, place them in a large saucepan or bowl and cover with 3 inches of water. Let stand, covered, for 6 hours or overnight. Do not soak beans longer than 12 hours or they may begin to ferment. Drain beans before cooking.

For the quick-soak method, place the beans in the pan in which they will be cooked. Cover with 3 inches of water. Bring to a boil and boil for 2 minutes. Remove from the heat; cover and let stand for 1 to 2 hours. Proceed with the recipe.

and to drink
$ 2003 Bergerac Rouge
Chateau Calabre, France
$$ 2000 Chateau Picard
Saint-Estèphe, France

WHERE TO BUY
Flageolets: Fox & Obel Food Market, 312-410-7301, www.fox-obel.com

spiaggia

1 MAGNIFICENT MILE   980 NORTH MICHIGAN AVENUE, LEVEL 2

CHICAGO, IL 60611   WWW.LEVYRESTAURANTS.COM

Spiaggia has been wowing critics and Chicagoans alike for more than twenty years, delivering what many agree is the very best Italian fine dining experience in town. Winner of the James Beard Foundation Award for best chef in the Midwest in 2005, chef and partner Tony Mantuano defines Spiaggia with his inspired interpretation of authentic Italian cuisine. The restaurant's name, which means "beach" in Italian, is a nod to its spectacular view over Lake Michigan and the Oak Street Beach. From its towering forty-foot windows to the custom-designed Italian chandeliers and champagne and black marble color scheme, Spiagga is a knockout. Then there's chef Mantuano's seasonally driven food, available à la carte or in a seven-course degustation menu. Examples of what might await include carpaccio of smoked Sicilian swordfish, wood-roasted loin of rabbit wrapped in lightly smoked pancetta, Venetian spaghetti with Maine lobster, pheasant-stuffed ravioli, and pumpkin risotto. Spiaggia's signature dessert is the baba all'arancia, a cake soaked in orange liqueur and served with orange cream, a perfect ending to a perfect meal.

This gnocchi recipe is a Mantuano family favorite for the traditional Italian dumpling made from potatoes. Don't be intimidated—gnocchi are not difficult to make. The key is to work quickly while the dough is just cool enough to handle. Also remember not to overwork the dough or it will become pasty, making for heavy dumplings. You can also buy gnocchi frozen at Italian gourmet stores, supermarkets, and by mail order (see Where to Buy, page 80).

gnocchi with braised beef

Beef

2 pounds chuck or other stewing beef, cut into 1-inch chunks

Coarse salt and freshly ground black pepper

5 tablespoons extra-virgin olive oil

2 onions, coarsely chopped

2 cloves garlic, crushed

2 cups dry white wine

1 cup canned plum tomatoes with their juices

8 cups chicken broth

4 sprigs fresh thyme

1 large sprig fresh rosemary

Gnocchi

2 russet potatoes (about 1 pound)

2 large egg yolks, beaten

Coarse salt and freshly ground white pepper

2 cups unbleached all-purpose flour

Grated Parmigiano-Reggiano, for serving

1. To make the beef, preheat the oven to 350ºF.

2. Season the beef generously with salt and pepper. In a large, deep ovenproof sauté pan with a tightly fitting lid or a Dutch oven, heat 3 tablespoons of the olive oil over medium-high heat. Add half the beef and brown on all sides, about 6 minutes. Remove the meat to a plate and repeat with the remaining meat. Set aside.

3. Reduce the heat to medium and heat the remaining 2 tablespoons olive oil in the same pan. Add the onions and garlic and cook, stirring frequently, until the onions begin to brown, 4 to 5 minutes. Add the wine and bring to a simmer, scraping the browned bits off the bottom of the pan. Simmer until the wine is reduced by half, about 5 minutes.

4. Stir in the tomatoes, broth, thyme, and rosemary. Return the beef to the pan, nestling it into the sauce, and bring back to a simmer. Cover the skillet tightly with a lid, transfer to the oven, and bake until the beef is very tender, 45 to 60 minutes.

5. Using a slotted spoon, transfer the beef to a platter. Discard the herb sprigs from the sauce. Strain the sauce into a bowl through a fine-mesh sieve and return to the pan. Bring to a boil over high heat, lower the heat, and simmer until it is thick enough to coat the back of a spoon, 20 to 30 minutes. Season to taste with salt and pepper, return the beef to the reduced sauce, and keep warm until ready to serve.

6. While the beef is cooking, make the gnocchi. Prick the potatoes all over with the tines of a fork and bake along with the beef until very tender, about 1 hour. While they are still hot (protect your hands with a folded kitchen towel), peel the potatoes and mash or pass them through a potato ricer into a bowl.

7. Spread the potatoes into a thin, even layer on the work surface without pressing them or compacting them. Let cool slightly.

8. When cool enough to handle, pour the egg yolks over the potatoes and sprinkle with a generous pinch of salt and white pepper. Toss the eggs with the potatoes and fold in the flour until combined and you have a smooth but slightly sticky dough. It should take no longer than 3 minutes to work the flour into the potato mixture; remember, the longer the dough is kneaded, the more flour it will require and the heavier it will become.

9. Pull off pieces of the dough and roll into ropes about ½ inch thick. Cut the ropes into 1-inch-long dumplings. Roll each dumpling gently in the palm of your hand, first into a ball, and then taper the ends so that it resembles a football. Place the gnocchi on a lightly floured cloth so that they are not touching and let dry for 15 minutes.

10. Bring a large pot of salted water to a boil. Add the gnocchi; they will sink, then rise to the surface as they cook. Allow them to cook 3 minutes after they rise to the surface, then drain. Add the gnocchi to the pan with the beef. Place over low heat for 1 to 2 minutes to allow the gnocchi to marry with the meat and sauce. Season with salt and pepper to taste.

11. Divide the pasta among warmed individual plates and spoon more sauce over the top. Serve immediately with Parmesan on the side.

and to drink

$ 2003 Promessa Negroamaro Puglia, Italy

$$ 2001 Cascina Val del Prete Barbera d'Alba "Carolina," Italy

chef's notes Gnocchi can be frozen for up to 1 month. Place the gnocchi on a sheet pan lined with wax or parchment paper and dusted with flour. Place the pan in the freezer until hard, about 20 minutes. Pack them in plastic bags and freeze until ready to cook. Bring 6 quarts salted water to a boil. Shake any excess flour from the frozen gnocchi, then stir gently as you add them to the boiling water. It is important that the water return to a boil as soon as possible; cover the pot if necessary. Cook 3 minutes. Drain the gnocchi as described above and serve according to the specific recipe.

WHERE TO BUY

Frozen gnocchi:

Alfonso Gourmet Pasta, 800-370-7278, www.alfonsogourmetpasta.com

Trader Joe's, multiple locations, 800-SHOP-TJS, www.traderjoes.com

tru

676 N ST CLAIR STREET   CHICAGO, IL 60611

312-202-0001   WWW.TRURESTAURANT.COM

Chef Rick Tramonto calls himself a blend of mad scientist and magician. And it's true that the culinary elixirs he conjures up at Tru are pure enchantment. Tramonto, who owns the restaurant with pastry chef Gale Gand, offers three, seven, or nine courses of inspired Mediterranean-influenced French cuisine. The food is simply exquisite, with presentations that are downright stunning. Case in point, the caviar service is offered on the steps of a miniature staircase of sparkling glass. A trio of tartare is served atop a fish bowl populated by a Japanese fighting fish. And roasted garlic soup with tomato basil chutney arrives in a gilded espresso cup. A fancier version of this risotto recipe, made with lobster, is presented on a square of marble. Gand's desserts are equally magical, including a creative pineapple "carpaccio" and a deconstructed lemon meringue pie that is pleasingly tart. Tru has won many awards over the years, perhaps most notably one of *Wine Spectator*'s Grand Awards, of which only four are handed out worldwide.

This recipe is adapted from *Tru: A Cookbook from the Legendary Chicago Restaurant* (Random House, 2004). We've substituted dried mushrooms for the truffle and shrimp for the lobster tail.

mushroom risotto
with shrimp and summer vegetables

SERVES 6

3 tablespoons
unsalted butter

1 cup sliced wild mushrooms

Coarse salt and freshly
ground black pepper,
to taste

3 tablespoons heavy cream

2 tablespoons dried
porcini mushrooms

16 cups (4 quarts)
vegetable broth

1 bulb fennel, thinly sliced

¼ cup haricots verts
or green beans, cut into
½-inch pieces

¼ cup fava or lima beans,
fresh or frozen

¼ cup corn kernels,
fresh or frozen

½ white onion, minced

1 clove garlic, minced

3 sprigs fresh thyme

1 pound (2⅓ cups)
arborio rice

1 pound peeled, cooked
shrimp, diced

½ cup grated Parmesan
cheese

2 plum tomatoes,
seeded and diced

1 tablespoon finely chopped
fresh flat-leaf parsley

1. In a small sauté pan, melt 1 tablespoon of the butter over medium-high heat. Add the mushrooms and cook, stirring, until softened and fragrant, about 3 minutes. Season with salt and pepper to taste and set aside.

2. With a whisk or handheld mixer, whip the cream until stiff peaks form. Cover and refrigerate until ready to use.

3. Place the porcini mushrooms in a small cup and cover with boiling water. Let sit 20 minutes, then drain and finely chop the mushrooms. Set aside.

4. In a large saucepan, bring the broth to a simmer. Add the fennel and green beans to the broth, along with the fresh fava beans and corn (if using frozen, don't add it at this point). Cook 2 minutes. Remove the vegetables from the broth with a slotted spoon and set them aside. Leave the broth in the pot over low heat for use in the risotto.

5. In a deep, heavy sauté pan over medium heat, melt 1 tablespoon of the remaining butter. Add the onion, garlic, and thyme and cook, stirring, until the onion is translucent, about 2 minutes. Remove and discard the thyme. Add the rice and stir until completely coated with the butter.

6. Add a ladleful of the hot broth and cook, stirring, until the rice absorbs all of the stock. Add another ladleful of stock and continue cooking in the same manner, adding broth as needed and stirring very frequently, until the rice is tender but still has a bit of crunch, about 25 minutes.

7. Stir in the wild mushrooms, fennel, green beans, lima beans, corn, porcini mushrooms, shrimp, cheese, and the remaining 1 tablespoon butter. Fold in the tomatoes, parsley, and whipped cream. Season to taste with salt and pepper and serve immediately.

and to drink
$ 2003 Di Bruno "Sanford and Benedict" Santa Maria Pinot Grigio, California
$$ 1996 Marc Colin, St-Aubin 1er Cru La Chatenière, France

chef's notes Risotto is a traditional Italian rice dish, made creamy from stirring frequently while cooking. You need fresh lobster to replicate Tru's risotto recipe, which uses lobster instead of shrimp. Most supermarket seafood departments will cook the lobsters for you. If you bring them home live, plunge the whole lobsters headfirst into a large pot of rapidly boiling, salted water. Cover and boil for 8 to 12 minutes, or until bright red and cooked through. Using a pair of long-handled tongs, remove the lobster from the pot and immediately submerge in cold water. Drain the lobster and allow to cool. Chop or break off the tail and remove the meat. Reserve the claw meat for another use.

WHERE TO BUY

Arborio rice: Gourmet Pasta Cheese, 800-386-9198, www.pastacheese.com
Wild and porcini mushrooms: Earthy Delights, 800-637-4709, www.earthy.com

topolobampo

445 NORTH CLARK STREET   CHICAGO, IL 60610

312-661-1434   WWW.FRONTERAKITCHENS.COM

Chef Rick Bayless is almost single-handedly responsible for convincing Americans that Mexico is home to one of the world's great cuisines. Bayless, host of PBS's *Mexico: One Plate at a Time* and author of five Mexican cookbooks, takes diners on a journey from Sonora to Yucatán, creating authentic dishes that demonstrate the country's remarkably diverse culinary style. His restaurants, the more casual Frontera Grill, opened in 1987, and the dressier Topolobampo (or Topolo to the locals), have spearheaded a national awakening to the breadth and refinement of true Mexican cooking.

Topolobampo, chosen by *Esquire* as one of the top new restaurants in America in 1991, boasts a hip South-of-the-border ambiance, with colorful artwork, blue-velvet curtains, and a brick-tile floor. The plates are works of art too, with their beautiful ingredients, often organic and custom grown for the restaurants by local producers. Try the boldly flavored tortilla soup, the salad sampler that includes marinated, shredded cactus spiked with habanero, and succulent chili-marinated pork. Bayless, a huge proponent of the slow food and sustainable agriculture movement, doled out nearly $80,000 in 2004 through his not-for-profit Frontera Farmer Foundation, giving grants to seven recipients to improve family farms.

The addition of serrano chiles, lime juice, and cilantro is what gives this salad a Mexican twist. Chef Bayless originally conceived this salad for Topolobampo, but it shows up at one time or another at all of his restaurants, including Frontera Grill. If the serrano chile isn't available, you can substitute a jalapeño.

topolobampo
caesar salad

SERVES 4 TO 6

1 cup extra-virgin olive oil

1½ tablespoons sherry vinegar

4 teaspoons Worcestershire sauce

1 fresh serrano or jalapeño chile, stemmed, seeded, and halved

Zest from 1½ limes

1 large egg

½ teaspoon salt, plus more to taste

2 medium heads of romaine lettuce, tough outer leaves removed, inner leaves rinsed and dried

½ cup chopped fresh cilantro

¾ cup finely crumbled Mexican queso anejo cheese or coarsely grated Parmesan cheese

2 cups store-bought croutons

1. Combine ½ cup of the olive oil, the vinegar, Worcestershire, chile, lime zest, egg, and ½ teaspoon salt in a food processor or blender and process 1 full minute. Scrape into a small bowl and slowly whisk in the remaining ½ cup olive oil. Taste and season with more salt if necessary.

2. In a large salad bowl, combine the lettuce, cilantro, and half of the cheese. Add ⅓ cup of the dressing (save the rest of the dressing for another use) and toss to coat. Divide among salad plates, top with the remaining cheese and the croutons, and serve.

chef's notes Queso anejo is a hard Mexican grating cheese that's coated with red chile paste. You can replace the lettuce in this recipe with sliced tomatoes. Drizzle them with some of the dressing and sprinkle with the cilantro, cheese, and croutons. An alternative to croutons is slices of grilled bread smeared with goat cheese.

and to drink

$ 2004 Hiedler Grüner Veltliner Löss, Austria

$$ 2003 Lucien Crochet Sancerre Le Chene, France

WHERE TO BUY

Queso anejo and other Mexican ingredients:

Casa Del Pueblo, 312-421-4640

Chile Guy, 800-869-9218, www.thechileguy.com

El Original Supermercado Cardenas, 773-525-5610

Jimenez Enterprises, Inc., 773-235-0999

Cheese: Specialty Cheese Company, Inc., 800-367-1711 x22, www.specialcheese.com

los angeles

laid back and ready to eat in L.CA.

Home to movie stars, palm trees, and perpetual sunshine, Los Angeles is also the stomping ground of those seeking some of the best restaurants and chefs in America. Wolfgang Puck, for one, has parlayed his Spago success into nationwide name recognition with a chain of restaurants and a packaged food business. And with the entrenchment of the contemporary California cooking style that Puck helped popularize, innovation has become an institution here, ensuring that you'll almost always find something new to eat in laid-back Los Angeles.

Unparalleled dining options continue to open up as a result of immigration from Central America, the Near East, Southeast Asia, and elsewhere. One consequence is that even going out for standard Mexican cooking is now an outdated concept. These days savvy diners seek out distinctive regional cuisines like Mexico's Jaliscan, Sonoran, and Oaxacan. Culinary diversity has spread far beyond immigrant neighborhoods. One of the city's best Indian restaurants is in Pasadena; first-rate Oaxacans have opened on the city's Westside; and several Hong Kong–style seafood houses have found homes far west of the San Gabriel Valley.

In this culinary melting pot, chefs don't have to look far to find the once-exotic ingredients that have become staples of contemporary cuisine in Los Angeles. Wasabi, lemongrass, phyllo pastry, bok choy, ginger, and Fuyu persimmons are just a few of the products now appearing regularly on the menus of the city's top restaurants.

California cuisine encompasses a wide range of cooking styles, but one element remains constant: The best chefs in town use only the freshest and finest ingredients, most locally sourced. Fortunately for them, thanks to California's rich agricultural legacy, they have plenty to work with.

In this chapter, we visit ten of the best kitchens in town, from the posh Belvedere in the Peninsula Beverly Hills to Valentino, hailed by former *New York Times* food critic Ruth Reichl as the best Italian restaurant in the United States. You'll love executive chef Ezio Gamba's recipe for rigatoni with eggplant, tomato, and broccoli rabe.

campanile restaurant

624 S. LA BREA AVENUE   LOS ANGELES, CA 90036

323-938-1447   WWW.CAMPANILERESTAURANT.COM

Housed in a rustically elegant space built by Charlie Chaplin in 1929, the building was adapted for chef and owner Mark Peel and his former business partners, pastry chef Nancy Silverton and wine buyer Manfred Kranki, and opened in 1989 as Campanile and La Brea Bakery. Reminiscent of a picturesque Mediterranean village, complete with a bell tower (*campanile* in Italian) and a court-yard with a bubbling fountain, the complex is home to chef Peel's earthy French- and Italian-influenced cuisine. Peel, who has worked with Wolfgang Puck and Alice Waters and earned multiple James Beard nominations, relies heavily on local and sustainable produce, meats, and fish, working closely with farms, including Campbell Farms in Sonoma County. A few of his specialties include grilled wild king salmon with roasted cauliflower and red onion, and veal scaloppine with sautéed porcini mushrooms and Marsala wine.

In all of his cooking, as this dish demonstrates, chef Peel never obscures an ingredient's true nature with fussy sauces or over-the-top presentation. His rosemary-charred leg of lamb is a match made in heaven: roasted lamb and bundles of fresh rosemary. Even if the rosemary didn't impart a wonderful flavor to the meat, the intoxicating aroma coming from the oven would be reason enough to use it in this quantity.

Have the butcher remove the small bone from the leg of lamb to make slicing easier, or use a boneless leg of lamb.

rosemary charred
leg of lamb

SERVES 6 TO 8

One 4-pound leg of lamb, trimmed of all but a thin layer of fat

3 large cloves garlic, thinly sliced

Olive oil

Coarse salt and coarsely ground black pepper, to taste

6 to 8 bunches rosemary sprigs

1. Using the tip of a paring knife, make 1-inch-long slits all over the lamb and insert a garlic slice into each slit. Rub the lamb well with olive oil and coat generously with salt and pepper. Wrap securely with plastic and set aside for several hours, or refrigerate overnight.

2. When ready to cook, preheat the oven to 500ºF.

3. Heat a large ovenproof skillet or heavy pan over medium-high heat. Add the lamb and brown it on all sides. Remove the lamb to a platter and pour off all but 1 tablespoon of fat. Cover the bottom of the pan with a bed of rosemary and place the lamb on top. Cover the lamb with more rosemary.

4. Place in the oven. After 20 minutes, turn the heat down to 375ºF. Roast for another 40 minutes, or until a meat thermometer inserted into the center registers 120°F for medium rare, 125°F for medium, or 130°F for medium well. Remove the pan from the oven.

5. When ready to serve, take the lamb outside, carefully ignite the rosemary on top of the lamb, and allow to burn itself out. (For safety, make sure you have a tight-fitting lid handy to cover the pot and extinguish the flames if necessary.) Brush off the woody stems.

6. Let the lamb rest 10 to 15 minutes and transfer to a serving platter. Slice and serve.

and to drink

$ 1998 Geoff Merrill Shiraz Reserve, Australia

$$ 2001 Vacqueyras, Montirius, Grenache/Syrah, Southern Rhone Valley, France

chef's notes ...esh rosemary is unavailable, soak 3 ounces of dried rosemary in water to cover for 30 minutes. Drain. Pat the wet rosemary on the lamb before placing it in the oven. Do not attempt to flame it.

WHERE TO BUY

Organic lamb: Lobel's, 877-783-4512, www.lobels.com

mélisse restaurant

1104 WILSHIRE BOULEVARD   SANTA MONICA, CA 90401

310-395-0881   WWW.MELISSE.COM

It's quite fitting that Mélisse Restaurant takes its name from the French word for lemon balm. Not only does chef Josiah Citrin have an amazing facility with fresh herbs and bright flavors (including citrus), but his restaurant is a soothing, elegant balm to the all-too-often overwrought dining experience. Decked out in Old World chic, from crystal chandeliers to hand-painted china and a gurgling fountain in the private Garden Room, the restaurant is an oasis of exquisite flavors and fine dining. Citrin brings local farm-fresh produce, line-caught seafood, and natural meats to center stage in dishes like white-corn ravioli infused with the earthy flavor of summer truffles, Maine lobster with a carrot emulsion, and smoked duck with crispy cannelloni and sour plum tart. Citrin and his wife, Diane, opened Mélisse in 1999, and it earned the coveted Mobil four-star rating after just eighteen months, a prestigious designation it has maintained ever since.

When morels are in season in the spring, chef Citrin features them in this delicately flavored white asparagus soup. You can omit the expensive morels and still wow your guests with a mini crab cake garnish.

white asparagus soup
with crab cakes

Soup

1 tablespoon vegetable oil

½ onion, thinly sliced

2 pounds white asparagus, peeled and trimmed of the woody lower stem

6 cups chicken broth

½ cup heavy cream

Coarse salt and freshly ground white pepper, to taste

1 tablespoon unsalted butter

Crab Cakes

10 ounces fresh or canned lump crabmeat

1 potato, baked, peeled, and mashed

1 tablespoon chopped fresh chives

1 tablespoon chopped fresh flat-leaf parsley

1 tablespoon thinly sliced shallot

5 tablespoons heavy cream

2 large eggs

1 teaspoon salt

½ teaspoon freshly ground black pepper

½ cup all-purpose flour

1 cup panko bread crumbs or plain bread crumbs

Vegetable oil, for frying

SERVES 6

1. To make the soup, heat a soup pot over medium-high heat. Add the oil and the sliced onion. Cook, stirring, until the onion is tender but not brown, about 4 minutes.

2. Meanwhile, chop the asparagus. Add to the pot with the onion. Add the broth and bring to a boil. Reduce the heat and simmer until the asparagus is very tender, about 15 minutes.

3. Add the cream and cook 5 more minutes. Working in small batches, transfer the soup to a blender and puree. Strain through a fine-mesh sieve, discard the solids, and return the soup to the pot. Season with salt and white pepper to taste and set aside.

4. To make the crab cakes, in a medium bowl, mix the crabmeat, potato, chives, parsley, shallot, 1 tablespoon of the cream, 1 egg, and the salt and pepper. Form the crab mixture into 12 patties, each about 2 inches in diameter and 1 inch thick.

5. Place 3 shallow bowls on a work surface. Put the flour in the first. Whisk together the remaining egg and cream in the second, and place the bread crumbs in the third. Dip each cake into the flour, shake off the excess, coat with the egg mixture, and then dredge in the bread crumbs. Dip a second time into the egg and then coat again with bread crumbs. Place on a sheet pan and refrigerate until needed.

6. When ready to serve, reheat the soup. While the soup is heating, place a large sauté pan over high heat. Pour in oil about ⅛ inch deep. When the oil is very hot, add the crab cakes and cook until browned on the outside and heated through, 2 to 3 minutes per side. Set aside and keep hot.

7. When the soup boils, whisk in the butter and remove from the heat. Place 2 crab cakes in the middle of each of 6 serving bowls and ladle the soup around the crab cakes.

White Asparagus Soup (*continued*)

chef's notes White asparagus is more tender and more expensive than its green cousin. Growers accomplish the milky hue by shielding the young stalks from the sun, thus preventing the production of chlorophyll and resulting in a more delicate vegetable. You can substitute green asparagus for the white in this recipe with no problem. The easiest way to remove the tough base of the stalk is to bend the asparagus in half—the stalk should break at the point where it starts to get tough.

Panko, or Japanese bread crumbs, are showing up more and more in recipes and on restaurant menus. Panko bread crumbs are coarser than the regular kind, making for a lighter and crunchier coating for fried foods. Look for panko in the Asian foods section of larger supermarkets.

and to drink

$ 2001 St. Supery Sauvignon Blanc, California

$$ 2001 Crossing Catherine's Run Sauvignon Blanc, New Zealand

WHERE TO BUY

Panko: Asian Food Grocer, 888-482-2742, www.asianfoodgrocer.com

lucques

8474 MELROSE AVENUE   WEST HOLLYWOOD, CA 90069

323-655-6277   WWW.LUCQUES.COM

Named for a briny French green olive and pronounced "Luke," this comfy Cal-Med restaurant features the earthy and inspired cooking of Suzanne Goin in a cozy setting that was once Harold Lloyd's brick carriage house. Goin, formerly of Campanile, and her partner Carolyn Styne, who also owns the L.A. wine bar A.O.C., deliver intelligent cuisine created with market-fresh ingredients and unpretentious service—the latter not that easy to come by in L.A. Standout dishes might include lime-marinated hamachi with avocado, tangelos, peppercress, mint, and pistachio oil, and braised beef short ribs with sautéed greens, pearl onions, and horseradish cream. The best deal is the three-course prix fixe on Sundays, still just $35 last time we checked. It's tough to choose between settling into the comfy leather couches around the wood-burning fireplace, or heading out to the high-walled patio out back with the stars for company.

For this dish, chef Goin shows off one of her favorite ingredients: the lovely kabocha squash. Wedges of squash are roasted until almost caramelized and woven into a salad of dandelion greens tossed in a tart sherry vinaigrette with smoky bacon, salty toasted pecans, and elegant shards of roncal, an earthy sheep's milk cheese from Spain.

You can substitute butternut or blue Hubbard for the kabocha if you need to. Arugula works fine in place of the dandelion and if you can't find roncal cheese, use manchego or pecorino.

warm kabocha squash salad
with bacon, roncal, and pecans

SERVES 4

1 medium kabocha squash, about 1¾ pounds

¼ cup plus 2½ tablespoons extra-virgin olive oil

1 tablespoon chopped fresh thyme, or 1 teaspoon dried

2½ teaspoons coarse salt, plus more to taste

Freshly ground black pepper, to taste

½ cup pecan halves

3 tablespoons sherry vinegar

⅔ pound thick-sliced apple-smoked bacon or regular bacon, cut into ½-inch pieces

¼ cup sliced shallots

½ pound young dandelion greens or arugula, tough stems discarded, leaves well rinsed

¼-pound piece roncal, manchego, or pecorino cheese

1. Preheat the oven to 475°F.

2. Cut the squash in half lengthwise and remove the seeds. Place the squash cut side down on a cutting board and use a sharp knife to remove the peel. Slice the squash lengthwise into ½-inch-thick wedges.

3. Toss the squash with ¼ cup of the olive oil, the thyme, 2 teaspoons of the salt, and some pepper. Place the squash flat on a baking sheet and roast until tender when pierced with the tip of a knife, about 20 minutes.

4. Turn the oven temperature down to 375°F.

5. Spread the pecans on a baking sheet and toast, stirring once, until they just begin to brown, about 5 minutes. Place in a small bowl and toss with ½ tablespoon of the olive oil and salt to taste. Set aside.

6. In a small bowl, whisk together the vinegar, remaining olive oil, and ¼ teaspoon of the salt.

7. Heat a large sauté pan over high heat for 1 minute. Add the bacon and cook, stirring occasionally, until it just begins to brown but is still tender, about 5 minutes. Leaving the bacon in the pan, pour off and discard all but about 2 tablespoons of the fat from the pan. Lower the heat to medium, add the shallots, and toss to combine. Remove from the heat and swirl in the sherry vinegar mixture to warm it.

8. Place the dandelion greens or arugula in a large bowl. Add the warm squash and the contents of the sauté pan to the greens. Season with the remaining ¼ teaspoon salt and a pinch of pepper and toss gently to coat the greens. Taste and season with more salt if necessary.

9. Arrange half the salad on a large platter. Using a vegetable peeler, shave some cheese over the salad and sprinkle with half the nuts. Top with the remaining salad, some more shavings of cheese, and the rest of the nuts.

and to drink

$ 2003 Gavi Villa Sparina, Italy

$$ 2002 Gewürztraminer
Grand Cru, Albert Mann,
Alsace, France

chef's notes Kabocha squash, also called Japanese pumpkin, is a sweet winter squash with a flavor reminiscent of sweet potatoes. Pumpkin-shaped, with a striated green rind and bright-orange flesh, kabocha is less fibrous than other winter squash. It's in season all winter and into the spring, but if you can't find it you can substitute butternut or acorn squash. Buy butternut squash in a bag, available in the produce department of your grocery store. You will have to slice the precut squash into smaller ½-inch pieces, but you'll still save time.

WHERE TO BUY

Artisanal cheese: 877-797-1200, www.artisanalcheese.com

Roncal cheese: Forever Cheese, 718-777-0772, www.forevercheese.com

Sherry vinegar: Gourmet Pasta Cheese, 800-386-9198,
   www.pastacheese.com

the belvedere in the peninsula beverly hills

9882 SOUTH SANTA MONICA BOULEVARD   BEVERLY HILLS, CA 90212

310-551-2888   WWW.BEVERLYHILLS.PENINSULA.COM

Voted Best Hotel Restaurant in the Continental US and Canada in 2005 by the readers of *Travel + Leisure* magazine, the Belvedere offers a head-turning dining experience in an ultra-posh setting. Frequented by celebs like Sly Stallone, Glenn Close, and Oprah, the hotel and restaurant boasts a staff well schooled in both gracious service and ultimate discretion. Executive chef Sean Hardy creates a menu of modern American cuisine, with specialties like Moroccan-spiced Peking duck with raisin couscous, lavender-braised halibut with English pea puree, and truffle-roasted chateaubriand of veal for one. The menu's option of small bites is alluring; taste teasers include a mini smoked salmon pancake, an espresso cup of clam chowder, and a baked baby golden potato topped with Russian caviar. Lunch on the patio is a pleasure, offering upscale interpretations of the shrimp po'boy and Cuban sandwich.

This grown-up version of mac and cheese comes in a small portion at lunch and dinner, but trust us on this, you'll want a full order. It really is that good. Taleggio is a rich, semisoft Italian cheese.

Chef Hardy gussies up this mac and cheese with shaved truffles, not usually an option for the home cook. A drizzle of truffle oil will work just fine.

macaroni with taleggio cheese sauce

SERVES 4

2 tablespoons
unsalted butter

1 leek (white part only),
thinly sliced

3 button mushrooms,
chopped

½ stalk celery, diced

2 shallots, minced

2 cloves garlic, minced

1½ cups white wine

3 cups heavy cream

4 sprigs fresh thyme

1 bay leaf

1 pound Taleggio
(or ½ pound each Gruyère
and Parmesan cheese)

¼ cup grated
Parmigiano-Reggiano

1 pound elbow macaroni

1 tablespoon truffle oil

Coarse salt and freshly
ground white pepper,
to taste

1 tablespoon chopped
fresh chives

and to drink

$ Beaulieu Vineyards Pinot
Noir Carneros Reserve,
California

$$ 2003 David Bruce Pinot
Noir, California

1. In a medium saucepan over medium heat, melt the butter. Add the leek, mushrooms, celery, shallots, and garlic and cook, stirring, until the vegetables are softened but not browned, about 6 minutes.

2. Add the white wine, bring to a boil, reduce the heat, and simmer, stirring occasionally, until almost all the wine has evaporated, about 10 minutes.

3. Stir in the cream, thyme, and bay leaf. Bring just to a simmer, lower the heat, and simmer, uncovered, for 20 minutes. Strain the sauce through a sieve. Discard the solids and transfer the sauce to a large saucepan.

4. Add the Taleggio and Parmigiano-Reggiano and stir until smooth. Set aside.

5. Cook the macaroni according to package directions. Drain and set aside.

6. Reheat the cheese sauce over low heat. Stir in the truffle oil and season with salt and white pepper to taste. Stir in the macaroni. Cook, stirring, until the pasta is heated through. Garnish with chives and serve.

chef's notes Dress up your presentation with Parmesan tuiles (pronounced *tweel*)—these thin, baked cheese crisps are easy to make. Simply place small rounds of grated Parmesan on a nonstick sheet pan and bake in a 400°F oven until lightly golden brown. Remove the pan from the oven, allow the cheese rounds to cool slightly, then lift them off with a spatula. Store in an airtight container for up to 3 days.

You can vary this dish by adding cooked shrimp, lobster, or ham just before serving.

WHERE TO BUY

Truffle oil: Trader Joe's, multiple locations, 800-SHOP-TJS, www.traderjoes.com

Taleggio cheese: Di Bruno Brothers, 888-322-4337, www.dibruno.com

josie restaurant

2424 PICO BOULEVARD   SANTA MONICA, CA 90405

310-581-9888   WWW.JOSIERESTAURANT.COM

When it comes to fine cooking, sometimes the apple doesn't fall far from the tart tatin. That's the case with chef Josie Le Balch, who learned fine French culinary arts from her father, chef Gregoire Le Balch, founder of one of the first French cooking schools in L.A. Some two decades into her career, Josie Le Balch remains a culinary original in her own right. Her résumé includes stints with Wolfgang Puck at Ma Maison and Jean Betranou at L'Ermitage, and an award-winning period as head chef at Saddle Peak Lodge.

At the helm of her own restaurant since 2001, along with her husband and partner Frank X. Delzio, Le Balch has successfully created an inventive menu of contemporary cuisine that is complemented by the restaurant's elegant, gracious ambiance. Her signature dishes include bacon-wrapped grilled quail, New Zealand snapper over Coleman Farms' pea tendrils, and cod served tagine style with preserved lemon and piquant carrot mustard.

Although chef Le Balch makes her own crust for her trademark quiches, if you're pressed for time, a frozen pie shell makes a fine substitute.

quiche
lorraine

Two 9-inch prepared
pie crusts

2 teaspoons olive oil

1 medium onion, finely diced

8 large eggs

1 teaspoon salt

1 tablespoon sour cream

2½ cups heavy cream

Dash freshly grated nutmeg

1½ cups Gruyère
or other Swiss cheese,
grated

½ cup finely diced
cooked ham

1. Thaw the pie crusts, if frozen. Using a fork, pierce the dough all over.

2. Preheat the oven to 375°F. Line the pie plates with parchment paper, weight with dry beans or metal pie weights, and bake until the dough is dried and just beginning to brown around the edges, 15 to 18 minutes. Remove from the oven, remove the parchment paper and weights, and set the crusts aside. (Leave the oven on.)

3. Meanwhile, place a medium skillet over medium heat and heat the oil. Add the onion and cook, stirring, until tender, about 4 minutes. Set aside to cool.

4. Whisk together the eggs and salt. Whisk in the sour cream, heavy cream, and nutmeg, whisking until smooth.

5. Spread half the grated cheeses over the bottom of the partially baked pie shells. Next, spread the onions on top of the cheese and top with the ham. Sprinkle with the remaining cheese. Slowly pour the custard over the top of the quiches until the custard comes up to within a ½ inch of the top of the crust.

6. Bake the quiches until the center is set and the top is lightly browned, about 45 minutes. Cool for at least 10 minutes, or to room temperature, before cutting and serving.

WHERE TO BUY

Imported cheeses: Cheese Store of Beverly Hills, 800-547-1515, www.cheesestorebh.com

and to drink
$ 2001 William Fèvre "Champs
Royaux" Chablis, France
$$ 2000 Chateau Maligny
Pre Cru Fourchaume Chablis,
France

chef's notes   Although quiche is associated with French cuisine, the popular baked egg pie actually originated in Germany, in the medieval kingdom of Lothringen, under German rule, and which the French later renamed Lorraine. The word *quiche* comes from the German word *Kuchen,* which means cake.

Wonderfully versatile, quiche works for breakfast, brunch, lunch, or dinner, as a first course and as an appetizer. Better yet, the busy home cook can prepare it ahead of time and serve it either hot or at room temperature.

You can dramatically reduce the fat in this recipe by using egg substitute instead of whole eggs, and low-fat sour cream and half-and-half instead of heavy cream. If you are sticking to a low-carb diet, just prepare the quiche without a crust: Spray a glass baking dish with cooking spray and coat with a fine dusting of flour; layer in the cheese and fillings, pour in the custard, and bake as above.

sona restaurant

401 N. LA CIENEGA BOULEVARD   WEST HOLLYWOOD, CA 90048

310-659-7708   WWW.SONARESTAURANT.COM

Chef David Myers, who co-owns Sona Restaurant with his wife, Michelle, embodies the Japanese concept of *kappo* in his approach to cooking. Kappo is all about capturing the exact moment when an ingredient is at its freshest, purest state. Myers, who created a sensation at the Raffles L'Ermitage Hotel's Jaan, maintains a firm commitment to California's artisanal farmers, a respect for the seasons, and a belief in spontaneity. His fluency in classic French traditions and technique allows him to blend multicultural flavors with his own innovative interpretations. The restaurant's decor combines Zen simplicity with elements of wood, granite, and earth tones, all dominated by a stunning wine decanting table, carved from a six-ton granite boulder by Japanese sculptor Yoshikawa. The ever-changing menu marries modern French fare with Asian sensibilities, as in the macadamia nut–crusted halibut with coconut milk, clams, and Chinese greens or the spiced pork belly with red wine, lentils, and parsnip puree. Michelle Myers, the restaurant's pastry chef, reinvents classic desserts like carrot cake, which she pairs with cream cheese ice cream and coriander granita. Sona's ninety seats are typically booked a month in advance, so make your reservation along with your travel plans.

In this clean-tasting appetizer, chef Myers pairs quick-seared tuna with crunchy Japanese radish, edamame, and spicy grapefruit. You can substitute regular red radishes for the daikon. You can also substitute canned grapefruit sections and grapefruit juice from concentrate, but fresh tastes better.

tuna with edamame puree
and spicy grapefruit

SERVES 4

Spicy Grapefruit

5 pink grapefruits, juiced, or 1½ cups pink grapefruit juice

2 tablespoons freshly grated lime zest

2 teaspoons cayenne

1 cup sugar

5 pink grapefruits, sectioned, or 2 cups canned grapefruit sections

3 serrano or jalapeño chiles, seeded and thinly sliced

Edamame Puree

1 pound frozen shelled edamame

2 cups cold water

2 tablespoons wasabi powder

Coarse salt, to taste

Tuna

Two 8-ounce tuna steaks

2 teaspoons fleur de sel sea salt or coarse salt

1 tablespoon olive oil

Ground turmeric, for garnish

1. To make the spicy grapefruit, put the grapefruit juice in a small saucepan with 1 tablespoon of the lime zest. Bring to a boil over high heat, reduce the heat, and simmer for 15 minutes.

2. Strain the juice and discard the zest. Return the juice to the pot and add the cayenne and sugar. Simmer, uncovered, until it becomes slightly syrupy. Remove from the heat and cool. Add the grapefruit segments, remaining tablespoon lime zest, and the chiles and set aside.

3. To make the edamame puree, bring a large pot of lightly salted water to a boil. Add the edamame and cook 1 minute. Drain.

4. Put the edamame in a blender with half the water and the wasabi. Blend, adding more water until the consistency is smooth and about as thick as applesauce. Strain through a fine sieve or chinois. Season to taste with salt and set aside.

5. When ready to serve, make the tuna. Season the steaks with the salt and drizzle with the olive oil. Heat a large sauté pan over high heat until very hot. Add the tuna steaks and cook until browned and to the desired doneness, about 3 minutes per side for medium rare.

6. Transfer the steaks to a cutting board and cut into ½-inch-thick slices.

7. To serve, reheat the edamame puree and make a pool of it on each of 4 plates. Alternate the tuna slices with grapefruit segments to cover the puree. Drizzle the spicy grapefruit juice on top and sprinkle turmeric around the plate for color.

chef's notes At the restaurant, this dish is served garnished with a salad of julienned daikon and basil. Daikon, also known as Chinese radish or watermelon radish, is larger and milder than its cousin, the red radish. It can be grated and served with sushi, stir-fried, or as in this case, served in salad. Japanese daikons tend to be longer and skinnier than their Chinese counterparts, but the two varieties can be used interchangeably.

WHERE TO BUY

Frozen, shelled edamame:

Asian markets, such as Hankook Market in Glendale, CA, 818-547-5932

Whole Foods, multiple locations, www.wholefoods.com

Fleur de sel sea salt: Penzey's Spices, 800-741-7787, www.penzeys.com

la cachette

10506 SANTA MONICA BOULEVARD   LOS ANGELES, CA 90025

310-470-4992   WWW.LACACHETTERESTAURANT.COM

French for "the hideaway," La Cachette is an award-winning showcase for chef and owner Jean-François Meteigner's country French food, prepared with boatloads of California style. Meteigner started his journey as a chef at a very young age at the three-star Troisgros restaurants in Roanne and his search for excellence led him to such restaurants as Le Chapon Fin in Bordeaux, and L'Archestrate and Le Chiberta in Paris.

His signature *cuisine naturelle* takes a lighter approach to traditional French fare, using little or no cream or butter to evoke every molecule of freshness in dishes like potato salad with homemade truffle vinaigrette, endive, walnuts, and Roquefort and Maine lobster salad served warm, with a medley of garden vegetables. True to its name, La Cachette is tucked away in Century City, a gem that shines brilliantly once it's discovered.

This simple squash and corn soup is made even simpler if you use peeled and cut squash-in-a-bag, available in the produce department of most supermarkets.

butternut squash and corn soup

SERVES 8

2 tablespoons grapeseed, canola, or olive oil

1 large onion, coarsely chopped

1 leek (white and light-green parts), coarsely chopped and thoroughly rinsed in a colander

One 2-pound butternut squash, peeled, seeded, and cut into 1-inch chunks (or 1 pound precut squash)

3 cups frozen corn

1 teaspoon coarse salt, plus more to taste

7 cups chicken or vegetable broth

1 tablespoon finely chopped chives, for garnish

Freshly ground black pepper

1. Place a large saucepan over medium heat and add the oil. Add the onion and leek and cook, stirring, until softened but not browned, about 5 minutes. Add the squash and corn and cook, stirring, for 10 minutes more.

2. Add 1 teaspoon salt and the broth. Bring to a boil over high heat, then lower the heat and simmer, uncovered, until the squash is very tender, about 45 minutes. Remove from the heat and let cool 15 minutes.

3. Ladle off and reserve about one third of the broth. Puree the remaining vegetables and broth in a blender in batches, filling the container only halfway and holding down the top securely with a folded towel. (Always start blending hot mixtures at the lowest speed and increase the speed gradually.)

4. Strain through a medium-mesh sieve into a clean saucepan, pressing hard to extract all the flavor, leaving the corn skins behind. Adjust the consistency by returning a little of the reserved broth to the soup, if desired (any broth you do not use for the soup may be frozen for future soups and sauces). Season to taste with more salt if necessary and reheat.

5. Ladle the soup into bowls and sprinkle with chives and a turn or two of the pepper mill.

chef's notes Grapeseed oil is prized for its health properties and its high smoke point, so it's perfect for frying or sautéing at high heat. Grapeseed oil is high in vitamin E and other antioxidants and has a milder taste than olive oil.

The skin on butternut squash is tough and very thick; use a sharp vegetable peeler and peel each squash twice to be sure you remove every last scrap of skin.

and to drink
$ Acacia Chardonnay, California
$$ Talbott Sleepy Hollow Chardonnay, California

WHERE TO BUY
Grapeseed oil: EuroGrocer, 201-476-1747, www.eurogrocer.com

valentino restaurant

3115 W. PICO BOULEVARD   SANTA MONICA, CA 90405

310-829-4313   WWW.WELOVEWINE.COM

If you visit just one Italian restaurant in L.A., make it Valentino. Hailed by former *New York Times* food critic Ruth Reichl as the best Italian restaurant in the United States, Valentino serves the kind of flavorful Italian cuisine you really do find in Italy. Opened by owner Piero Selvaggio as his flagship restaurant more than thirty years ago, Valentino is now also in Las Vegas at the Venetian Hotel. The seasonal menu includes favorites like carpaccio with capers, pappardelle with mushrooms and garlic, and seafood risotto, along with a killer osso buco and a veal chop with Marsala wine sauce that you'll be dreaming about for years. Known as much for its wine as for its cuisine, the wine cellar ranks number one in L.A., according to *Wine Spectator*, with a voluminous wine list and a cellar holding somewhere around 150,000 bottles, including a stellar collection of Italian wines. Gentlemen, take note: Although not strictly required, you'll be most comfortable wearing a jacket in this elegant dining room.

This quick pasta dish makes a perfect summer supper, or serve it on the side with grilled meat or chicken.

rigatoni with eggplant,
tomato, and broccoli rabe

SERVES 4

1 bunch broccoli rabe,
well rinsed

6 Japanese eggplants

8 tablespoons olive oil,
plus extra for drizzling

1 clove garlic

2 tablespoons
unsalted butter

1 large shallot, minced

Red pepper flakes, to taste
(optional)

$\frac{1}{4}$ cup dry white wine

One 14$\frac{1}{2}$-ounce can
chopped plum tomatoes

3 sprigs fresh rosemary

2 sprigs fresh thyme

1 bay leaf

Coarse salt and freshly
ground black pepper,
to taste

$\frac{3}{4}$ pound rigatoni

$\frac{1}{2}$ cup grated ricotta salata
or Parmesan cheese

1. Discard the tough broccoli rabe stems and coarsely chop the tops. Bring a large pot of salted water to a boil, add the tops, and cook 2 minutes. Immediately drain and cool the rabe in a large bowl of ice water. Drain, pat dry, and set aside.

2. Cut the tips off the eggplants and partially peel them by cutting off strips with a vegetable peeler; the eggplants will look striped. Cut the eggplants into $\frac{1}{2}$-inch cubes. Set aside.

3. In a medium sauté pan over medium-high heat, heat 5 tablespoons of the olive oil. Add the garlic and cook until it just begins to brown, about 3 minutes. Lift out and discard the garlic. Add the eggplant and cook until golden, about 4 minutes. Transfer the eggplant to a strainer to remove any excess oil and set aside.

4. In a large sauté pan set over medium heat, combine the butter and remaining 3 tablespoons olive oil. When the butter has melted, add the shallot and cook, stirring, until the shallot is translucent. Add the pepper flakes and cook, stirring, another minute. Add the white wine and boil until evaporated. Stir in the tomatoes, rosemary, thyme, bay leaf, and salt and pepper. Add the eggplant and broccoli rabe and simmer over medium-low heat, uncovered, until the vegetables are very tender, about 5 minutes. Discard the herbs.

5. Meanwhile, bring a large pot of salted water to a boil. Cook the pasta until just al dente and add to the sauce in the sauté pan, tossing to combine. Drizzle with olive oil to taste, top with ricotta salata or Parmesan, and serve.

WHERE TO BUY

Ricotta salata: A.G. Ferrari Foods, 877-878-2783, www.agferrari.com

and to drink

$ 2002 Librandi Ciro Rosso
Classico, Italy

$$ 2000 Trefethen Cabernet
Franc, California

chef's notes Widely available in large supermarkets and Asian grocery stores, Japanese eggplants are longer, thinner, and sweeter than the Italian variety. The reason for partially peeling the eggplant in this recipe is that too much skin imparts a bitter taste to the dish, but you need some for color and texture.

Ricotta salata is a hard, imported Italian sheep's milk cheese. The milk curds and whey used to make this cheese are pressed and dried even before the cheese is aged, giving this pure white cheese a dense but slightly spongy texture and a salty, milky flavor—it's something like the Italian version of feta.

the restaurant at hotel bel-air

701 STONE CANYON ROAD   LOS ANGELES, CA 90077

310-472-1211   WWW.HOTELBELAIR.COM

The rich and famous have been hiding away at the five-diamond Hotel Bel-Air since 1946. A home away from home to the likes of Cary Grant, Elizabeth Taylor, and Marilyn Monroe back in the studio era, these days it's not unusual to find celebrities like Robert De Niro, Brad Pitt, or Kate Winslet in a corner of The Restaurant, the hotel's newly renovated country French–style dining room. Voted Most Romantic Hotel Restaurant and Most Appealing Decor in the *Zagat* guide, The Restaurant offers a combination of French-California and Mediterranean cuisine along with a 40,000-bottle wine cellar with more than 1,250 varieties of wine. Executive chef Douglas Dodd and chef de cuisine Bruno Lopez create Mediterranean-inspired specialties made with California products, including artisanal cheeses, poultry, and produce. A daily special of fresh egg pasta, homemade in the Bel-Air kitchen, is served with farmers' market vegetables. We like the porcini-dusted diver scallop, wild mushroom risotto with Oregon truffles, and the ever-so-satisfying lobster club sandwich, best paired with a glass of California bubbly at lunch.

For this market-fresh salad, use vegetables that are in season or whatever's in your garden. It's a great accompaniment to grilled steak, chicken, or fish—the grill is already fired up, so why not use it for your veggies?

grilled farmers' market
vegetable salad

SERVES 4

Herb Vinaigrette

¼ cup chopped mixed fresh
herbs (such as parsley,
thyme, rosemary, chives)

¼ cup champagne or
white-wine vinegar

1 tablespoon finely
chopped shallot

1 tablespoon honey

1 teaspoon freshly ground
black pepper

¾ cup canola oil

½ teaspoon coarse salt

Vegetable Marinade

1 cup olive oil

¼ cup balsamic vinegar

1 tablespoon
chopped shallot

1 tablespoon minced garlic

¾ teaspoon coarse salt

½ teaspoon freshly ground
black pepper

Vegetables and Salad

2 large portobello
mushroom caps

1 bunch green asparagus,
ends trimmed

1 red bell pepper, cut into
1-inch-wide strips

1 yellow bell pepper, cut into
1-inch-wide strips

1 bunch baby carrots,
trimmed and peeled

1. To make the herb vinaigrette, in a small bowl, whisk together the herbs, vinegar, shallot, honey, and pepper. Pouring in a very slow stream, whisk in the oil. Set aside.

2. To make the vegetable marinade, whisk together all the ingredients in a small bowl. Set aside.

3. To make the vegetables and salad, toss the mushrooms, asparagus, bell peppers, carrots, zucchini, squash, eggplants, and artichokes separately with the vegetable marinade to coat and let them stand for 20 minutes.

4. Prepare a charcoal or gas grill for medium-high heat cooking. Grill the vegetables until each is tender and nicely browned, 5 to 10 minutes.

5. Meanwhile, toss the baby greens with enough herb vinaigrette to coat them well. Arrange the greens on a large serving platter.

6. Once the vegetables are cooked, dice them into large pieces and toss with some of the herb vinaigrette. Mound the vegetables in the center of platter over the greens and arrange some of the larger pieces of vegetable around the sides of the platter.

7. Sprinkle the goat cheese and pistachios over the salad. Serve the salad immediately—it's best when the vegetables are still warm.

WHERE TO BUY

Artisanal goat cheese: Redwood Hill Farm, 707-823-8250,
    www.redwoodhill.com
Organic produce: Diamond Organics, 888-ORGANIC (888-674-2642),
    www.diamondorganics.com

1 zucchini, cut into
thick slices

1 summer squash,
cut into thick slices

4 Japanese baby eggplants,
cut into thick slices

2 artichokes
(see Chef's Notes for
instructions)

4 cups baby greens

½ pound goat cheese,
crumbled

¼ cup pistachios,
toasted and chopped

chef's notes Flavorful fresh artichokes are readily available in the supermarket and well worth the little bit of time it takes to get them ready to cook. Buy artichokes with firm, compact heads and evenly colored green leaves. Start by trimming the stem so the artichoke stands upright on its own.

Pull off the tough, dark outer leaves, then, using kitchen shears, cut off the sharp tips of the remaining leaves. Sprinkle the artichoke with lemon juice to keep it from turning dark. Now it's ready to be steamed or grilled. After the artichoke is cooked, cut it in half lengthwise. With a small knife or teaspoon, scoop out the fuzz or choke at the center. Cut the artichoke into quarters lengthwise, then cut each quarter in half across the middle. Enjoy!

and to drink
$ 2001 Erath Pinot Blanc,
Oregon
$$ 2002 Kreydenweiss Pinot
Gris Moenchberg, Alsace,
France

saddle peak lodge

419 COLD CANYON ROAD   CALABASAS, CA 91302

818-222-3888   WWW.SADDLEPEAKLODGE.COM

Part roadhouse, part Pony Express stop, hunting lodge, European auberge, and even bordello, Saddle Peak Lodge has been many things to many people for more than a hundred years. Located about thirty miles west of L.A., in the Malibu hills under the dramatic Saddle Peak rock formation, the Lodge has evolved from cowboy outpost to rustic country retreat and top-rated restaurant. Under the direction of executive chef Mark Murillo, Saddle Peak Lodge continues to win accolades, including the *Zagat* Award of Distinction, the *Wine Spectator* Award of Excellence, the AAA Four-Diamond Award, and the DiRoNA award as a Distinguished Restaurant of North America. The chef specializes in game, including buffalo tartare with whole-grain mustard aïoli, pheasant breast with roasted purple Peruvian potatoes, and roasted elk tenderloin with bacon-wrapped salsify.

This elegant appetizer is an easy start to a special-occasion dinner party.

seared diver scallops with
potato chive puree and frisée salad

SERVES 4

2 russet potatoes, peeled and cut into 1-inch cubes

½ cup heavy cream

1 tablespoon crème fraîche or sour cream

1 tablespoon unsalted butter

Coarse salt and freshly ground white pepper, to taste

1 tablespoon chopped chives

1 slice bacon, diced

1 head frisée lettuce, well rinsed

1 teaspoon finely chopped shallot

12 teardrop tomatoes, halved

1 tablespoon extra-virgin olive oil, plus more for drizzling

12 sea scallops

1. Place the potatoes in a medium saucepan with cold salted water to cover by 1 inch. Bring to a boil over high heat, reduce the heat, and simmer until the potatoes are just fork-tender, about 10 minutes. (If the potatoes are cooked too long they will absorb too much water and give you a thin, watery puree.)

2. Drain the potatoes and transfer them to a medium bowl. Add the cream, crème fraîche, and butter to the bowl and use a handheld mixer to whip the potatoes just until smooth. Stir in salt and pepper to taste, then stir in the chives.

3. In a small sauté pan, cook the bacon until crispy and drain on paper towels. Set aside.

4. Cut away and discard the core and the tips of the frisée leaves. In a bowl, mix the frisée, bacon, shallot, and tomatoes. Lightly drizzle with olive oil and season with salt and pepper to taste.

5. Season the scallops with salt and pepper. In a large sauté pan, heat the remaining tablespoon olive oil over medium-high heat. When very hot, add the scallops and cook until just seared on both sides, about 2 minutes.

6. To serve, make a circle of potato puree in the center of each of 4 plates. Place the greens in the center and set 3 scallops around the salad.

and to drink

$ Acacia Chardonnay, California

$$ Talbott "Sleepy Hollow" Chardonnay, California

chef's notes Saddle Peak Lodge features applewood smoked Nueske bacon in this salad, produced by the Nueske family in Wisconsin since 1933.

WHERE TO BUY

Nueske bacon: 800-392-2266, www.nueskes.com

Sea scallops: Browne Trading Company, 800-944-7848, www.brownetrading.com

miami

miami's new world cuisine

The idea of Miami as a culinary destination dates back to the late 1980s and the birth of a new style of cooking: "New World" cuisine, also known as Floribean, Tropical Fusion, and Nuevo Latino. A quartet of star chefs dubbed the Mango Gang, aka Mark Militello (Mark's South Beach), Allen Susser (Chef Allen's), Douglas Rodriguez (Deseo, Phoeniz, Alma de Cuba, Philadelphia, Ola Miami), and Norman Van Aken (Norman's in Coral Gables and Mundo at Merrick Park), pioneered this contemporary cuisine, which combines the freshest local ingredients and influences from the Caribbean and Latin America with time-honored European cooking techniques.

High in flavor and low in fat, Floribean cuisine showcases clean flavors derived from ingenious combinations of fresh seafood and tropical fruits and vegetables. Local waters offer a bounty of fresh seafood including snapper, grouper, lobster, stone crabs, shrimp, and conch. Exotic fruits and spices grown in Miami's backyard in the agricultural breadbasket of South Dade include citrus, yuca, mango, cherimoya, hearts of palm, avocado, guava, papaya, coconut, banana, cilantro, ginger, garlic, coriander, carambola, litchi, and Scotch bonnet peppers. Intriguing entrées are simply prepared:

marinated, grilled, and steamed with tropical sauces and accents to create dishes that delight the palate. Mango Gang members have received their industry's highest honors and distinctions, authored cookbooks, created empires, and developed product lines. They continue to hold diners in thrall, constantly refining and reinventing this seminal cuisine, all the while inspiring a new generation of talented young chefs.

From New World specialties like Norman Van Akens's popcorn-crusted crispy shrimp with warm citrus mojo to Jonathan Eismann's lobster pancake at Pacific Time; from guava pastels in Little Havana to pastrami on rye at Rascal House, Miami's culinary scene is a vibrant expression of this diverse and inviting city.

In this chapter, we deliver the best of Miami's dining scene, including such exciting dishes as potato tacos with avocado salsa from Norman's, a rainbow of fried oysters from Azul, the hotspot in the Mandarin Oriental hotel, and from chef Cindy Hutson's popular Ortanique on the Mile in Coral Gables, snapper with escovitch sauce.

azul, mandarin oriental miami

500 BRICKELL KEY DRIVE   MIAMI, FL 33131

305-913-8288   WWW.MANDARINORIENTAL.COM

The only restaurant in Miami to earn the prestigious AAA Five-Diamond Award, the 120-seat waterfront Azul, overlooking Biscayne Bay, is the showstopping dining venue for the elegant Mandarin Oriental hotel. With chef Clay Conley at the helm, Azul's dramatic white marble open kitchen delivers rustic Mediterranean fare with Asian influences. Sample dishes from the frequently changing menu might include grilled Colorado lamb with harissa, lobster salad with hearts of palm and avocado served in a coconut shell, and miso-marinated hamachi tuna with edamame-studded rice and shrimp dumplings. Conley, who joined Azul in January 2005, honed his culinary reputation at Todd English's acclaimed Olives restaurant in Boston, where he served as executive chef and culinary director for eight years.

This colorful appetizer is simple to make and elegant to behold. If you'd prefer to sear your tuna and beef instead of serve it raw, that would work too. But chef Conley likes the contrast between the coolness of the carpaccio and the heat of the fried oysters.

rainbow of fried oysters

SERVES 4

Avocado Salad

1 avocado, peeled, pitted, and cut into ½-inch dice

2 tablespoons minced red onion

1 tablespoon chopped fresh cilantro leaves

½ jalapeño, seeded and minced

Juice of 1 lime

Coarse salt and freshly ground black pepper, to taste

Oysters

1½ cups all-purpose flour

¾ cup semolina flour

1 teaspoon coarse salt

1 teaspoon freshly ground black pepper

1 cup buttermilk

12 oysters, shucked

⅓ cup vegetable oil

Four 1 x 4-inch slices smoked salmon

Four 1 x 4-inch very thin slices raw top round or London broil

Four 1 x 4-inch very thin slices raw tuna

3 tablespoons mayonnaise

and to drink

$ 2003 Kenwood Sauvignon Blanc, California

$$ 2001 Tement Sauvignon Blanc, Grassnitzberg Sud Steiermark, Austria

1. To make the avocado salad, combine all the ingredients and toss. Let sit at room temperature for 1 hour.

2. To make the oysters, place the all-purpose flour, semolina, salt, and pepper in a shallow bowl and mix well. Place the buttermilk in another shallow bowl. Dredge the oysters in the flour mixture, shake off the excess, then dip in the buttermilk. Dredge again in the flour mixture.

3. In a medium sauté pan, heat the oil over medium-high heat until very hot. Fry the oysters until crispy, 1 to 2 minutes per side. Use a slotted spoon to transfer the oysters to paper towels to drain.

4. On a work surface, lay out the slices of salmon, beef, and tuna. Put a little dab of mayonnaise in the center of each slice. Place a warm fried oyster on top of the mayonnaise and wrap the slice around the oyster.

5. To serve, divide the avocado salad among 4 plates. Place 3 rolls (1 beef, 1 tuna, 1 salmon) on top of the avocado salad.

chef's notes   The easiest way to cut thin slices of beef or tuna for carpaccio is to start with a partially frozen piece of meat or fish. Wrap the beef or tuna in plastic, place in the freezer until just beginning to firm, ½ hour to 1 hour. Unwrap and use a very sharp knife to thinly slice it.

This recipe is a variation of traditional carpaccio. As the story goes, carpaccio was first made by Giuseppe Cipriani in 1950 at Harry's Bar in Venice, Italy. Carpaccio is usually served on a bed of greens, often arugula or watercress, and usually with a vinaigrette.

Semolina is roughly milled flour made from durum wheat. In this recipe, it adds a bit more texture to the oyster's coating than using just all-purpose, finely ground flour.

WHERE TO BUY

Fresh Florida seafood: Gary's Seafood, 407-423-8550, www.garyseafood.com

norman's

21 ALMERIA AVENUE   CORAL GABLES, FL 33134

305-446-6767   WWW.NORMANS.COM

Chef and author Norman Van Aken arguably tops the list of influential chefs, not just in the state of Florida, but nationwide. One of the chefs credited with creating New World Cuisine, Van Aken, a Chicago native who moved to Key West at age twenty, brings a sense of discovery to every dish that leaves the impressive open kitchen at his eponymous Coral Gables restaurant. The menu, which changes daily, presents a vibrant blend of Caribbean, Latin American, Asian, and American cuisine, served with picture-perfect flair. A few of the chef's mouth-watering dishes include Key West yellowtail with garlicky mashed potatoes, Mongolian barbecued veal chop with grilled Chinese eggplant and Thai fried rice, and cheese blintz with rum, pepper-braised bacon, and pineapple moonshine chutney. Chef Van Aken's facility with both local ingredients and classic European technique makes Norman's a highpoint of any Miami experience.

This recipe is a surprising combination of mashed potatoes, avocado salsa, and corn tortillas. It can work as either a hearty appetizer or a vegetarian main course.

potato tacos
with avocado salsa

SERVES 4

Avocado Salsa

1 large, ripe avocado, peeled, pitted, and diced

1 large tomato, diced, or 1 cup canned diced tomatoes, drained

1 jalapeño, seeded and minced

2 tablespoons chopped fresh cilantro

1 tablespoon minced Spanish onion

Juice of 1 lime

1 tablespoon extra-virgin olive oil

Coarse salt, to taste

Potato Tacos

1 head garlic

Olive oil, for drizzling

1½ pounds red bliss potatoes

2 tablespoons extra-virgin olive oil

4 tablespoons (½ stick) unsalted butter

1 medium Spanish onion, sliced

1 tablespoon sugar

1 tablespoon red-wine vinegar

1 jalapeño, seeded and minced

1 cup shredded cabbage

(continued)

1. To make the avocado salsa, in a small bowl, toss together all the salsa ingredients. Refrigerate until chilled, 1 to 2 hours.

2. To make the potato tacos, preheat the oven to 375ºF.

3. Slice off the top of the head of garlic to expose the cloves. Drizzle the cloves with olive oil and wrap the entire head in foil. Set aside.

4. Place the potatoes in a roasting pan and bake for 30 minutes. Add the foil-wrapped garlic to the pan with the potatoes and continue to bake until the potatoes are very tender when pierced with the tip of a knife and the garlic cloves are buttery soft, about 30 minutes more.

5. In a medium sauté pan over medium-high heat, combine 1 table-spoon of olive oil and 1 tablespoon of the butter. When the butter melts, add the onion and cook, stirring, for 1 minute. Add the sugar and vinegar and continue to cook, stirring, until the onion begins to caramelize and is completely soft, about 4 minutes more. Add the jalapeño and cook 1 more minute. Remove the mixture from the pan and set aside.

6. Wipe the pan out with paper towels and return it to medium-high heat. Add the remaining tablespoon oil. When hot, add the cabbage and cook, stirring, until it wilts, about 2 minutes. Season with salt and pepper to taste and set aside.

7. Remove the potatoes from the oven. When they are cool enough to handle, peel and discard the skins. Squeeze the garlic cloves out of their papery skins. With a potato masher, mash the potatoes together with the roasted garlic. While the potatoes are still hot, stir in the remaining 3 tablespoons butter, the cheese, onion mixture, and cabbage. Season with salt and pepper to taste.

8. Fill each shell generously with the potato mixture (it can be warm or room temperature, whichever you prefer). Serve with the avocado salsa on the side.

Coarse salt and freshly
ground black pepper,
to taste

1 cup grated (unaged)
manchego or
cheddar cheese

8 taco shells

chef's notes   Handling hot peppers can be a painful business if you don't take precautions. Consider wearing disposable latex gloves to protect yourself from the pepper's oily residue that can really burn if you get it in your eyes or into an open cut. At the restaurant, chef Van Aken uses habaneros (pronounced ha-BAHN-air-ohz) in this recipe, one of the hottest chile peppers on the market. Chiles are measured by Scoville heat units, with a green bell pepper at 0 units, jalapeños scoring about 5,000 units, and a typical habanero at 300,000 units. Now, that's hot!

In this recipe, the manchego is not the aged, hard version of the La Mancha cheese, but the young, semifirm white manchego that is ideal for melting.

and to drink

$ 2002 Dyed-in-the-Wool
Pinot Noir, New Zealand
$$ 2001 Acacia Pinot Noir,
California

WHERE TO BUY

Manchego cheese: Di Bruno Brothers, 888-322-4337, www.dibruno.com

pascal's on ponce

2611 PONCE DE LEON BOULEVARD   CORAL GABLES, FL 33134

305-444-2024   WWW.PASCALMIAMI.COM

The food takes center stage at Pascal's on Ponce, an intimate, fifty-five-seat restaurant known for its impeccable French cuisine. Chef and owner Pascal Oudin, a native of Bourbon Lancy in France, has worked with such masters of haute French cuisine as Alain Ducasse, Roger Verge, Joseph Rostang, and Jean-Louis Palladin. Realizing a lifelong dream, Oudin opened Pascal's on Ponce in 2000, earning raves, including Best French Food in America from *Bon Appétit*. Oudin's cuisine eschews fusion and fads, choosing instead to emphasize local ingredients, prepared to order with classic French techniques. Specialties include creamy lobster bisque flavored with brandy; sautéed duck breast with leg confit, apple, glazed turnip, beet, and orange gastrique; and rack of lamb with an herb and grain mustard crust and cranberry beans. Pascal's signature dessert is his traditional bittersweet chocolate soufflé with chocolate ganache.

For this dish, chef Oudin recommends using fresh grouper, halibut, cod, or monkfish if Florida black grouper is not available. Although he uses a whole fish and reserves the head for the sauce, fillets work fine. For the salsify, substitute celery root, and for the chanterelles, use the mushroom of your choice. Oudin uses 2 tablespoons of canned truffles and 4 tablespoons of truffle juice to add flavor to the sauce, but this can be omitted.

florida black grouper
with salsify and chanterelles

Salsify

3 tablespoons extra-virgin olive oil

1 clove garlic, minced

1 salsify or $\frac{1}{2}$ celery root, peeled and cut into $\frac{1}{2}$-inch dice

Coarse salt and freshly ground white pepper, to taste

2 cups dry white wine

2 cups chicken broth

$\frac{1}{2}$ cup beef broth or beef bouillon

2 cups spinach leaves

Sauce

1 tablespoon olive oil

2 tablespoons unsalted butter

2-ounce piece grouper fillet

2 cloves garlic, crushed

Leaves from 1 bunch basil, rinsed and patted dry

2 cups white wine

Coarse salt and freshly ground white pepper, to taste

Mushrooms

1 tablespoon olive oil

2 cups chanterelles or other mushrooms, stems trimmed

1 clove garlic, minced

$1\frac{1}{2}$ tablespoons unsalted butter

1. To make the salsify, in a large sauté pan set over medium heat, heat the oil. Add the garlic and cook, stirring frequently, until soft, about a minute. Add the salsify or celery root, season with salt and white pepper to taste, and cook, stirring, for 5 minutes.

2. Add the wine and simmer until the liquid is reduced by about half. Add the chicken broth and beef broth. Simmer 5 minutes more.

3. Strain; reserve the liquid for use in the sauce. Return the vegetables to the sauté pan and place over low heat. Add the spinach and cook, stirring, just until it wilts. Remove from the pan and set aside.

4. To make the sauce, place a large heavy pot over medium-high heat. Add the olive oil and 1 tablespoon of the butter. When the butter has melted, add the grouper and cook until just browned on both sides. Add the garlic and basil, cover the pot, and simmer over low heat for 5 minutes.

5. Uncover the pot and stir in the white wine, stirring to incorporate any browned bits from the bottom of the pan. Adjust the heat and simmer, uncovered, until the liquid is reduced by about half.

6. Add the reserved liquid from the salsify to the pot and continue simmering, uncovered, for 20 minutes. Strain through a fine-mesh sieve, discard the solids, and set the sauce aside.

7. To make the mushrooms, heat the olive oil in a small saucepan over medium heat. Brush the mushrooms to remove any grit and cut large mushrooms in half lengthwise. Add the mushrooms and garlic to the pan. Cover and cook for 3 minutes. Uncover the pan, add the butter, reduce the heat to low, and continue to cook until the mushrooms are tender, about 10 minutes.

8. To make the grouper, preheat the oven to 350ºF.

Grouper

Four 6-ounce grouper fillets

Coarse salt and freshly ground white pepper

2 tablespoons extra-virgin olive oil

9. Season the fillets on both sides with salt and white pepper. Heat the oil in a large ovenproof skillet over medium heat. Add the fillets and cook until browned, about 2 minutes per side. Place in the oven and bake just until the fish is opaque all the way through, about 8 minutes.

10. Meanwhile, reheat the sauce over medium heat. When simmering, remove from the heat and whisk in the remaining tablespoon butter. Season to taste with salt and pepper.

11. Reheat the salsify and mushrooms over low heat. When hot, place on a platter. Place the grouper fillets on top of the vegetables and cover with the sauce.

chef's notes   Although this recipe has a few steps, it's not difficult, as long as you have all of your ingredients close at hand. Chefs call this *mise en place* (MEEZ ahn plahs), a French term for having all ingredients prepared and ready to go.

Salsify is a root vegetable that has the taste and texture of an artichoke heart when it's cooked. Celery root, also called celeriac, is a cousin of ordinary celery and is prized for its mild celery flavor. Popular in France and elsewhere in northern Europe, celery root can be served both cooked and raw. Although still underrated in the United States, it's available in most supermarket produce sections and is a good substitute for salsify.

and to drink

$ 2003 Chehalem Willamette Valley Pinot Gris Reserve, Oregon

$$ 2002 Bourgogne Cuvée des Forgets Cuvée Speciale, France

WHERE TO BUY

Chanterelles: Earthy Delights, 800-637-4709, www.earthy.com
Grouper: Keys Fisheries, 866-743-4353, www.keysfisheries.com

cacao

141 GIRALDA AVENUE   CORAL GABLES, FL 33134

305-445-1001   WWW.CACAORESTAURANT.COM

Chef Edgar Leal creates the sun-kissed cuisine of the Americas at his highly regarded restaurant Cacao, located on a waterfront estate along Giralda Avenue's trendy restaurant row.

Leal, a native of Caracas, Venezuela, worked in kitchens from Seville to Paris and Barcelona before settling in along Florida's south coast in 2002. The stylish restaurant sets the stage for his intriguing and complex treatment of traditional Latin fare. Menu choices might include black tamal filled with spicy shrimp, blackened salmon with pineapple chutney and tequila-lime beurre blanc, and rabbit with yuca gnocchi in mango sauce. A glass-enclosed wine room at the center of the restaurant is filled with South American wines and a selection of Cakebread Cellars wines, handpicked by Dennis Cakebread himself. Leal deals with Venezuelan chocolatier Chocolates El Rey, lending the dessert list an authentic patina of South American cocoa.

Chef Leal uses quail for this dish at the restaurant, but Cornish hen works just as well. Wild rice makes a nice accompaniment. As for the rose essence he uses to perfume the sauce, Hendrick's gin does the trick.

stuffed cornish hens
in gin essence

SERVES 4

1 cup cooked diced chicken, preferably dark meat

1 large egg

1 tablespoon cognac

1 teaspoon coarse salt

¾ teaspoon freshly ground black pepper

¼ teaspoon nutmeg

¼ cup heavy cream

4 Cornish hens

3 tablespoons unsalted butter

2 cups dry red wine

2 cups beef broth

2 tablespoons cornstarch

1½ tablespoons cold water

2 tablespoons gin, preferably Hendrick's

1. Preheat the oven to 350ºF.

2. In a food processor, combine the cooked chicken, egg, cognac, salt, pepper, and nutmeg. Process until finely chopped. With the motor running, slowly pour the cream in through the feed tube. Process until you have a smooth mousse.

3. Stuff the mousse inside the hens. Melt 1 tablespoon of the butter and drizzle over the skins of the hens. Wrap each in heavy-duty aluminum foil. Roast the wrapped hens in the oven for 30 minutes.

4. Meanwhile, in a medium saucepan set over medium heat, bring the red wine to a boil. Reduce the heat and simmer, uncovered, until reduced to 1 cup. Add the broth and simmer until the mixture is reduced to 1½ cups.

5. In a small cup, combine the cornstarch and water. Whisk the mixture into the wine and beef broth mixture and cook, whisking, until the sauce thickens, about 2 minutes. Whisk in the gin. Keep warm.

6. After the hens have baked 30 minutes, remove them from the oven and unwrap them. Place 2 large sauté pans over medium heat. Melt 1 tablespoon of the remaining butter in each pan. Add the hens and cook, turning occasionally, until golden brown on all sides and cooked through, about 15 minutes.

7. Serve each hen with the red wine sauce.

and to drink

$ 2004 Bodegas Sabato Bec, Malbec Nuevo, Argentina

$$ 2001 Dolium Mendoza Reserva Malbec, Argentina

chef's notes Hendrick's gin (www.hendricksgin.com) is a small-batch, hand-crafted gin distilled with rose petals in Ayrshire, Scotland.

WHERE TO BUY

Hendrick's gin: ABC Wine & Spirits, multiple locations in Florida, 800-942-9463, www.abcfws.com

carmen the restaurant

700 BILTMORE WAY   CORAL GABLES, FL 33134

305-913-1944   WWW.CARMENTHERESTAURANT.COM

Located in the posh David Williams Hotel, Carmen the Restaurant is the brainchild of chef and owner Carmen Gonzalez, a stylish showcase for her New American-meets-Latino cuisine. Named One of America's Best New Restaurants by *Esquire* magazine in 2003, Carmen the Restaurant was included in *Zagat*'s America's Top Restaurants lineup for 2005. A graduate of the New York Restaurant School, Gonzalez connects with her Puerto Rican heritage with dishes that include yuca, mofongo, plantains, and island mojito sauce. The menu is chock-full of bold inspirations, like the double Colorado lamb chops with yuca-potato croquette and baby spinach salad tossed with cilantro oil, and this version of chef's pan-seared red snapper fillet with white water clams and chorizo stew.

Fresh clams are widely available at supermarket seafood counters; mussels would work as well. Look for chorizo in the meat department with other smoked meats and sausages. (Palacios is an excellent brand.) Turkey chorizo, which cuts the fat but is made with the same blend of Spanish spice, can be substituted for the pork variety.

snapper, clam, and **chorizo stew**

SERVES 4

8 fingerling potatoes, peeled

½ cup extra-virgin olive oil

1 cup thinly sliced leeks
(white part only)

2 dozen littleneck
clams, scrubbed
(discard any that are open)

Twelve 1½-inch slices
Spanish chorizo

4 cloves garlic, thinly sliced

1 cup canned chopped
tomatoes, drained

3 cups white wine

¼ cup fresh cilantro leaves

3 cups clam juice
(preferably low-sodium)

Four 5-ounce red snapper
fillets, skin on

2 tablespoons unsalted
butter (preferably
Plugrá brand)

8 chives

1. Place the potatoes in a medium saucepan and cover with salted water by 1 inch. Bring to a boil over high heat, reduce the heat, and simmer until the potatoes are just tender when pierced with the tip of a knife, 10 to 15 minutes. Drain and set aside.

2. Preheat the oven to 350°F.

3. In a large sauté pan over medium heat, heat ¼ cup of the oil. Add the leeks, clams, chorizo, and garlic and cook for 2 minutes.

4. Add the potatoes and tomatoes. Pour in the white wine and cook, stirring, until all the ingredients are combined. Stir in the cilantro leaves and the clam juice. Cover, reduce the heat, and simmer until the clams open, about 2 minutes more. (Discard any clams that do not open.) Set the pan aside, covered.

5. In a large ovenproof skillet, heat the remaining ¼ cup oil over medium-high heat. Add the snapper, skin side down, and cook until just browned. Turn the fish and place the skillet in the oven until the fish is just opaque all the way through, 3 to 4 minutes.

6. Uncover the stew and swirl in the butter. Remove the fish from the oven.

7. Place 6 clams around the sides of each of 4 wide bowls. Mound 2 potatoes and 3 pieces of chorizo in the center of each. Place the fish on the potatoes, skin side up, and sauce with the remaining stew mixture. Garnish each serving with 2 chives.

and to drink

$ 2000 Three Rivers
Chardonnay, Washington

$$ 2002 Bonterra Chardonnay,
California

chef's notes Chorizo is pork sausage made with smoked Spanish paprika, giving it a deep-red color and rich smoky flavor.

Plugrá is a rich European-style butter sold in many supermarkets.

WHERE TO BUY

Spanish chorizo: La Tienda, 888-472-1022, www.tienda.com

chef allen's

19088 NE 29TH AVENUE   AVENTURA, FL 33180

305-935-2900   WWW.CHEFALLENS.COM

Hard to imagine now, but twenty-five years ago, the notion of pairing fish with, say, tropical fruit, was unheard of. That's one reason why the *New York Times* called chef Allen Susser "the Ponce de Leon of New Floridian cooking." Susser, whose iconic Chef Allen's restaurant has been a dominant force both in South Florida and the national food scene since 1986, saw vast potential in his adopted state's natural resources. His visionary cross-cultural tropical cuisine draws influences from the Caribbean, Latin America, the Pacific Rim, and the tropical Mediterranean to create sweet, spicy, and aromatic harmony. Chef Allen's menu is positively bracing: Tuna tartare is topped with pummelo (Malaysian cousin to the grapefruit), avocado, and mango and dressed with a coconut-lime-ginger vinaigrette. Bahamian lobster and crab cakes arrive gussied up with tropical fruit chutney and vanilla beurre blanc. And the pistachio-crusted black grouper is sauced with a fricassee of rock shrimp, mango, leeks, and coconut rum. Sassy indeed.

Rum shows up in this easy-to-make fish sauté spiked with coriander, garlic, and lime. Chef Susser prepares this dish with mahi mahi, but you can substitute any firm white fish that is readily available. If you don't have the whole spices, skip the toasting step and just season the fish. Mojo is a spicy, olive oil–based sauce used in many Latino dishes.

mahi mahi

with orange, thyme, and rum mojo

SERVES 4

2 teaspoons ground cumin

1 teaspoon ground coriander

1 teaspoon freshly ground black pepper

Four 6-ounce mahi mahi fillets

1 tablespoon coarse salt

1 teaspoon dried thyme

2 tablespoons extra-virgin olive oil

1 cup diced sweet onion

1 tablespoon minced garlic

1 cup fresh orange juice

1/4 cup fresh lime juice

4 tablespoons spiced dark rum

1 seedless orange, peeled and chopped

1 tablespoon chopped fresh cilantro leaves

1. Heat a small skillet over medium heat. Add the cumin, coriander, and pepper and toast, shaking the pan, just until the spices are fragrant, about 30 seconds. Remove the spices from the pan and cool a few minutes.

2. Reserve 1 teaspoon of the toasted spices for the mojo. Sprinkle the rest over the fish fillets. Sprinkle the fillets with the salt and thyme as well. Drizzle the fish with 1 tablespoon of olive oil and set aside.

3. In a medium saucepan over medium heat, heat the remaining tablespoon oil. Add the onion and garlic and cook, stirring frequently, until the onion is translucent, about 3 minutes. Stir in the remaining teaspoon toasted spices, the orange juice, lime juice, and 1 tablespoon of the rum. Bring to a boil, lower the heat, and simmer 10 minutes. Set aside.

4. When you're ready to cook, heat a large nonstick skillet over medium-high heat. Cook the fish on one side until well browned, about 3 minutes. Use a spatula to flip the fish over, then add the remaining 3 tablespoons rum to the pan. Cook the fish until just opaque all the way through, about 3 minutes more.

5. Transfer the fish to 4 serving plates. Garnish each piece with orange pieces and cilantro and serve with the sauce.

and to drink

$ 2003 Ferrari-Carano Fumé Blanc, California

$$ 2003 Conundrum California, California

chef's notes Toasting spices releases their aromatics and gives them a deeper, nuttier flavor. While kitchenware stores like Williams Sonoma and Kitchen Kapers sell mortars and pestles for grinding toasted spices, the cheapest place to buy them is an Asian supermarket. Or you can use an electric coffee grinder dedicated only to spices.

WHERE TO BUY

Mahi mahi: Keys Fisheries, 866-743-4353, www.keysfisheries.com

chispa

225 ALTARA AVENUE   CORAL GABLES, FL 33146

305-648-2600   WWW.CHISPARESTAURANT.COM

Chispa, which means "spark" in Spanish, is a contemporary Latin restaurant and bar inspired by the history and traditions of Hispanic culture. Chispa features innovative dishes reflective of the Hispanic heritage, such as masitas de mahi mahi, sour orange mojo, wood-roasted shrimp, spit-roasted young suckling pig, ceviche, and this recipe for lechon asado risotto. The restaurant's dramatic forty-foot bar is the place for drinks including mojitos, caipirinhas, specialty martinis, and more than twenty wines by the glass. Chef and owner Robbin Haas's creative flair and culinary expertise has been showcased in such South Florida restaurants as the Four Seasons Ocean Grand, Turnberry Isle Resort & Club, the Colony Bistro, and Bang. He was executive and consulting chef for China Grill Café and Red Square, opened the highly successful Baleen, and supervised several restaurants at Noble House Hotels, Resorts, & Hideaways. He opened Chispa in October 2003.

Lechon asado is Spanish for "roast suckling pig." Leftover pork tenderloin works well, but sliced roast pork from the deli counter is a good substitute.

lechon asado (roast pork)
risotto

SERVES 4

1 tablespoon olive oil

1 teaspoon minced shallot

1 cup arborio rice

5 cups chicken broth, or as needed

1 cup shredded roast pork

½ cup grated aged manchego or pecorino cheese

2 tablespoons unsalted butter

Coarse salt and freshly ground black pepper, to taste

1. In a large sauté pan, heat the oil over medium-high heat. Add the shallot and cook, stirring, until translucent, about 2 minutes. Add the rice and stir until the grains are coated in the oil. Stir in 1 cup of the chicken broth. Bring to a simmer, lower the heat to medium, and cook, stirring, until the broth is almost completely absorbed, about 5 minutes.

2. Add the shredded pork and another cup of the broth to the pan. Continue stirring until the broth is once again almost absorbed, about 5 minutes more. Add more broth, a cup at a time and stirring constantly, until the rice is tender and very creamy, 10 to 15 minutes more.

3. Add the cheese, butter, and a little more broth to moisten, stirring to incorporate the butter and cheese. Season to taste with salt and pepper and serve immediately.

and to drink
$ 2001 Cline Zinfandel Bridgehead, California

$$ 2001 Frog's Leap Zinfandel, California

chef's notes Aged manchego cheese, a yellow Spanish cheese that comes from La Mancha, is an excellent grating cheese. Don't confuse it with unaged manchego cheese, which is lighter in color, semifirm, and typically melted.

WHERE TO BUY

Manchego cheese: Di Bruno Brothers, 888-322-4337, www.dibruno.com

ortanique on the mile

278 MIRACLE MILE   CORAL GABLES, FL 33134

305-446-7710   WWW.CINDYHUTSONCUISINE.COM

Chef Cindy Hutson's cuisine of the sun shines brilliantly at Ortanique on the Mile, a mix of bold Caribbean, Floridian, Asian, and Latin flavors that sparkle with indigenous, fresh ingredients. Decked out in a riot of tropical color, Ortanique provides a lush backdrop for a glowing menu that might include South American ceviche, hearts of palm and mango salad, roasted garlic and lemon Caesar, guava soy–barbecued Norwegian salmon, or pan-sautéed Bahamian black grouper with Ortanique orange liqueur sauce. Named best new restaurant in 2000 by *Bon Appétit*, Ortanique is now also in Las Vegas and Washington, D.C. Exotic tropical drinks are a specialty of the house, and the wine list boasts an extensive range of California chardonnays and cabernets.

Escovitch is a style of cooking using vinegar, onions, and spices that is popular on the island of Jamaica. For this recipe, chef Hutson uses snapper, but fresh swordfish, halibut, or cod also works well. Rice and peas is a good accompaniment to this dish. To julienne means to cut into thin, matchstick strips.

snapper

with escovitch sauce

SERVES 6

¼ cup mild olive oil

2 cups thinly sliced yellow onions

2 teaspoons ground allspice

½ cup all-purpose flour

2 cups peeled carrots, julienned

½ cup apple-cider vinegar

2 cups fish stock or bottled clam juice

2 cups chayote (peeled) or zucchini, julienned

1 large red bell pepper, seeded and julienned

1 Scotch bonnet pepper, seeded and finely chopped

1 tablespoon coarse salt, plus more to taste

Chopped leaves from 1 bunch fresh thyme, or 1 teaspoon dried

1 cup canola oil

Six 8-ounce, skin-on snapper fillets

Freshly ground black pepper, to taste

1. Heat the olive oil in a large sauté pan set over high heat. When hot, add the onions and 1 teaspoon of the allspice. Cook, stirring, until the onions are softened, about 4 minutes. Stir in ¼ cup of the flour and turn the heat down to medium.

2. Add the carrots, vinegar, and fish stock. Cook, stirring, until the mixture begins to thicken, about 1 minute. Add the chayote or zucchini, bell pepper, Scotch bonnet, salt, thyme, and remaining teaspoon allspice. Reduce the heat to low and simmer 2 to 3 minutes more, then remove from the heat. The sauce should taste spicy and pickled and the vegetables will be slightly tender. Keep warm.

3. Heat the canola oil in a large, deep sauté pan set over high heat. Sprinkle the fillets with salt and pepper and dust them with the remaining flour. When the oil is very hot, add them to the pan, skin side down. Cook until the skin is golden brown and crisp, about 4 minutes.

4. Using a large spatula, carefully turn the fish over and cook until just opaque in the center (do not overcook), about 3 minutes more.

5. To serve, place the fish on a platter and top with the escovitch sauce.

chef's notes   Chayote, also called christophene, is a mild squash that looks like a pale-green wrinkled pear. Peel it before cooking and there's no need to remove the edible seed, which is quite tasty. Zucchini is a fine substitute.

If you can, substitute 6 allspice berries for the final teaspoon of allspice. Allspice berries have a pungent flavor that tastes like a mixture of cinnamon, cloves, and nutmeg.

and to drink

$ 2002 Sterling Vintners Collection Chardonnay, California

$$ 2000 Ferrari-Carano Reserve Chardonnay, California

WHERE TO BUY

Allspice berries: Penzey's Spices, 800-741-7787, www.penzeys.com

talula

210 23RD STREET   MIAMI BEACH, FL 33139

305-672-0778   WWW.TALULAONLINE.COM

This inviting restaurant is the brainchild of chef and co-owner Andrea Curto-Randazzo and her husband and partner, chef Frank Randazzo. Located in the heart of Miami Beach's burgeoning arts district since 2003, Talula manages to be both an upscale dining destination and a comfy neighborhood restaurant. Encompassing flavors from the Caribbean, Asia, Latin America, Italy, and America, Talula's cuisine is an eclectic blend of both chefs' influences, tastes, and culinary approaches. Appetizers range from the signature shrimp tamale to grilled Sonoma Valley foie gras with caramelized pears and blue corn cakes. Entrées include lime and marisol chile–glazed black grouper with sweet sake broth, udon noodles and bok choy, and grilled Atlantic salmon served with potato-smoked bacon hash, asparagus, and a Dijon-garlic vinaigrette.

Chef Curto-Randazzo's manchego tart works well as a side dish with grilled meat or chicken. Manchego cheese is available at any gourmet cheese store and at some supermarket specialty cheese counters. You can also substitute pecorino Romano.

manchego and vidalia onion tart
with shaved fennel and mixed greens

SERVES 4

1 prepared 9-inch pie crust

8 tablespoons (1 stick) unsalted butter

3 pounds Vidalia onions, thinly sliced

½ cup heavy cream

2 large eggs

1 large egg yolk

1 teaspoon coarse salt

2 teaspoons freshly ground black pepper

¾ pound aged manchego or pecorino Romano cheese, grated

½ cup chopped fresh herbs (parsley, chives, thyme)

1 bulb fennel, thinly sliced

1 red onion, thinly sliced

3 cups baby greens

¼ cup balsamic vinaigrette dressing (store-bought is fine)

¼ cup drained, diced, pickled beets from a can or jar

Chopped fresh chives, for garnish

1. Preheat the oven to 375°F. Thaw the pie crust, if necessary.

2. In a large skillet over medium heat, melt the butter. Add the onions and cook, stirring frequently, until they are very tender and just beginning to caramelize, about 15 minutes. Set aside to cool.

3. In a large bowl, whisk together the cream, eggs, egg yolk, salt, and pepper. Stir in the cheese and herbs. Spread the cooled onions evenly in the bottom of the pie crust. Pour in the egg mixture. Bake until the egg is just set, 25 to 30 minutes. Remove from the oven and cool 5 minutes before slicing.

4. Meanwhile, toss the fennel, onion, and greens in a bowl with the vinaigrette. Divide among 4 serving plates. Place a spoonful of the beets to the side on each plate. Place a slice of the warm tart next to the salad and garnish with chopped chives.

chef's notes Manchego cheese is made exclusively from the milk of the manchego strain of ewes found in the high plateau of central Spain, called La Mancha. Aged manchego cheese takes more than a year to achieve its full nutty flavor.

and to drink

$ 2001 Erath Pinot Blanc, Oregon

$$ 2002 Pinot Blanco Carneros, Robert Sinskey Vineyards, California

WHERE TO BUY

Manchego cheese: La Tienda, 888-472-1022, www.tienda.com

wish

801 COLLINS AVENUE   MIAMI BEACH, FL 33139

305-531-2222   WWW.WISHRESTAURANT.COM

This chic SoBe eatery merges contemporary American cuisine with Asian flavors in a lush indoor-outdoor setting designed by fashion guru Todd Oldham. Located on prime real estate along Collins Avenue, Wish draws a mix of tourists and locals for its Mobil four-star dining. Chef Michael Bloise's food manages to surprise at every bite. Pan-seared foie gras is stacked on slices of cascabel-infused roasted banana, then topped with a toasted black pepper marshmallow, an eclectic touch that balances sweetness with the bite of the chile pepper. A deconstructed gazpacho is poured around a salad of chilled Maine lobster, avocado, grilled chayote squash, and toasted corn. And vegetarians everywhere will thank the chef for his vegetarian platter, which is created based on what five vegetables the diner selects. Mushrooms may show up in a spiced mushroom soup and asparagus in a creamy risotto. Chef Bloise describes his food much like he describes himself: half Italian American and half Vietnamese—hence his American menu with Italian and Asian influences.

This recipe uses lop chong, a dried Chinese sausage that looks and feels like a sweeter version of pepperoni. Dried chorizo, salami, or ham can substitute. Lop chong is available at Chinese grocery stores.

sautéed shrimp
with chinese sausage

SERVES 4

1 tablespoon canola oil

4 links Chinese-style sausage (such as lop chong), diced (or 2 cups diced chorizo or salami)

½ pound large shrimp, peeled and deveined

1 clove garlic, minced

1 teaspoon brown sugar

1 tablespoon soy sauce

¼ cup sake or white wine

Leaves from 2 sprigs fresh basil, torn or chopped

Leaves from 2 sprigs fresh cilantro, torn or chopped

Leaves from 1 sprig fresh mint, torn or chopped

2 bunches scallions, chopped

Coarse salt and freshly ground black pepper, to taste

Rice, for serving

1. In a medium sauté pan over medium-high heat, heat the oil. Add the sausage and cook, stirring, 1 minute. Add the shrimp and cook, stirring, another minute. Stir in the garlic and let it toast for about 10 seconds, then sprinkle the brown sugar and soy sauce into the pan. Pour in the sake and let reduce until slightly thickened and syrupy, about 2 minutes.

2. Add the basil, cilantro, mint, and scallions and toss until just wilted. Season to taste with salt and pepper and serve with rice.

chef's notes When using fresh herbs, consider chopping or ripping them into irregular pieces. Chopping herbs so fine that they mix into the dish can weaken their impact and fresh flavor.

WHERE TO BUY

Chinese sausage:

Culinaire Specialties, 305-635-1249

Sun Hing Foods, 800-258-6669, www.sunhingfoods.com

and to drink

$ 2001 Grove Mill Sauvignon Blanc, New Zealand

$$ 2001 Chalk Hill Sauvignon Blanc, California

new orleans
dining big easy style

If you've never dined in New Orleans (pronounced NAWlins by the locals), then the sad truth is, you've never dined at all. Here, people don't eat to live, they live to eat. As soon as they finish one meal, it's time to talk about what's on the menu next. And the choices are enough to make a person dizzy. From po'boys, the local (but better) version of Philly's hoagies and Manhattan's subs, to Gulf oysters Rockefeller, crawfish étouffée, and shrimp rémoulade, New Orleans is a dining destination second to none. A gumbo of cultures, from African to Spanish, Cajun, and French, came together over the last three centuries to cook up gastronomy so diverse that it truly stands alone. Although Hurricane Katrina took a toll on the restaurant and hospitality industry in this completely original American city, dining in New Orleans will always be something special.

A few chefs really helped put New Orleans on the international map as a dining destination, most notably Chef Paul Prudhomme, who learned to cook at home in Opelousas, Louisiana, in the heart of Cajun country. While at Commander's Palace, chef Prudhomme revolutionized the use of fresh seafood and regional products in his kitchen, a philosophy that wasn't common back in the early 1970s. Another Commander's Palace alumnus, Emeril Lagasse, brought New Orleans' cooking to the Food Network, eventually putting the "Bam!" into a string of restaurants that stretch from the French Quarter to Las Vegas, Atlanta, and Miami Beach.

A new generation of kitchen luminaries, including John Besh of August, Susan Spicer of Herbsaint, and Frank Brigtsen of Brigtsen's, continue innovating and refining the city's restaurant scene. Dining is nothing short of a passionate art form in New Orleans and the word's out. The millions of tourists who visit New Orleans every year come hungry. And they've surely come to the right place.

In this chapter, ten of the city's finest restaurants, including Commander's Palace, Brigsten's, August, and Herbsaint, open their kitchens to share recipes that bring true New Orleans flavor to your table.

brigtsen's restaurant

723 DANTE STREET   NEW ORLEANS, LA 70118

504-861-7610   WWW.BRIGTSENS.COM

Take the St. Charles streetcar all the way uptown to Maple Street, walk two blocks toward the river, and you'll find Brigtsen's, a family-run restaurant located in a cozy nineteenth-century Victorian cottage. Owned by chef Frank Brigtsen and his wife, Marna, this relaxed eatery delivers updated versions of classic Cajun, Creole, and American specialties. The menu changes daily, but you might enjoy everything from sautéed soft-shell crab with spiced pecans and lemon bordelaise sauce to braised rabbit in phyllo pastry with creamed spinach, bacon, mushrooms, leeks, and white truffle oil. In a city dripping with shrimp rémoulade, Brigtsen's version, with deviled egg, guacamole, and mirliton corn relish, is one of the best in town.

And no wonder—Brigtsen, named best chef in the Southeast at the 1998 James Beard awards, learned many of his moves during his seven-year tenure with Paul Prudhomme, first at Commander's Palace, then at K-Paul's Louisiana Kitchen. If you want to know more, take one of Brigtsen's cooking classes. He teaches Louisiana cuisine at the New Orleans Cooking Experience (504-945-9104; www.neworleanscookingexperience.com), a unique cooking school that offers intimate half-day culinary classes for six to ten students, culminating in an elegant four-course dining experience.

This easy-to-make side dish showcases black-eyed peas, a favorite ingredient in the South, where they're traditionally eaten on New Year's Day or combined with rice and sausage to make Hoppin' John. Unlike most dried legumes, they don't need soaking and they cook in no time.

black-eyed pea
succotash

SERVES 8

6 cups frozen
black-eyed peas

2 bay leaves

2¾ teaspoons salt,
plus more to taste

½ cup Steen's cane vinegar
or rice-wine vinegar

2 tablespoons honey

1½ teaspoons Coleman's
mustard powder

1½ teaspoons Zatarain's
Creole mustard or
whole-grain mustard

¼ teaspoon Tabasco®

¼ teaspoon minced garlic

¾ cup extra-virgin olive oil

6 cups thawed, frozen corn

1 cup finely diced red onion

1 cup finely diced bell
pepper (preferably a mixture
of red and green)

1. In a large saucepan, combine the black-eyed peas, bay leaves, and 2 teaspoons of the salt. Cover with water by 2 inches and bring to a boil over high heat. Reduce the heat to low and simmer until the peas are tender, about 10 minutes. Drain, discard the bay leaves, and set the peas aside.

2. In a small bowl, whisk together the vinegar, honey, mustard powder, mustard, Tabasco, garlic, and ¾ teaspoon of the salt. Pouring in a slow stream and whisking constantly, whisk in the olive oil. Set aside.

3. In a very large mixing bowl, combine the peas, corn, onion, and bell pepper. Toss well with the vinaigrette and season to taste with more salt if needed. Refrigerate until ready to serve.

chef's notes   The succotash is best made a day ahead, so that the flavors marry. It will last for up to a week in the refrigerator.

Zatarain's is a favorite full-flavored mustard in New Orleans. A suitable alternative is Pommery-style whole-grain brown mustard.

Steen's cane vinegar is made from Louisiana sugarcane and has a distinctive sweet aftertaste. Rice-wine vinegar makes a fine substitute.

and to drink

$ 2003 Rosemount Shiraz, Australia

$$ 2003 Bonny Doon Le Cigare Volant, California

WHERE TO BUY

Steen's Louisiana Cane Vinegar: Steen's, 800-725-1654,
www.steensyrup.com

Zatarain's Creole mustard:
The Cajun Connection, 504-914-8371, www.thecajunconnection.com
Zatarain's, 888-264-5460, www.zatarain.com

broussard's

819 CONTI STREET   NEW ORLEANS, LA 70112

504-581-3861   WWW.BROUSSARDS.COM

Local foodies went into mourning when chef Gunter Preuss shuttered his much-revered Versailles restaurant in the Garden District more than a decade ago. The Berlin-born chef had spent twenty years elevating Creole fare to its most elegant level, and in a town where good restaurants are as common as street buskers, that's saying something. Fortunately, chef Preuss and his gracious wife, Evelyn, touched down at Broussard's, taking over the French Quarter restaurant, with its formal dining room and lovely courtyard complete with its century-old wisteria vine, in 1995. Today, with youngest son Marc as general manager, the restaurant offers a true New Orleans dining experience. Chef Preuss works magic with sweet Gulf crabmeat in dishes like crabmeat Broussard's, baked in artichoke-Brie béchamel with spinach. Another local favorite is the redfish Ponchartrain, panfried and served on shrimp, crabmeat, and oyster mushroom étouffée. Forget your diet when you visit Broussard's; chef Preuss isn't stingy with the cream and butter. The desserts are equally decadent, especially the double chocolate marquise Nelly Melba, dripping with bittersweet chocolate sauce. The restaurant backs up to the historic Hermann-Grima House, and frequently utilizes the shared space for glittering parties. Ask to see a cigar and cognac menu after dinner.

The secret to this wonderfully simple chicken dish is using apple brandy in the sauce. Either French Calvados or applejack brandy does the trick.

sautéed free-range chicken breast
with calvados and thyme

SERVES 6

6 tablespoons (¾ stick) unsalted butter

Six 5- to 6-ounce boneless, skinless chicken breast halves

Coarse salt and freshly ground white pepper, to taste

½ cup Calvados or applejack brandy

¼ cup chopped scallions

2 shallots, chopped

1 clove garlic, chopped

1 teaspoon chopped fresh thyme, or ½ teaspoon dried

1 cup chopped mushrooms

1 cup heavy cream

1. In a large sauté pan over medium-high heat, melt the butter. Season the chicken breasts with salt and pepper and cook, turning once, until cooked through, 3 to 4 minutes per side. Remove the chicken to a plate, cover, and keep warm.

2. Add the Calvados to the hot pan, place over medium heat, and cook, stirring with a wooden spoon and scraping up any browned bits from the bottom of the pan. Add the scallions, shallots, garlic, thyme, mushrooms, and cream and cook until the cream just comes to a boil. Lower the heat and simmer, uncovered, until the sauce has thickened slightly and reduced by about one third, about 10 minutes.

3. Return the chicken breasts to the pan, season, and simmer for 2 minutes longer. Season the sauce with salt and pepper to taste and serve.

chef's notes   Calvados is a dry apple brandy aged in oak casks and made in the town of Calvados, located in the Normandy region of northern France. Calvados lends a fruity note to chicken, veal, and pork dishes.

When chopping fresh thyme, carefully strip off the small leaves from the woody stem; discard the stem and chop the thyme as directed.

and to drink
$ Pinot Gris Trimbach, Alsace
$$ 2004 Cakebread Sauvignon Blanc, California

WHERE TO BUY
Calvados: 67 Wine & Spirits, 888-671-6767, www.67wine.com

herbsaint

701 ST. CHARLES AVENUE   NEW ORLEANS, LA 70130

504-524-4114   WWW.HERBSAINT.COM

Talented chef Donald Link has officially taken over for owner Susan Spicer at this understated bistro in the Warehouse District, a perfect backdrop for Link's gutsy, flavorful Franco-American menu. Rooted in down-home sensibility—he's a Louisiana son after all—his fricasseed rabbit with homemade pappardelle and wild mushrooms, muscovy duck leg confit with dirty rice, and a Spanish-inspired dish of shrimp with Romesco are all divine. Link's menu reflects the bounty of near and far with rabbits and suckling pigs from nearby southern Mississippi, locally caught wild shrimp, and regular shipments of fresh seafood from the West and East coasts. The restaurant's minimalist decor and cool lighting sets off a jazzy likeness of music legend Buddy Bolden in the dining room. Its name, Herbsaint, refers to a brand name of anise-flavored liqueur, made in New Orleans in the mid-nineteenth century as a cheaper domestic alternative to the French-made absinthe popular in intellectual and artistic circles.

These short ribs marry well with mashed potatoes flavored with horseradish and sour cream.

cane-braised
beef short ribs

SERVES 6

5 pounds beef short ribs,
trimmed of excess fat

Coarse salt and freshly
ground black pepper,
to taste

1¼ cups all-purpose flour

3 tablespoons canola oil

3 stalks celery, chopped

2 onions, chopped

2 carrots, chopped

1 cup red wine

2 teaspoons tomato paste

2 cups canned chopped
tomatoes, drained

4 cups chicken broth

1 tablespoon Steen's cane
vinegar or rice-wine vinegar

2 teaspoons Steen's cane
syrup or light corn syrup

3 cloves garlic

2 sprigs fresh thyme,
or ¾ teaspoon dried

1 sprig fresh rosemary,
or ½ teaspoon dried

1 tablespoon unsalted butter

1. Preheat the oven to 300°F.

2. Sprinkle the ribs generously with salt and pepper. Place ½ cup of the flour on a plate and dredge the ribs in the flour, coating thoroughly. Shake off the excess flour. Set the ribs aside; discard any remaining flour.

3. In a large skillet, heat 2 tablespoons of the oil over medium-high heat. Add half the ribs to the skillet and cook until golden brown on all sides, about 6 minutes. Transfer the ribs to a roasting pan. Repeat with the remaining ribs, adding more oil to the pan if needed.

4. Add the celery, onions, and carrots to the skillet the ribs cooked in. Lower the heat to medium and cook, stirring, until the vegetables are lightly browned, about 5 minutes. Sprinkle ¼ cup of the remaining flour over the vegetables and stir to incorporate. Pour in the wine and use a wooden spoon to scrape up any browned bits from the bottom of the skillet. Stir in the tomato paste and chopped tomatoes and cook until the mixture begins to thicken, about 20 minutes.

5. Stir in the chicken broth, vinegar, cane syrup, garlic, thyme, and rosemary. Bring to a simmer, season with salt and pepper, and pour over the ribs in the roasting pan. (The sauce should come halfway up the short ribs but not cover them.) Cover the dish with aluminum foil and bake until the ribs are fork-tender, 3 to 4 hours.

6. Remove the short ribs from the oven and allow to cool. When cool enough to handle, remove the meat from the bones. Discard the bones and refrigerate the meat until ready to cook. Using a spoon, skim off and discard any fat from the braising liquid. Strain the liquid through a sieve and discard the solids. Place the liquid in a heavy-bottomed saucepan and bring to a boil over high heat. Lower the heat and simmer, uncovered, until the sauce thickens enough to coat the back of a spoon, 15 to 20 minutes. Whisk in the butter, season to taste with salt and pepper, and keep warm.

7. Place the remaining ½ cup flour on a plate. Dredge the cold short rib meat in the flour and shake off the excess. Heat the remaining tablespoon oil in a large skillet set over medium-high heat. Add the meat and cook until crispy on the outside and warmed all the way through. Return the meat to the sauce and serve.

and to drink

$ 2001 Chateau Valcombe Cotes de Ventoux, France

$$ 2001 Les Forts de Latour, Bordeaux, France

chef's notes If you have the time, season the ribs the day before cooking and let them sit overnight in the fridge. This will really impart the flavor of the seasoning to the meat. When you're searing the short ribs, use moderate heat so you don't burn them.

WHERE TO BUY

Beef short ribs: Lobel's, 877-783-4512, www.lobels.com

Steen's 100% Pure Cane Syrup and Steen's Louisiana Cane Vinegar:
Steen's, 800-725-1654, www.steensyrup.com

restaurant august

301 TCHOUPITOULAS STREET   NEW ORLEANS, LA 70130

504-299-9777   WWW.REST-AUGUST.COM

Bayou-born chef John Besh creates extraordinary European-style cuisine with Gulf Coast ingredients in an atmospheric circa-1800s French building, brought back to its original splendor thanks to a $3.5-million renovation in 2001. Besh, a graduate of the Culinary Institute of America, worked at Michelin-starred restaurants in Germany and France before returning to his Louisiana roots. Recognized as one of *Condé Nast Traveler*'s fifty "Hot Tables" the year it opened, August was joined by Besh's second enterprise, the Besh Steakhouse at Harrah's, in 2003. The chef's frequently changing menu, divided into "To Begin," "To Continue," and "To Finish," always includes his signature BLT— buster crabs, lettuce, and tomatoes on pain perdu, a Cajun take on French toast that means "lost bread" in French. Dinner might also include tongue and cheek (a combination of foie gras, veal cheeks, and beef tongue terrine); Moroccan spiced duck with polenta, duck foie gras, and cherries tempura; or crispy red snapper with a crab-stuffed piquillo pepper, edamame, and truffle vinaigrette. The restaurant is located right outside the French Quarter in the Central Business District, just three blocks from Canal Street.

This shrimp and squash risotto can be served either as an appetizer or a main course. Chef Besh uses a small pumpkin for the squash, but any winter squash works well, including butternut or acorn. Save time by using peeled and cut squash-in-a-bag, available in the produce department of most supermarkets.

shrimp and butternut squash
risotto

SERVES 4

2 tablespoons sugar

2 cups ½-inch cubes peeled butternut squash

2½ tablespoons unsalted butter

1 pound large shrimp, peeled and deveined

2 cloves garlic, minced

Coarse salt and freshly ground black pepper, to taste

8 cups (2 quarts) reduced-sodium chicken broth

1 small yellow onion, finely diced

2 cups arborio rice

½ cup grated Parmesan cheese

¼ cup heavy cream

¼ cup chopped fresh chives

1. Bring a medium pot filled two thirds full of lightly salted water to a boil. Add the sugar and stir until dissolved. Add the squash and cook 1 minute. Drain and set aside.

2. In a heavy-bottomed medium sauté pan over medium heat, melt 1 tablespoon of the butter. Add the shrimp and garlic, season with salt and pepper, and cook, stirring, until the shrimp is just cooked through, about 5 minutes. Remove from the heat and cool. Refrigerate until ready to use.

3. Pour the chicken broth into a medium pot and place over medium-high heat at the back of the stove. Bring just to a simmer, then lower the heat so that the broth stays very hot but just below a simmer.

4. In a large heavy-bottomed saucepan over medium heat, melt the remaining 1½ tablespoons butter. Add the onion and cook, stirring, until just translucent, about 4 minutes. Add the rice and stir until all the grains are coated with butter.

5. Add the chicken broth, 1 cup at a time, and stir continuously until the broth is absorbed. Repeat, adding more broth 1 cup at a time and stirring, until the rice is firm to the bite but not crunchy, about 25 minutes.

6. Add the squash and continue cooking, stirring, until the squash is heated through; add more broth if necessary. Add the reserved shrimp and heat through. Stir in the Parmesan and cream. Remove from the heat and stir in the chives. Season to taste with salt and pepper and serve immediately.

WHERE TO BUY

Risotto rice: Gourmet Pasta Cheese, 800-386-9198, www.pastacheese.com

chef's notes Risotto is the rice dish of northern Italy, especially popular in Piedmont, Milan, Lombardy, and Venice. Best made with imported Italian rice grown in the Po Valley, the most popular types for risotto are arborio, carnaroli, Roma, and violone nano, with "superfino" indicating the best quality. Risotto rice is large-grained and releases its creamy starches while stirred with broth. Don't rinse risotto rice—you'll wash off the starch that gives it such a creamy consistency.

commander's palace

1403 WASHINGTON AVENUE   NEW ORLEANS, LA 70130

504-899-8221   WWW.COMMANDERSPALACE.COM

With its signature green-and-white awning and beautiful Victorian mansion setting, Commander's Palace is a New Orleans landmark of iconic proportions, the circa-1880 grand dame of the Garden District. Both Emeril Lagasse and Paul Prudhomme started here, and the Brennan family has maintained a tradition of culinary excellence within these hallowed walls since 1969, with standout menu items including turtle soup laced with sherry, trout wrapped in crispy pecan crust, and shrimp rémoulade. Rated number one in *GQ*'s 2005 list of 10 Restaurants That Still Matter, Commander's is a hallmark of fine Creole cuisine—never served Cajun cuisine and never will. Sunday jazz brunch is a must, complete with a Bloody Mary, egg Sardou (poached egg with creamed spinach and hollandaise sauce on an artichoke bottom), a version of the following recipe, made with quail instead of game hen, and one of the best bread puddings in town.

Coffee and molasses give these hens a shiny brown sheen. For the stuffing, the chef recommends Stove Top Stuffing®, or you can use another favorite kind.

chicory coffee–lacquered
game hens

SERVES 4

Stuffing

One 6-ounce box stuffing mix

Leaves from 1 sprig thyme, chopped, or ½ teaspoon dried

Creole or Season-All® seasoning, to taste

Sauce

2 tablespoons unsalted butter

¼ cup peeled, diced carrot

¼ cup diced onion

¼ cup diced celery

1½ cups chicken broth

½ cup brewed and cooled chicory or regular coffee

½ cup molasses

1 tablespoon black peppercorns

1 sprig fresh thyme, or ½ teaspoon dried

Cabbage

½ cup diced bacon

½ cup diced onion

2 green apples, peeled, cored, and diced

1 small head purple cabbage, shredded

2 tablespoons apple-cider vinegar

(*continued*)

1. To make the stuffing, prepare the stuffing mix according to package directions, omitting the seasoning packet. Stir in the thyme leaves and Creole seasoning. Let cool.

2. To make the sauce, heat a medium saucepan over high heat for 3 minutes. Add the butter, carrot, onion, and celery and cook until the vegetables are soft, about 4 minutes, stirring occasionally. Stir in the chicken broth, coffee, molasses, peppercorns, and fresh thyme. Simmer until the sauce is reduced by about half and thickens slightly, about 15 minutes. Strain and set aside.

3. To make the cabbage, heat a large sauté pan over medium-high heat. Add the bacon and onion and cook, stirring frequently, for 3 minutes. Add the apples and cook for 1 minute. Add the cabbage and vinegar and season with salt and pepper. Cook, stirring frequently, until the cabbage is tender, about 10 minutes. Add the brown sugar. Season to taste again with salt and pepper and set aside.

4. To make the hens, preheat the oven to 350°F. Place the hens in a large roasting pan. Sprinkle the birds all over with the Creole seasoning. Spoon the prepared stuffing loosely into the cavity of each hen. Rub the melted butter onto the breast of each to prevent them from drying out. Roast the hens for 45 minutes.

5. Remove the hens from the oven. Using a pastry brush, coat the birds with the sauce. Return to the oven and continue to cook until the skin is shiny and the birds are cooked through (an instant-read thermometer inserted into the thickest part of a thigh but not touching the bone should register 170°F), 5 to 10 minutes more. Remove the birds from the oven and let rest for 10 minutes.

6. Meanwhile, make the salad. In a large bowl, toss together the apple, sprouts, and vinegar. Season to taste with salt and pepper and set aside.

Coarse salt and freshly
ground black pepper,
to taste

2 tablespoons brown
sugar

Hens

4 Cornish hens

1½ tablespoons Creole or
Season-All seasoning

1 tablespoon unsalted
butter, melted

Salad

1 green apple, peeled,
cored, and cut into thin
matchsticks

¾ cup mixed sprouts

1 tablespoon
apple-cider vinegar

Coarse salt and freshly
ground black
pepper, to taste

7. When ready to serve, reheat the cabbage. Spoon the cabbage onto the center of each of 4 serving plates. Place a hen on top of the cabbage and top each with a quarter of the apple salad. Drizzle some of the remaining sauce around the hens and serve.

chef's notes At Commander's this dish is made with quail, prized for its delicately flavored meat. Cornish hens make a fine substitution.

It's a little-known fact that coffee first came to America by way of New Orleans in the mid-1700s. The French brought coffee to America with them from Martinique as they settled new colonies along the Mississippi. During the Civil War, when coffee was hard to come by, French New Orleanians began adding chicory to stretch their precious grounds. Chicory is the root of the endive plant, which, when roasted and ground, softens the bitter edge of dark-roasted coffee and imbues it with a chocolaty flavor. To this day, chicory-flavored coffee is served at all the best coffeehouses in town, usually with the addition of steaming milk for café au lait.

and to drink

$ 2003 Bodegas Borsao
Garnacho, Spain

$$ 1998 Badia a Coltibuno,
Chianti, Italy

WHERE TO BUY

Chicory coffee: French Market Coffee, 800-554-7234,
www.frenchmarketcoffee.com

peristyle

1041 DUMAINE STREET   NEW ORLEANS, LA 70116

504-593-9535   WWW.WOLFESOFNEWORLEANS.COM

It's not easy taking over a legend. But that's what chef Tom Wolfe did in 2004, when he bought the venerable Peristyle from Anne Kearney in 2004. Wolfe and Kearney go back a ways—they worked together many moons ago at Mr. B's Bistro and Emeril's. Wolfe has so far trod lightly with Kearney's contemporary French menu, preserving signature dishes, such as the onion, roasted garlic, and white anchovy pissaladière and Gulf drum amandine with leek and potato hash. Return guests will find the setting comfortably familiar. The nineteenth-century building and the no-nonsense dining room fitted with dark woods, terrazzo floors, bentwood chairs, white linens, and flickering candles set a handsome backdrop for the cuisine. Note Alonzo Lansford's huge oil paintings of architectural structures in City Park, including the restaurant's namesake Peristyle. The paintings were created in the 1930s for the old Gentilich family restaurant that used to occupy the premises.

This updated pork and cabbage recipe incorporates local New Orleans Abita beer into its sauce.

beer-braised pork
and crisp herb cabbage

SERVES 4

Pork

¼ cup soy sauce

2 tablespoons minced shallots

1 tablespoon chopped garlic

1 tablespoon Dijon mustard

¾ teaspoon coarse salt

¾ teaspoon freshly ground black pepper

1 pound pork shoulder, cut into 2-inch-thick slices

2 tablespoons vegetable oil

2 cups Abita amber beer or other lager-style beer

1 tablespoon unsalted butter

1 red bell pepper, cut into thin strips

Cabbage

½ cup rice-wine vinegar

¼ cup white vinegar

Juice of 2 lemons

1 tablespoon sugar

2 teaspoons minced garlic

1 teaspoon crushed red pepper flakes

½ teaspoon ground allspice

½ teaspoon ground coriander

1 tablespoon coarse salt

½ head cabbage, shredded

1 red onion, thinly sliced

1. To make the pork, in a large nonreactive bowl, whisk together the soy sauce, shallots, garlic, mustard, salt, and pepper. Add the pork, turn to coat, and marinate, refrigerated, for at least 1 hour and up to overnight.

2. Remove the pork from the marinade and pat dry. Reserve the marinade.

3. In a large sauté pan, heat the oil over medium-high heat. Add the pork slices and brown lightly on both sides.

4. Add the reserved marinade, the beer, and butter to the pan. Bring to a boil, lower the heat, and simmer, uncovered, until the sauce is reduced by half, 25 to 30 minutes.

5. Using a slotted spoon, lift the pork out of the pan and place it on a cutting board. Using a sharp knife, finely chop it. Put the pork back in the pan with the sauce. Add the red bell pepper and set the pan aside.

6. To make the cabbage, in a large bowl, whisk together the rice vinegar, white vinegar, lemon juice, sugar, garlic, red pepper flakes, allspice, coriander, and salt. Add the cabbage, onion, parsley, basil, and thyme and toss well.

7. Reheat the pork and serve alongside the cabbage.

WHERE TO BUY

Abita beer: 800-737-2311, www.abita.com

Snake River Ranch pork: 800-657-6305, www.snakeriverfarms.com

½ cup chopped fresh
flat-leaf parsley leaves

¼ cup chopped fresh
basil leaves

1½ teaspoons chopped
fresh thyme leaves

and to drink

$ Abita Springs Amber

$$ 2001 Riefle Tokay Pinot
Gris Grand Cru Steinert,
Alsace

chef's notes Abita beer is made locally in Abita Springs, across the Ponchartrain Causeway in the piney woods thirty miles north of New Orleans. A favorite brew among the locals, Abita amber is a Munich-style lager brewed with crystal malt and Perle hops. It has a smooth, malty, slightly caramel flavor and a rich amber color that blends perfectly with pork.

Peristyle's menu features Kurobuta Snake River Ranch pork, considered the "Kobe" of pork. This all-natural Berkshire pork, prized for its superior taste, texture, and marbling, has a darker color and richer flavor than traditional American white pork.

the new orleans grill at the windsor court

30 GRAVIER STREET   NEW ORLEANS, LA 70130

504-522-1992   WWW.WINDSORCOURTHOTEL.COM

Located in the *très* elegant Windsor Court Hotel, the New Orleans Grill, formerly the Grill Room, sets the standard for high-end, over-the-top dining in New Orleans. Dress to impress (gents must wear a jacket in the evening) and settle in for quite a gastronomic ride. Chef Jonathan Wright, formerly of Raffles in Singapore and his own restaurant, La Gousse D'Ail ("the garlic clove"), in the U.K., constructs artful European dishes with seemingly endless creativity. Who knew that partnering crab ravioli with cilantro and preserved Meyer lemon poached in crab and ginger bisque would be this perfect? Humble boudin—locally made Cajun sausage that tastes like spicy scrapple in a casing—is paired magically with a quail and porcini salad with fried quail eggs and crispy pancetta. Roasted duck is enhanced beautifully by slow-cooked Louisiana peaches topped with a slab of seared foie gras. Chef Wright gets it right just about every time, designing contemporary European cuisine supported by his French training and brought to life with a bounty of Louisiana products. Serious food has a home right here at the New Orleans Grill.

This recipe uses a slow cooker to braise the lamb shanks for six hours until they're fall-off-the-bone tender.

slow-cooked lamb shanks
with carrots, turnips, and shallots

SERVES 4

2 tablespoons unsalted butter

½ cup olive oil

Four 10- to 12-ounce lamb shanks, trimmed of excess fat

2 cups white wine

2 cups chicken broth or water

8 large shallots (4 cut into 1-inch dice, 4 left whole)

12 carrots, peeled (6 cut into 1-inch dice, 6 cut into thirds)

8 small turnips, peeled (4 cut into 1-inch dice, 4 cut into thirds)

8 cloves garlic, chopped

1 celery heart or 3 tender inner celery ribs, cut into 1-inch dice

3 sprigs fresh thyme

2 sprigs fresh rosemary

1 bay leaf

Dash Worcestershire sauce

1 teaspoon coarse salt

1 teaspoon freshly ground black pepper

1. In a large sauté pan set over medium heat, heat 1 tablespoon of the butter and ¼ cup of the olive oil. When the butter begins to foam, add the lamb shanks and cook until browned on all sides, about 8 minutes. Transfer the shanks to the container of a slow cooker.

2. Pour off the excess fat from the pan and place over medium heat. Add the wine and chicken broth to the pan and use a spatula to scrape up any browned bits from the bottom of the pan. Reduce the heat and simmer the mixture until it is reduced by about one third, about 15 minutes, then pour over the lamb in the slow cooker.

3. Wipe the pan out with paper towels and return it to medium heat. Add the remaining tablespoon butter and the remaining ¼ cup olive oil. When the butter has melted, add the diced shallots, diced carrots, diced turnips, garlic, and celery and cook, stirring occasionally, until they just begin to soften, about 6 minutes.

4. Scatter the cooked diced vegetables around the meat in the slow cooker. Add 2 sprigs of the thyme, 1 sprig of the rosemary, the bay leaf, Worcestershire, salt, and pepper. Turn the slow cooker to the low setting and cook, covered, for 6 hours.

5. Remove the lamb carefully from the pot and set aside. Strain the liquid in the pot through a sieve into a large saucepan. Discard the solids. Add the remaining shallots, carrots, and turnips to the pan and simmer until the vegetables are just tender, 10 to 15 minutes.

6. Remove the vegetables from the pan with a slotted spoon and place them back in the slow cooker. Cover and turn the cooker to low heat to keep warm.

7. Place the saucepan with the sauce in it back over medium heat and simmer until it is thick enough to coat the back of a spoon, about 20 minutes. Pour the sauce over the meat and vegetables, add the remaining sprigs of thyme and rosemary, and serve.

and to drink

$ 1999 Voss Vineyards Shiraz, Napa, California

$$ 1996 Chateau Haut Bages Averous Bordeaux, France

chef's notes Searing the shanks caramelizes their outsides, giving the meat wonderful color and flavor. When you buy your lamb shanks, ask for the shoulder cut, which is more tender and flavorful than shanks from the leg.

WHERE TO BUY

Organic lamb: Whole Foods, multiple locations, www.wholefoods.com

victor's grill at the ritz-carlton

921 CANAL STREET   NEW ORLEANS, LA 70112

504-524-1331   WWW.RITZCARLTON.COM

Victor's Grill showcases the talents of Irish-born chef Matthew Murphy in a sumptuous setting of tufted velvet banquettes, rich brocade, fine linens, and silk upholstery. (Ask for the Cheater's Booth—a private dining area enclosed in peek-a-boo velvet draperies.) Chef Murphy, who studied culinary arts at the prestigious Cathal Brugha College in Dublin, honed his skills at two- and three-star Michelin restaurants in Europe and worked at Commander's Palace before coming to the Ritz. A proponent of sustainable agriculture, Murphy buys local when he can, creating seasonal Louisiana-inspired dishes like pan-seared striped sea bass with squash-asparagus flan, crab claw salad and rémoulade beurre blanc, and roasted duck breast with a duck and apple beignet, braised greens, tomato-raisin fondue, and preserved fig-orange sauce. The best table in the house? A four-top in the kitchen, smack in the middle of all the action. Chef Murphy discusses food preferences with his guests, and prepares a personalized six- to ten-course feast on the spot—he calls it reality dining.

Chef Murphy uses pork broth for a deeper pork flavor in this recipe, but chicken broth will do in a pinch.

pork chops
with country dressing

SERVES 4

1 tablespoon canola oil

Four 8-ounce pork chops

Coarse salt and freshly ground black pepper, to taste

¼ cup (½ stick) unsalted butter

⅓ cup sliced mirliton (chayote) or fennel

⅓ cup chopped celery

⅓ cup chopped onion

⅓ cup chopped green bell pepper

¼ cup chopped garlic

¼ pound andouille sausage, diced

6 canned smoked oysters, chopped

1½ cups plain bread crumbs

1 tablespoon chopped fresh thyme, or 1 teaspoon dried

1 tablespoon chopped fresh rosemary, or 1 teaspoon dried

1 cup chicken broth, plus more if needed

1. Preheat the oven to 350° F.

2. In a heavy ovenproof skillet, heat the oil over medium-high heat. Season the pork chops with salt and pepper. Add the pork chops to the pan and cook until just browned, about 1 minute per side. Transfer the pan to the oven and cook until the pork chops reach 165°F on an instant-read thermometer, about 15 minutes.

3. Meanwhile, melt the butter in a medium skillet over medium heat. Add the mirliton, celery, onion, bell pepper, and garlic and cook, stirring, until tender, about 10 minutes. Stir in the andouille and then the oysters. Fold in the bread crumbs, thyme, and rosemary. Stir in enough chicken broth until the dressing holds together.

4. Season the dressing with salt and pepper to taste. Scrape it onto a serving platter and top with the pork chops.

WHERE TO BUY

Mirliton:

Robért Fresh Market, 504-885-7005, www.robertfreshmarket.com

Whole Foods, multiple locations, www.wholefoods.com

and to drink:

$ 2005 Firestone Vineyard
Select Riesling, California

$$ 2003 Schloss Vollrads
Rheingau Riesling Spätlese,
Germany

chef's notes Mirliton, a favorite vegetable in New Orleans and elsewhere in the South, is also called chayote (chi-OH-tay) or christophene. A mild-flavored squash that looks a little like a wrinkled, pale green pear, mirliton needs to be cooked longer than other summer squash. To prepare, peel the mirliton and chop it. Don't worry about the seed—it's tasty and edible.

rené bistrot

817 COMMON STREET   NEW ORLEANS, LA 70112

504-412-2580   WWW.RENEBISTROT.COM

This Central Business District gem, named a best new restaurant of the year by *Esquire* magazine when it opened in 2002, manages to be both chic and cozy, with its bold contemporary color scheme, copper accents, and metallic tile tableaux. Chef René Bajeux, one of fifty French master chefs living in America, mines the cuisine of his native France, offering his contemporary interpretation of classics like bouillabaisse and a velvety French onion soup topped with Gruyère custard, escargot, and roast duck. Formerly chef at the Windsor Court's (then-named) Grill Room, chef Bajeux does everything from smoking his own salmon to butchering his own meat and creating homemade sausages and pâtés that are truly to die for. The deeply sophisticated menu is reflected in a gorgeous setting dominated by an art-glass mural suggestive of the hills of Provence. Don't miss scrumptious desserts by pastry chef Joy Jessup, notably her chocolate-infused beignets with warm praline sauce.

diver scallops with braised fennel, porcini broth, and parmesan crisps

SERVES 6

Parmesan Crisps

2 cups freshly grated
Parmesan cheese

Broth

1 cup dried porcini
mushrooms

2 tablespoons olive oil

1/4 cup minced shallots

1/2 cup white wine

2 bay leaves

2 cups chicken broth

Coarse salt and freshly
ground black pepper

Fennel

1 tablespoon olive oil

1/2 medium fennel bulb,
quartered lengthwise
and thinly sliced

1 Vidalia onion, finely
chopped

1 cup frozen, shelled
edamame beans

2 tablespoons
chopped chives

Coarse salt and freshly
ground black pepper

Scallops

1 tablespoon olive oil

2 pounds sea scallops

Coarse salt and freshly
ground black pepper

6 sprigs fresh herbs
(thyme, parsley, tarragon)

1. Preheat the oven to 350° F.

2. To make the Parmesan crisps, line a baking sheet with aluminum foil. Spread the cheese over the foil in a thin, even layer. Bake until golden brown, about 10 minutes. Remove from the oven and let cool 5 minutes. Break the sheet of crisp cheese into large pieces. Set aside.

3. To make the broth, place the mushrooms in a small bowl and cover with boiling water. Let soak 20 minutes. Drain, reserving the liquid, and chop the mushrooms. Set aside.

4. Heat the olive oil in a medium sauté pan over medium heat. Add the shallots and cook, stirring, until just tender, about 3 minutes. Add the mushrooms and cook another 2 minutes. Add the white wine and bay leaves and simmer until most of the liquid has evaporated, about 5 minutes.

5. Add the chicken broth and reserved mushroom liquid and simmer over medium heat until reduced by half, about 15 minutes. Remove the bay leaves and season the liquid with salt and pepper to taste.

6. To make the fennel, heat the olive oil in a large sauté pan over medium heat. Add the fennel and onion and cook, stirring, until golden, about 10 minutes. Stir in the edamame and chives and season to taste with salt and pepper. Keep warm.

7. To make the scallops, in a large sauté pan, heat the olive oil over medium-high heat. Sprinkle the scallops with salt and pepper. When the oil is very hot, add the scallops and cook, turning once, until just browned, about 1 minute per side. Remove from the heat and let them rest in the pan for a few minutes.

8. To assemble the dish, reheat the broth if necessary. Place 1 crisp in each of 6 bowls and top with the fennel mixture and scallops. Pour some of the broth into each bowl, garnish each with an herb sprig, and serve.

chef's notes Drying has long been used to preserve fruits and vegetables, including mushrooms, to enjoy their flavor year-round. Dried mushrooms must be reconstituted, or softened in liquid, to bring their pungent, earthy flavor back to life. Add reconstituted mushrooms at the beginning of the cooking process, to allow their highly concentrated flavors to permeate the entire dish.

Dried mushrooms will keep for months without refrigeration, and for a year or more if frozen. To reconstitute, soak the mushrooms in warm water for 20 to 30 minutes, saving the water for soups or sauces. (It freezes well.)

If you can't find dried porcini mushrooms, you can substitute fresh portobello or oyster mushrooms.

and to drink
$ 2001 Stone Cellars Sauvignon Blanc, California
$$ 2001 Chalk Hill Sauvignon Blanc, California

WHERE TO BUY

Dried porcini mushrooms: Earthy Delights, 800-367-4709, www.earthy.com

stella!

1032 CHARTRES STREET   NEW ORLEANS, LA 70116

504-587-0091   WWW.RESTAURANTSTELLA.COM

Lake Charles native chef Scott Boswell brings training in France, Italy, and Asia to the table at Stella!, the restaurant named for Stanley Kowalski's bellow in *A Streetcar Named Desire*. Prior to opening Stella! in 2004, Boswell worked at a diverse group of impressive restaurants, from Enoteca Pinchiorri (home of the Italian Iron Chef) in Florence, Italy, to the Windsor Court's Grill Room and the well-regarded Rainbow Ranch Lodge in Big Sky, Montana. The chef, a CIA graduate, uses Louisiana ingredients in such globally accented dishes as tandoori-spiced salmon, tomato curry puree with cumin-grilled shrimp, and cayenne-cured pork loin. The atmosphere is crisply Old World rustic, with functional antiques and clean lines setting an understated tone. A thoughtful wine list earned the restaurant the *Wine Spectator* Award of Excellence in 2004 and 2005.

This global take on traditional tomato soup borrows exotic flavors from East Indian curry and Thai chile sauce.

tomato curry puree with
cumin-grilled shrimp

3 tablespoons olive oil

⅓ cup chopped garlic

3 tablespoons peeled finely chopped ginger

4 pounds diced pear tomatoes (or two 28-ounce cans chopped tomatoes, drained)

2 cups ketchup

2 cups chicken broth

2 tablespoons sriracha chili sauce (or 1 teaspoon cayenne)

1 tablespoon garam masala, or to taste

2 cups heavy cream

Sugar, to taste

Coarse salt and freshly ground black pepper, to taste

2 pounds large shrimp, peeled and deveined

1 teaspoon ground cumin

Chopped fresh chives, for garnish

1. In a large saucepan, heat the oil over medium-high heat. Add the garlic and ginger and cook, stirring, until they are lightly browned, about 2 minutes. Add the tomatoes, ketchup, and chicken broth. Bring to a boil, lower the heat, and simmer for 15 minutes.

2. Stir in the sriracha, garam masala, and cream and bring just to a simmer. Remove from the heat. Working in small batches, puree the soup in a blender. Season to taste with sugar, salt, and pepper. Add more garam masala if you'd like a stronger curry flavor.

3. Sprinkle the shrimp with cumin and salt. Set a nonstick grill pan or cast-iron skillet over high heat. When very hot, add the shrimp and cook until seared and just cooked through, about 2 minutes per side. Remove from the pan and keep warm.

4. Reheat the soup if necessary and ladle into bowls. Garnish the soup with a generous portion of shrimp and fresh chives.

WHERE TO BUY

Garam masala: Import Food, 887-618-8424, www.importfood.com
Sriracha: Asian Food Grocer, 888-482-2742, www.asianfoodgrocer.com

and to drink

$ Trimbach Gewürztraminer, Alsace, France

$$ Hugel Gewürztraminer Cuvée Jubilee, Alsace, France

chef's notes Masalas, different in every Indian kitchen, can be made up of more than a dozen spices: black or green cardamom pods, cayenne, cinnamon, cloves, coriander, cumin, mustard seed, star anise, and turmeric to name a few. While curried dishes are ubiquitous, it's important to know that curry is a blend of spices, not a single spice, and many chefs blend their own top-secret combination by hand. Sriracha chili sauce, made from vinegar, red chiles, sugar, salt, and garlic, is an intense Thai sauce, delicious in everything from curries to Buffalo-style chicken wings.

If you're feeling ambitious, here is chef Scott Boswell's recipe for garam masala.

• • •

Garam Masala

1 tablespoon cumin seeds

1 tablespoon coriander seeds

1 tablespoon mustard seeds

1 teaspoon whole black peppercorns

3 whole cloves

3 whole green cardamom pods

1 cinnamon stick

3 bay leaves

Heat a dry skillet or sauté pan over medium heat. When the pan is hot, add the spices, then quickly stir the mix until they release their rich aromas, about 1 minute. Cool the spices and grind in a spice grinder or coffee grinder dedicated only to spices.

new york city

take a bite out of the big apple

The city that never sleeps is also the city that never stops eating. New York's food scene is as frenetic and diverse as its population. With nearly 40 percent of its more than eight million residents foreign-born, New York City sets an international table. From Sicilian slices on Arthur Avenue in the Bronx to Middle Eastern meze on Atlantic Avenue in Brooklyn, the Big Apple boasts eclectic neighborhoods full of fabulous food, bustling markets, and colorful festivals.

If you're hungry, New York City will satisfy, with more than 18,000 restaurants serving up delicious dishes from every corner of the globe. From haute French cuisine, Brazilian *feijoada*, and New York pizza to sushi, souvlaki, and sandwiches, there is a dish to tempt every palate.

Some of the eating you'll do is neighborhood driven. New York's Chinatown, America's largest, is the obvious destination for everything from soup dumplings to pad thai. And in Little Italy, streets are crowded with mom-

and-pop spaghetti joints, pizza parlors, and Italian pastry shops. South Street Seaport, despite its touristy sheen, is still a great place for fresh seafood and oysters on the half shell.

But what makes New York a true foodie mecca is the sense that around every corner, a great meal might await. The best chefs in the world want to work in Manhattan, and many of them do. The glamour, the pace, the sheer excess of it all invigorates a restaurant scene that is second to none.

In this chapter, ten of the city's finest restaurants, including Daniel Boulud's Daniel, Charlie Palmer's Aureole, and Jean-Georges Vongerichten's Jean Georges, offer recipes you'll actually be able to re-create at home, without first taking a crash course at the Culinary Institute of America.

annisa

13 BARROW STREET   NEW YORK, NY 10014

212-741-6699   WWW.ANNISARESTAURANT.COM

Annisa is an upscale contemporary American restaurant with a small, elegant bar and an extensive wine list. The airy, minimally adorned room features creamy walls and polished wood floors. A large white curtain gathers along one wall. Flickering candlelight and comfortable banquettes create an atmosphere of whispered intimacy.

Chef and co-owner Anita Lo was named one of America's ten best new chefs by *Food & Wine* magazine the year after the restaurant opened in 2000. Located in the heart of the West Village, Annisa offers a seasonally changing, eclectic menu that reflects Lo's multicultural Chinese-American upbringing and her solid foundation in French technique. The ninety-bottle wine list, drawn solely from women vintners, was created by master sommelier Roger Dagorn and is maintained by co-owner Jennifer Scism. If you can't decide, there are thirty fortified wines and sakes poured by the glass. Dishes might include seared foie gras with soup dumplings and jícama, uni (sea urchin) with celeriac rémoulade, miso-marinated sablefish with crispy deep-fried silken tofu in a bonito-kelp broth, and grilled noisette of lamb with Chinese broccoli. The food is exquisitely prepared, with chef Lo's careful attention to color, texture, and flavor apparent at every turn.

Halibut or cod can be used in place of the wild striped bass in this simple grilled entrée.

wild striped bass

with braised endive and hazelnuts

SERVES 4

Braised Endive

4 large heads endive

2 cups water

1½ tablespoons fresh lemon juice

1 tablespoon unsalted butter

1 tablespoon sugar

1 teaspoon coarse salt

Hazelnut Butter and Fish

4 tablespoons (½ stick) unsalted butter

¼ cup chopped toasted hazelnuts

Coarse salt and freshly ground black pepper, to taste

Four 6-ounce pieces wild striped bass, halibut, or cod fillet, skin on

1 tablespoon vegetable oil

2 teaspoons chopped fresh chives

2 teaspoons chopped fresh tarragon

½ lemon

1. To make the braised endive, trim off the discolored ends and any wilted leaves from the endive and cut each head in half lengthwise. Place in a single layer, cut side down, in a large sauté pan and add the water, lemon juice, butter, sugar, and salt. Bring to a boil, adjust the heat, and simmer until all the water has evaporated and the endive has turned a deep brown on the cut bottoms, 12 to 15 minutes. Transfer to a plate and keep warm.

2. To make the hazelnut butter and fish, place the butter in a small saucepan and cook over medium-high heat until lightly browned and fragrant. Add the hazelnuts and remove from the heat. Season to taste with salt and pepper and keep warm.

3. Preheat an outdoor grill or place a grill pan over high heat. Season the fish on both sides with salt and pepper and brush with the oil. Place skin side down and cook until the skin is crisp. Turn and finish cooking on the other side until just opaque all the way through, 3 to 4 minutes more.

4. Add the chives and tarragon to the hazelnut butter and divide among 4 plates. Top with the endive and the fish. Squeeze a little extra lemon over the fish and serve immediately.

chef's notes Bring out the best in any nut simply by toasting it. Toast shelled hazelnuts in a 325°F oven for 10 to 15 minutes, stirring occasionally. As soon as you take them from the oven, rub the nuts vigorously with a towel to remove their brown skins.

and to drink

$ 2002 Villa Maria Private Bin Sauvignon Blanc, New Zealand

$$ 2000 Sauvignon Blanc Selene "Hyde Vineyards," Carneros, California

WHERE TO BUY

Wild striped bass:

Prawn Corporation of America: 866-772-9626, www.prawnco.com

Whole Foods, multiple locations, www.wholefoods.com

aureole

34 EAST 61ST STREET   NEW YORK, NY 10021

212-319-1660   WWW.CHARLIEPALMER.COM

Nestled in a sophisticated brownstone on Manhattan's Upper East Side, Aureole is celebrity chef Charlie Palmer's gastronomic tribute to progressive American cuisine. With his protégé, executive chef Dante Boccuzzi, in the kitchen, the emphasis is on sharply focused ingredient pairings, striking architectural presentation, and deeply flavored food. The modern and elegant menu is reflected in a dining room to match, accented by theatrical flower arrangements, a romantic garden open in season, and intimate seating. Chef Boccuzzi's global reach includes signature dishes firmly rooted in the classical style, like a sesame-seared Atlantic salmon with orange-miso vinaigrette; ginger-marinated magret of moulard duck with sugar snap peas, mango, and wild mushroom roulade; and foie gras with port-glazed Bing cherries and young onions. Give the chef free rein and opt for a six-course market or vegetarian tasting menu, the ultimate for the truly adventurous palate.

Halibut can stand in for sole and regular shrimp for rock shrimp in this stylish variation of broiled sole.

crusted sole
with sautéed shrimp and couscous

SERVES 6

Crust

2 cups dried brioche or other bread crumbs

14 tablespoons unsalted butter, softened

Bouillabaisse Sauce

1½ cups clam juice

½ cup finely diced carrot

½ cup diced onion

½ cup diced celery

3 cloves garlic, chopped

⅛ teaspoon coarse salt, plus more to taste

3 tablespoons tomato paste

1 cup white wine

½ cup Pernod (optional)

1 bulb fennel, sliced

Pinch saffron, or to taste

2 sprigs fresh parsley

2 sprigs fresh thyme

2 bay leaves

Couscous

2 tablespoons unsalted butter

¼ cup finely diced carrot

¼ cup finely diced celery

¼ cup finely diced onion

4 cups chicken stock

½ teaspoon coarse salt

2 cups couscous

4 large eggs, lightly beaten

(continued)

1. To make the crust, mix together the brioche crumbs and softened butter. Cover and refrigerate.

2. To make the bouillabaisse sauce, in a medium saucepan, combine the clam juice, carrot, onion, celery, garlic, and salt. Bring to a boil over high heat, lower the heat, and simmer 5 minutes. Stir in the tomato paste and simmer for 5 minutes more.

3. Add the white wine, Pernod, fennel, saffron, parsley, thyme, and bay leaves. Simmer until reduced by two thirds, about 10 minutes. Strain the sauce through a fine-mesh sieve, pressing on the solids to extract all the liquid. Discard the solids. Return the sauce to the pan, season with more salt if needed, and set aside.

4. To make the couscous, melt the butter in a medium saucepan over medium heat. Add the carrot, celery, and onion and cook, stirring, until the vegetables are just tender, about 5 minutes. Add the chicken stock and salt and bring to a boil. Put the couscous in a medium bowl and pour the boiling stock mixture over the couscous. Stir once, cover the bowl with plastic wrap, and let rest for 10 minutes.

5. After the couscous has absorbed all of the liquid, mix in the eggs and herbs. Set aside.

6. Meanwhile, to make the shrimp, in a medium bowl, toss the shrimp with the olive oil, zest, chives, salt, and pepper and marinate for 10 minutes.

7. Heat a nonstick sauté pan over medium-high heat. Cook the shrimp, stirring, until just cooked through, 3 to 4 minutes. Set aside and keep warm.

8. To make the sole, preheat the broiler.

9. Season the fillets with salt and white pepper on both sides. Spread the butter over the bottom of a large ovenproof baking pan. Lay the

2 tablespoons mixed finely
chopped fresh herbs
(parsley, chives, tarragon)

Shrimp

1½ pounds medium shrimp,
peeled and deveined

1 tablespoon extra-virgin
olive oil

1 tablespoon grated
fresh lemon zest

3 tablespoons chopped
fresh chives

½ teaspoon coarse salt

¼ teaspoon pepper

Sole

Six 6-ounce fillets sole or
any firm, flat, white fish like
turbot or halibut

Coarse salt and freshly
ground white pepper,
to taste

3 tablespoons unsalted
butter, softened

and to drink

$ 2000 Chablis, Domaine
de l'Orme, France

$$ 2000 Michaud Chardonnay,
The Pinnacles, California

fillets in a single layer in the pan. Top each fillet with 2 tablespoons of the chilled crust mixture. Broil until the fish flakes easily with a fork and the crust is golden, 8 to 10 minutes.

10. To serve, place a spoon of couscous on each of 6 serving plates. Top with the fish and shrimp and a few spoons of the bouillabaisse sauce.

chef's notes   Pernod (per-NO) is an anise-based spirit that has been a favorite in France for some two hundred years, both as a before-dinner beverage that stimulates the appetite and a zestful cooking ingredient. For cooking, Pernod is a natural companion to fish and seafood. It is included, for instance, in New Orleans oysters Rockefeller, a signature American dish.

WHERE TO BUY

Wild and line-caught fish:

Citarella, 212-874-0383, www.citarella.com

Wild Edibles, 212-687-4255, www.wildedibles.com

café gray

TIME WARNER CENTER   10 COLUMBUS CIRCLE, THIRD FLOOR   NEW YORK, NY 10019

212-823-6338   WWW.CAFEGRAY.COM

Legendary chef Gray Kunz took New York by storm when he opened Café Gray in 2004, a 200-seat brasserie designed by David Rockwell in the Time Warner Center. With its leafy Central Park views and high-profile address, Café Gray is the perfect showcase for Kunz's synthesized cuisine, a product of his international upbringing and stints in the illustrious kitchen of Fredy Girardet in Lausanne, Switzerland, and the Regent Hotel in Hong Kong. *New York* magazine described Kunz's cuisine as "not so much fusion as the product of a man fluent in the food languages of Europe, India, China, and Southeast Asia." After all, this is the same chef who earned a four-star rating from the *New York Times* while at Lespinasse, which *Zagat* rated as New York's Best Overall Restaurant for three years in a row. In 2003 the Culinary Institute of America heralded him as a Master of Aesthetics, an award given to only a handful of culinary professionals.

Chef Kunz creates layered dishes composed of intriguing ingredients that add up to a single, bold statement. A few cases in point are his bouquet of pencil asparagus with fresh peas, mint, and yogurt; black bass with ancho chiles, coriander, and mussel-clam broth; or coconut-coated red snapper with crabmeat and green papaya. Ask for a seat in the showcase kitchen, where the chefs dance the well-choreographed waltz of impeccable gastronomy.

Chef Kunz uses concentrated tamarind paste to give an exotic jolt to the barbecue glaze for this steak.

tamarind-glazed flank steak
with mango-jícama salsa

Tamarind Glaze

1 cup tamarind paste
(or 1 cup pureed mango)

2 plum tomatoes,
roughly chopped
(or 1 cup canned
diced tomatoes)

½ cup coarsely chopped
fresh ginger

½ cup honey

1 tablespoon ground cumin

1 tablespoon ground
coriander

1 cup water

Coarse salt

Salsa

2 tablespoons vegetable oil

½ red bell pepper, seeded
and cut into ½-inch dice

½ cup peeled jícama,
cut into ½-inch dice

1 mango, peeled, pitted,
and cut into ½-inch dice

1 tablespoon white vinegar

1 tablespoon sugar

Cayenne, to taste

Coarse salt, to taste

Freshly ground white
pepper, to taste

Flank Steak

1½ pounds flank steak

1. To make the tamarind glaze, in a medium saucepan, combine the tamarind paste, tomatoes, ginger, honey, cumin, coriander, and water. Place over low heat and simmer, stirring frequently, for 10 minutes.

2. Strain the mixture through a fine-mesh sieve, discard the solids, and return the sauce to the pan. Simmer again, stirring occasionally, until the mixture is syrupy, 5 to 7 minutes. Season with salt and set aside.

3. To make the salsa, in a large sauté pan over high heat, heat the oil. Add the bell pepper and jícama and cook, stirring occasionally, until warmed but still crisp, about 2 minutes. Add the mango and remove from the heat. Stir in the vinegar and sugar. Season to taste with cayenne, salt, and white pepper. Set aside.

4. To make the flank steak, brush the steak with the oil and season with cayenne, salt, and black pepper. Preheat an outdoor grill or heat a grill pan over high heat. Grill the steak, turning once, until it reaches the desired doneness, 6 to 8 minutes for medium rare.

5. Let the steak rest 5 minutes, then slice into thin slices on the bias. Coat the steak with the tamarind glaze, garnish with the salsa and chopped cilantro, and serve.

WHERE TO BUY

Tamarind paste: Import Food, 888-618-8424, www.importfood.com

2 tablespoons vegetable oil

Cayenne, to taste

Coarse salt, to taste

Freshly ground black
pepper, to taste

½ cup roughly chopped
fresh cilantro leaves

and to drink

$ 2004 Jezebel Willamette
Valley Blanc, Oregon
$$ 2003 Domaine Weinbach
Gewürztraminer Cuvée
Laurence, Alsace, France

chef's notes Tamarind paste is made from the pods of the feathery tamarind tree native to Latin America and the Caribbean. The pulp of these pods is mixed with water, and the resulting liquid is used as a souring agent in beverages, curries, soups, and other dishes. Tamarind is a very common ingredient in Thai and Indian cuisines. It is available in Asian markets and in some large supermarkets.

Jícama is a large, bulbous root vegetable that is popular in Mexican and other Latino cuisines.

blue hill

75 WASHINGTON PLACE   NEW YORK, NY 10011

212-539-1776   WWW.BLUEHILLNYC.COM

Named for a farm in the Berkshires that belongs to co-chef and owner Dan Barber's grandmother, Blue Hill is an intimate restaurant located just below street level in a landmark old speakeasy off Washington Square in the West Village. With a menu that reflects a passion for local, seasonal food, simply prepared and beautifully presented, Barber and co-chef Alex Urena deliver well-conceived dishes like asparagus soup topped with Parmesan foam and a side terrine of smoked eel, foie gras, and green apples, and poached breast of tender duck served with crisp confit. Savory foams often find their way onto Blue Hill plates, probably because Urena apprenticed with Spanish foam impresario Ferran Adria.

Chef Barber is also an owner at Blue Hill at Stone Barns, located at Pocantico, the 4,000-acre country estate in Westchester County established by oil magnate John D. Rockefeller, Sr. Barber and executive chef Michael Anthony head up a seasonally driven 125-seat restaurant and working farm.

To draw the most flavor out of this garden-fresh gazpacho recipe, it's best to marinate the vegetables overnight. But if you're in a pinch, steep the veggies in the oil, lemon, and vinegar mixture for at least an hour, and proceed with the recipe.

178 IMPRESS FOR LESS!

garden
gazpacho

SERVES 6 TO 8

2 small zucchini

2 small cucumbers, peeled

1 green bell pepper, seeded

2 stalks celery

½ scallion

1 jalapeño, seeded

Leaves from
½ bunch parsley

2 cloves garlic, chopped

Coarse salt and freshly
ground black pepper,
to taste

1 cup extra-virgin olive oil,
plus more for drizzling

¼ cup rice vinegar

¼ cup sherry vinegar

2 tablespoons fresh
lemon juice

Few dashes Tabasco

2 pounds fresh tomatillos, or
two 16-ounce cans roasted

2 avocados, peeled
and pitted

8 cups vegetable broth,
or as needed

Coarse salt and freshly
ground black pepper,
to taste

and to drink

$ 2003 Belle Pente Reserve
Pinot Gris, Oregon

$$ 2003 Roger Sabon
Chateauneuf du Pape Blanc
Cuvée Renaissance, Rhone,
France

1. In the bowl of a food processor, combine half the zucchini, half the cucumbers, the green pepper, celery, scallion, jalapeño, parsley, and garlic. Pulse just until the vegetables are finely chopped (do not over-process). Place in a large nonreactive bowl and season with salt and pepper. Pour in ½ cup of the oil, the rice vinegar, sherry vinegar, lemon juice, and Tabasco. Cover and refrigerate overnight.

2. If using fresh tomatillos, preheat the oven to 400°F. Place the tomatillos in a small roasting pan and drizzle with a little olive oil. Roast until the skins blister, about 20 minutes. Set aside. If using canned tomatillos, skip this step.

3. In the bowl of a food processor, combine the tomatillos, remaining zucchini and cucumber, remaining ½ cup oil, and the avocados. Process until smooth. Pour the avocado mixture into the bowl with the vegetables. Stir in the vegetable broth until the desired consistency is reached. Season to taste with salt and pepper and chill until ready to serve.

chef's notes Tomatillos are small fruits that look like green or yellow tomatoes wrapped in a papery husk. The fruit's yellow color indicates ripeness, although green tomatillos are firmer and easier to slice. There is evidence that the Aztecs first grew tomatillos as far back as 800 B.C., and they remain popular in Mexico and other Latin American countries. Fresh tomatillos are available year-round in supermarkets and specialty markets. Canned tomatillos are available at specialty markets and are often used in sauces.

WHERE TO BUY

Canned tomatillos: 858-459-0577, www.mexgrocer.com

Seasonal and organic produce: Diamond Organics, 888-ORGANIC
    (888-674-2642), www.diamondorganics.com

chanterelle

2 HARRISON STREET   NEW YORK, NY 10013

212-966-6960   WWW.CHANTERELLENY.COM

Owners Karen and David Waltuck blazed a trail to fine French dining in Tribeca when they opened Chanterelle in 1979. More than a quarter century later, Chanterelle is as relevant as ever. Against a backdrop of simple elegance, David Waltuck's market-driven, prix-fixe dinner menu combines French inspiration with New American innovation. Timeless dishes on the menu, which changes monthly, might include grilled seafood sausage, arctic char with a citrus sauce, loin of lamb in a cumin salt crust, or grilled foie gras with portobellos. Sommelier Roger Dagorn's wine list is excellent. Chanterelle received the 2004 James Beard Foundation award for outstanding restaurant.

With a few adaptations, this satisfying treatment of striped bass replicates chef Waltuck's original recipe. Most notably, we used fillets instead of whole fish. The finished plates can be garnished with a green vegetable such as haricots verts (French green beans).

striped bass

with red wine and fresh sage

SERVES 6

4 tablespoons softened unsalted butter

¼ cup chopped sage leaves

¼ teaspoon chopped garlic

1 tablespoon fresh lemon juice

2 cups red wine

2 tablespoons red-wine vinegar, plus more to taste

2 tablespoons finely chopped shallots

1 cup (2 sticks) cold unsalted butter, cut into small pieces

Coarse salt and freshly ground black pepper, to taste

Six 6-ounce pieces striped bass fillet, skin on

Wondra extra-fine flour, or regular all-purpose flour, for dredging

½ cup extra-virgin olive oil

1. In a small bowl, combine the softened butter, sage, garlic, and lemon juice. Stir until blended. Cover and refrigerate.

2. In a medium nonreactive saucepan over medium heat, combine the wine, vinegar, and shallots. Simmer until reduced to ½ cup, about 20 minutes. Reduce the heat to low and whisk in the cold butter a chunk at a time, whisking constantly. Season to taste with salt, pepper, and additional vinegar if needed. (The sauce may be prepared up to 2 hours in advance. However, be certain to keep the sauce warm until it is ready to serve. It can be rewarmed over low heat, whisking constantly, but do not allow it to cool completely or the sauce may separate. You can also store it in a small insulated thermos to keep it warm.)

3. Dredge the bass fillets in flour and season with salt and pepper. Heat the butter-and-sage mixture and the olive oil in a large sauté pan over medium-high heat. When the butter has melted, add the fillets, skin side first, and cook until browned and crisp and just opaque in the center, about 4 minutes per side.

4. Spoon some of the wine sauce over 6 plates. Top each plate with a fish fillet.

and to drink

$ 2003 Frecciarossa Uva Rara, Lombardy, Italy

$$ 1993 Volnay-Santenots Robert Ampeau Red, Burgundy, France

chef's notes For this recipe, we deleted the chef's addition of 2 tablespoons of demi-glace (DEHM-ee glahs) from the red wine sauce, making the flavor just slightly less complex, but the difference is negligible. Demi-glace, a rich brown reduction made from concentrated veal or beef stock is available at specialty gourmet markets.

WHERE TO BUY

Demi-glace: D'Artagnan, 800-327-8246, www.dartagnan.com

gotham bar and grill

12 EAST 12TH STREET   NEW YORK, NY 10003

212-620-4020   WWW.GOTHAMBARANDGRILL.COM

It doesn't get more New York than the expansive Gotham Bar and Grill. Under the watchful eye of chef Alfred Portale, Gotham has been leading Manhattan's culinary revolution for more than two decades. The creator of food as architectural as the city's skyline, Portale is a master of dishes that are at once intensely flavored and accessible. The intense jewelry designer–turned–chef (he was first in his class at CIA in 1981), Portale approaches each plate with an artist's clarity of purpose. One of the founders of New American Cuisine, Portale's seasonally changing menu might offer creamy asparagus and morel mushroom risotto; a salad of skate and white asparagus with caramelized fennel, hazelnuts, and Meyer lemon brown butter; and a burnished roast squab with crisp pancetta, sautéed greens, and a balsamic caper raisin sauce.

At Gotham, this cold pea soup is garnished with everything from lobster and caviar to a warm custard made with spring morels and peas. Even stripped down, this fresh-tasting pea soup is outstanding. Dress it up with a little crème fraîche or sour cream garnished with fresh mint. A drizzle of extra-virgin olive oil is also a good way to finish.

chilled
pea soup

SERVES 4

1 tablespoon olive oil

2 tablespoons
unsalted butter

1 onion, chopped

½ stalk celery, chopped

8 cups chicken broth

4 cups fresh peas
(or two 10-ounce packages
frozen petits pois
[baby peas])

2 tablespoons sugar,
or to taste

Coarse salt and freshly
ground white pepper,
to taste

1. In a large soup pot over medium heat, heat the oil and butter. When the butter has melted, add the onion and celery and cook, stirring frequently, until the vegetables are softened, 3 to 4 minutes. Add the chicken broth, raise the heat to high, and bring to a boil. Add the peas. Return to a boil and cook until the peas are tender, about 12 minutes for fresh peas or 3 to 4 minutes for frozen.

2. While the soup is simmering, set up the equipment to puree the soup. You will need a blender, a ladle, and a bowl set in ice water (to chill the puree quickly and preserve its brilliant green color).

3. When the peas are tender, taste the soup and season with the sugar, salt, and white pepper. Strain the soup, reserving the stock. Put the peas into the blender in batches and puree, adding only enough stock to create a thick puree. Pour the contents of the blender into the bowl set in ice water, and continue until all the peas have been pureed.

4. Add some of the reserved stock a little at a time to the pea puree until your soup has a nice, thick consistency. Taste again and add more sugar, salt, or pepper if needed. When the soup has cooled, cover and refrigerate. Serve chilled.

and to drink

$ 2003 Bernardus Monterey
Sauvignon Blanc, California
$$ 2002 Chalk Hill Estate
Sonoma Sauvignon Blanc,
California

chef's notes Using an ice bath in this recipe assures that the peas will hold their bright green color and the soup will chill quickly.

WHERE TO BUY

Seasonal and organic produce:
Diamond Organics, 888-ORGANIC (888-674-2642),
    www.diamondorganics.com
Union Square Farmers' Market, Union Square (17th Street at Broadway),
    212-633-2026

daniel

60 EAST 65TH STREET   NEW YORK, NY 10021

212-288-0033   WWW.DANIELNYC.COM

Chef Daniel Boulud's renowned seasonal French cuisine is served in a stunning setting reminiscent of a Venetian renaissance palazzo, formerly the lobby of the Mayfair Hotel. Daniel's elegant ambiance, gracious service, and delectable food and wine epitomizes *la grande restauration Française* in the heart of Manhattan's Upper East Side. Signature specialties are accompanied by a 700-option wine list of world-class vintages. The private Bellecour Room occupies the site of the original Le Cirque, where Boulud presided in the kitchen for a decade. For a less formal experience (jackets are required at Daniel for gentlemen in the dining room), settle into the plush Bar & Lounge, with its ruby color scheme and intimate seating. Daniel is one of only five Manhattan restaurants to hold the *New York Times*'s coveted four stars as well as NYC's top food rating in the *Zagat Survey*. Boulud learned his abiding respect for ingredients on his family farm in Lyon. That love for fresh and seasonal fare is reflected in dishes like chilled carrot soup with cilantro cream, kataifi-wrapped Carolina shrimp and lime coulis (kataifi is shredded phyllo dough), peekytoe crab salad with mango-tomato gazpacho, and roasted striped bass stuffed with chanterelles.

This recipe is adapted from *Daniel's Dish: Entertaining at Home with a Four-Star Chef* (Filipacchi Publishing, 2003).

caramelized bay scallops
with clementines and cauliflower

SERVES 4

1 head cauliflower, cut into 1-inch florets, stems peeled and cut into $\frac{1}{2}$-inch-thick slices

Coarse salt and freshly ground black pepper, to taste

8 tablespoons (1 stick) unsalted butter

2 tablespoons extra-virgin olive oil

2 pounds large bay scallops

Juice of 1 lemon

2 navel oranges, segmented

Zest removed in strips from 4 kumquats or 2 navel oranges

3 tablespoons capers, soaked in cold water for 20 minutes, rinsed, and drained

1 tablespoon finely chopped fresh flat-leaf parsley

1. Bring a medium saucepan of salted water to a boil. Add the cauliflower and cook until tender, 7 to 9 minutes. Drain well.

2. Put the cauliflower in a food processor and process just until smooth, taking care not to overprocess the mixture. Season with salt and pepper and stir in 4 tablespoons of the butter. Set aside.

3. In a large sauté pan set over high heat, heat the remaining 4 tablespoons butter and the olive oil. Pat the scallops dry, season with salt and pepper, and slip them into the pan. Cook, turning the scallops as necessary, until they are golden on all sides and just cooked through, 4 to 5 minutes. Transfer to a plate and cover to keep warm. Pour off the excess butter from the pan.

4. Return the pan the scallops cooked in to medium heat. Add the lemon juice to the pan, stirring to scrape up any browned bits from the bottom of the pan. Add the orange segments, zest, capers, and parsley. Cook, stirring, until heated through, about 1 minute. Season with salt and pepper to taste.

5. Reheat the cauliflower. To serve, divide the cauliflower among 4 warmed soup plates. Arrange the scallops on top and spoon the orange mixture on top. Serve immediately.

WHERE TO BUY

Scallops: Browne Trading Company, 800-944-7848, www.brownetrading.com

Sicilian capers and imported Italian ingredients: Buonitalia, 212-633-9090, www.buonitalia.com

and to drink
$ 2003 Lynmar Chardonnay
Russian River Valley, California
$$ 2003 Aubert
Chardonnay Quarry Vineyard
Sonoma Coast, California

chef's notes   To segment an orange, trim a small slice of peel from both ends so the flesh is exposed and the orange will sit flat. Place the orange cut side down on a cutting board. Remove the peel with a sharp knife, cutting down and around the flesh and leaving as little pith as possible. Over a small bowl, cut on either side of the membranes to release the segments.

Zest is the fragrant outermost skin layer of citrus fruits like oranges, lemons, or limes. Removed with the aid of a citrus zester, grater, or vegetable peeler, the zest possesses aromatic oils that add bright flavor to food. Only the colored portion of the skin, not the bitter white pith, should be used.

gramercy tavern

42 EAST 20TH STREET   NEW YORK, NY 10003

212-477-0777   WWW.GRAMERCYTAVERN.COM

Danny Meyer's and Tom Colicchio's contemporary American restaurant has been a destination for New Yorkers and their out-of-town guests since 1994.

Colicchio, who also owns the spectacular Craft and CraftBar restaurants on 19th Street and CraftSteak in Las Vegas, is a master at marrying the finest ingredients available with the highest level of culinary craftsmanship, letting each dish speak for itself without a hint of fanciness. His style simply lets the integrity of the raw materials shine through. At Gramercy Tavern, dine in the airy first-come-first-serve bar, perfumed by the aroma of the wood-burning oven, or in the main dining room, where special-occasion diners enjoy a more formal ambiance. Choose from an à la carte or a three- or seven-course menu, with dishes like smoked paprika-rubbed quail atop buttery polenta, a stellar braised lamb with summer beans and leeks, and rabbit roasted with shallots, garlic sausage, olives, rosemary, and potato puree.

Chef Colicchio braises artichokes with extra-virgin olive oil, fresh herbs, garlic, lemon, and vegetables to pair with chicken in this easy-to-make recipe. Canned artichoke hearts will work just fine when you're in a hurry. This recipe is adapted from his book *Think Like a Chef* (Clarkson Potter, 2000).

slow-braised chicken
with artichokes

SERVES 4

2 tablespoons peanut oil

Coarse salt and freshly ground black pepper, to taste

4 chicken drumsticks

4 chicken thighs

1 large yellow onion, cut into 8 pieces

3 carrots, each cut into 4 pieces

3 stalks celery, each cut into 4 pieces

4 cloves garlic

4 sprigs thyme, plus more for garnish

4 sprigs fresh tarragon, plus more for garnish

1¼ cups chicken broth, plus more as needed

One 8.5-ounce can artichoke hearts, drained

2 tablespoons unsalted butter

1. Preheat the oven to 350°F.

2. Heat the oil in a large, ovenproof sauté pan over medium-high heat until it shimmers. Salt and pepper the drumsticks and thighs on all sides. Working in batches, brown the chicken, about 7 minutes per side. Transfer the chicken to a plate.

3. Pour off all but enough fat to coat the bottom of the pan (about 2 tablespoons) and place over medium heat. Add the onion, carrots, celery, and a little salt. Cook, stirring occasionally, until the vegetables begin to brown, about 15 minutes. Add the garlic and 2 sprigs each of the thyme and tarragon and cook for 5 minutes more.

4. Arrange the chicken, skin side up, over the vegetables. Add enough stock to come up to but not over the chicken and bring to a simmer on top of the stove. Transfer the pan to the oven and bake, uncovered, for 1½ hours, adding more stock if the pan begins to look dry.

5. Add the artichokes, butter, and remaining sprigs of thyme and tarragon. Bake for another 15 minutes, basting the chicken frequently. Check the chicken; when it is done it will be very tender and the braising liquid will have thickened slightly. Serve the chicken with the braising liquid.

WHERE TO BUY

Organic poultry: Lobel's, 877-783-4512, www.lobels.com

and to drink
$ 2002 Michel Thomas
Sancerre, France
$$ 2003 Lucien Crochet
Sancerre Croix du Roy, France

chef's notes Dried herbs are really no substitute for fresh. The drying process changes the essential flavor of herbs, causing them to lose some of their delicacy and nuances. Nowadays, fresh herbs can be purchased in just about any supermarket. Although most recipes call for only one sprig or two, use them liberally. Unlike with dried, you run little risk of overpowering a dish with most fresh herbs.

To wash fresh herbs, dip them into a bowl of cool water or under a gentle stream of tap water. Always use a very sharp knife to chop herbs and do so only at the last moment—never in advance.

jean georges

1 CENTRAL PARK WEST   NEW YORK, NY 10023

212-299-3900   WWW.JEAN-GEORGES.COM

When he opened his eponymous restaurant on Central Park West in 1997, chef and owner Jean-Georges Vongerichten brought a new breed of four-star dining to Manhattan. With its neutral palette and austere design, the restaurant puts the focus completely on the Asian-accented French food at hand. And what food it is. From the moment the complimentary *amuse bouche* arrives, a trio of treats presented on a slim, rectangular plate, it's apparent that an extraordinary experience awaits. The tantalizing starter might include a tiny waffle of goat cheese bonneted with thin slices of white peach and cornichon; a frothy shot of sweet truffle-enriched corn soup, textured with beads of curried tapioca; and a spoonful of peekytoe crab, topped with cucumber gelée and fiery wasabi. And that's just the beginning. Vongerichten's mastery of innovative pairings and earthy flavors greets diners at every turn. One outstanding signature dish features sliced sea scallops atop caramelized cauliflower in a puddle of raisin and caper emulsion. Nougatine, in the front of the restaurant, serves a more moderate à la carte menu, with a view of the open kitchen.

Serve this dish over rice or on a bed of greens. You can substitute chicken legs for the duck in this recipe, although chicken doesn't have the fat content or flavor of duck legs. Many supermarkets sell duck with other upscale meat items.

braised duck legs
with asian spices

SERVES 4

1 onion

1 stalk celery

1 carrot

½ stalk lemongrass, peeled, or 1 teaspoon grated fresh lemon zest

2 tablespoons plus 2 teaspoons peeled, minced fresh ginger

2 tablespoons grapeseed or canola oil

6 duck or chicken legs, excess fat removed

Coarse salt

2 teaspoons five-spice powder

1 scallion, minced

Soy sauce, to taste

1. In the bowl of a food processor, combine the onion, celery, carrot, and lemongrass. Pulse until minced.

2. Preheat the oven to 350°F. In the bottom of a large, heavy sauté pan, make a bed of the minced vegetables and 2 tablespoons of the minced ginger. Drizzle with the oil.

3. Sprinkle the duck or chicken legs with salt and five-spice powder. Place the legs on top of the vegetables. Roast for 2 hours, undisturbed.

4. Remove from the oven and let sit until cool. Remove the meat from the bones; discard the skin and bones, and shred the meat with your fingers. Combine the meat with the cooked vegetables, the scallion, and the remaining 2 teaspoons ginger. Season to taste with soy sauce.

chef's notes Five-spice powder is a pungent mix of five ground spices—cinnamon, cloves, fennel seed, star anise, and Szechuan peppercorns. It's used extensively in Chinese cooking. Five-spice powder is available in supermarkets and Asian markets.

and to drink

$ 2002 Bishops Peak Pinot Noir Central Coast, California

$$ 2003 Lemelson Vineyards Pinot Noir Thea Selection, Willamette Valley, Oregon

WHERE TO BUY

Duck legs:

D'Artagnan, 800-327-8246, www.dartagnan.com

Prawn Corporation of America, 866-772-9626, www.prawnco.com

l'impero

45 TUDOR CITY PLACE   NEW YORK, NY 10017

212-599-5045   WWW.LIMPERO.COM

Scott Conant's Italian food is truly emperor-worthy. His restaurant, L'Impero, tucked away in Midtown's Tudor City, purveys sensual dishes that highlight Conant's skill with textures and deep flavors. From his years of mastering *alta cucina* at New York City's famed San Domenico to his explorations of *cucina rustica* in the trattorias of the Italian countryside, Conant has long demonstrated a single-minded determination to understand the full spectrum of Italian cuisine. Named one of *Food & Wine*'s Best New Chefs in 2004, Conant creates a changing menu of rousing, Italian-inspired dishes that include such signatures as foie gras-duck agnolotti, garlicky gnocchi adorned with snails and porcini, succulent roasted and seared branzino with rosemary-scented lentils and oven-dried tomatoes. The thoughtful wine list includes headings like "Powerful, Elegant . . . Contemplative" and "Sweet & Sexy," with plenty of options in both price and region.

If possible, buy wild salmon rather than farm-raised; the flavor is much better.

slow-roasted salmon
with smoked bacon and escarole

2 pounds wild salmon fillet

¾ cup plus 2 tablespoons extra-virgin olive oil

Crushed red pepper flakes, to taste

Coarse salt and freshly ground black pepper, to taste

1 scallion, thinly sliced

1 shallot, thinly sliced

4 leaves escarole, chopped

2 tablespoons chopped, smoked bacon

8 porcini or other wild mushrooms, chopped

3 tablespoons clam juice or water

SERVES 4

1. Marinate the salmon in ¾ cup of the olive oil for about 15 minutes and season with the red pepper, salt, and pepper.

2. Preheat the oven to 150°F.

3. Top the salmon with the scallion and half the shallot. In a nonreactive roasting pan, roast until the flesh is just warmed through, 1 hour or more, basting with the olive oil about every 10 minutes.

4. Meanwhile, heat the remaining 2 tablespoons olive oil over medium heat in a medium sauté pan. Add the remaining half of the shallot and the escarole and cook, stirring, until the vegetables soften, about 3 minutes. Add the bacon, mushrooms, and clam juice and cook until the mushrooms and escarole are tender and the bacon is cooked through, about 8 minutes.

5. To serve, form a bed with the escarole mixture. Place the salmon on top and spoon some of the olive oil the fish cooked in over the top.

and to drink

$ 2003 Alto Adige Lagrein Rosato, Italy

$$ 2001 Trebbiano D'Abruzzo, Valentini, Italy

chef's notes The flesh of wild salmon is firmer than that of farm-raised salmon because the fish swim free rather than being penned. Wild salmon also have a higher content of omega-3 fatty acids and a lower saturated-fat level than farm-raised salmon. If you buy farm-raised, look for organic salmon that is free from chemicals, antibiotics, and colorants. While wild salmon gets its pink color from pigments in its food, such as shrimp, most farmed salmon are fed a coloring additive called canthaxanthin, in the beta-carotene family. Canthaxanthin is also added to chicken feed to make egg yolks and chickens more yellow.

WHERE TO BUY

Wild salmon: Wild Edibles, 212-687-4255, www.wildedibles.com

philadelphia

philadelphia's bountiful table

*I*f you think Philadelphia's dining scene is defined by cheese-steaks, hoagies, and soft pretzels, think again. The city long known for American history, passionate sports fans, and, yes, cheesesteaks, continues to emerge as one of the country's finest culinary destinations. More than a decade of development has transformed the region's dining scene from merely memorable to absolutely abundant. Throughout the city and beyond, four-star dining rooms coexist with unassuming neighborhood bistros; boisterous upscale taprooms counterbalance romantic foodie hideaways; and bring-your-own-bottle (BYOB) establishments share the sidewalk with swanky restaurants owned by high-profile restaurateurs.

In this town, food is serious business. Restaurants are at the forefront of urban development, transforming ignored intersections and outlying neighborhoods into pockets of trendy nightlife and vibrant residential enclaves. Ethnic dining has fueled much of this growth. A visit to Chinatown delivers everything from Vietnamese to Malaysian, Thai, and regional Chinese cuisine. In South Philadelphia, traditional spaghetti houses have made way for taquerias, sushi bars, and pho cafés along Washington Avenue.

Foodies can't leave town without visiting two of the city's most colorful market destinations, Reading Terminal Market in Center City and the Italian Market in South Philly. Reading Terminal Market, housed in the former train shed of what was once the city's commuter rail station, dates back to 1892,

a colorful mix of fishmongers, Amish poultry purveyors, family-owned butchers, and fresh produce stands, along with food kiosks proffering everything from soul food to sushi. At the Italian Market visitors will find everything from whole pigs hanging in butcher shop windows to three-feet-long wheels of provolone and vats of olives in Italian delis

along a lively five-block stretch of open-air stalls and specialty stores.

In this chapter, chefs from ten of the city and region's finest restaurants share their recipes for everything from crab ceviche to smoked rib eye.

alma de cuba

1623 WALNUT STREET   PHILADELPHIA, PA 19103

215-988-1799   WWW.ALMADECUBARESTAURANT.COM

Douglas Rodriguez, the oft-cited godfather of haute Nuevo Latino cuisine and the son of Cuban immigrants, joined forces with Philadelphia's high-profile restaurateur Stephen Starr to create Alma de Cuba, the "soul of Cuba," with its invigorated menu of Cuban classics and luscious mojitos. Rodriguez, whose Phoenix restaurant Deseo is featured in our Phoenix chapter, is a master of strong, bold flavors, found in variations on classic dishes, like his slow-roasted pork shank and short rib empanada. This easy-to-make ceviche uses crabmeat in a tangy mustard-citrus sauce to create an exotic appetizer or the centerpiece for a light summer supper.

Ceviche is a popular Latin American appetizer generally made with raw fish marinated in citrus juice, although this recipe applies the technique to crabmeat.

crab ceviche

SERVES 4

3 tablespoons fresh
lime juice

2 tablespoons fresh
orange juice

2 tablespoons heavy cream

1½ tablespoons
Dijon mustard

½ teaspoon prepared
horseradish

Dash Tabasco

1 pound jumbo lump
crabmeat, picked through
to remove any bits of shell
or cartilage

½ bunch scallions,
thinly sliced on the bias

Leaves from
½ bunch cilantro

½ bunch chives,
thinly sliced

½ yellow or red
tomato, diced

Coarse salt to taste

In a large mixing bowl, whisk together the lime juice, orange juice, cream, mustard, horseradish, and Tabasco. Add the crabmeat, scallions, cilantro, chives, and tomato and mix gently until blended. Season to taste with salt and refrigerate at least 1 hour before serving.

chef's notes Alma de Cuba uses meat from stone crab claws when they're in season (October 15 to May 15). The claws yield flaky white meat that is extremely sweet. In the United States, only one of the crab's claws is removed during the fishing season, and the animal is returned to the ocean, where it regenerates its claw in about a year.

Cracking open a stone crab claw is messy business, but well worth the effort. Lay the claw in the palm of your hand and whack it with the heavy end of an all-stainless butter knife. With a little practice, you'll eventually be able to pull the meat out of the shell in one piece. Another, less messy option is to place the claw in a resealable plastic bag and hit it with a wooden mallet. Either way, be careful handling the cracked claws, since their broken edges can be very sharp.

and to drink

$ Corona Light with lime

$$ 2002 Casa Lapostolle
Sauvignon Blanc, Chile

WHERE TO BUY

Stone crabs:

Anastasi Seafood, 215-462-0550

Legal Sea Foods, 800-343-5804, www.legalseafoods.com

Seafood World, 877-276-CRAB (2722), www.beststonecrabs.com

dilworthtown inn

1390 OLD WILMINGTON PIKE   WEST CHESTER, PA 19382

610-399-1390   WWW.DILWORTHTOWN.COM

Located thirty miles west of Philadelphia, the elegant Dilworthtown Inn has witnessed key events in Philadelphia's history since James Dilworth built it as his home in 1754. Nearly destroyed by the British in the 1777 Battle of Brandywine, the residence was converted to an inn in 1780, and remained a fixture in the Village of Dilworthtown until the nineteenth century. Proprietors Jim Barnes and Bob Rafetto, who extensively restored the inn's three floors and fifteen dining rooms, opened the inn as a fine restaurant in 1972. Well-crafted New American cuisine, a romantic Old World setting, and a 900-bottle award-winning wine cellar make this destination restaurant truly something special.

This zesty appetizer can be made with a variety of soft cheeses, including Boursin, a flavorful triple-cream cheese.

spice-rubbed crostini
with warm boursin mousse

SERVES 10

½ pound Boursin cheese, at room temperature

¾ cup cream cheese, at room temperature

Freshly ground white pepper

9 large eggs

3 cups heavy cream

2 tablespoons thinly sliced chives

1 loaf French bread

½ cup clarified butter

Coarse salt, to taste

2 tablespoons McCormick's Grill Mates® Montreal Chicken Seasoning

2 tablespoons finely chopped fresh thyme

1. Preheat the oven to 325°F. Butter ten 6-ounce ovenproof ramekins and have ready a roasting pan that can hold the ramekins comfortably.

2. In a food processor, combine two thirds of the Boursin with the cream cheese. Add white pepper to taste and process until the mixture is very smooth. Add the eggs, 1 cup of the cream, and half the chives. Pulse until the ingredients are blended.

3. Divide the mixture among the ramekins. Place the ramekins in the roasting pan. Pour boiling water into the pan until it comes about halfway up the sides of the ramekins. Transfer to the oven and bake until a knife inserted near the center of a ramekin comes out clean, about 15 minutes. Remove the ramekins from the water and cool for a few minutes before serving.

4. Meanwhile, cut the bread into thin slices. Heat the clarified butter in a large sauté pan over medium heat. Working in batches, fry the bread slices, turning once, until browned on both sides, about 4 minutes. Drain well on absorbent toweling. Sprinkle with chopped thyme while the bread is still hot.

5. To make the sauce, in a small saucepan over medium heat, simmer the remaining 2 cups cream until reduced by half, about 10 minutes. Season with salt and pepper to taste. Add the remaining chives.

6. Unmold each custard by running a small knife around the inside of each ramekin, then inverting the ramekins onto serving plates. Drizzle with some warm cream sauce. Serve with a toasted crostini (piece of fried bread) or two, each spread lightly with some of the reserved Boursin cheese.

WHERE TO BUY

Brillant-Savarin: Di Bruno Brothers, 888-322-4337, www.dibruno.com
Mesa Rosa Rub: Dilworthtown Inn, 610-399-1390, www.dilworthtown.com

Spice-Rubbed Crostini (*continued*)

chef's notes The Dilworthtown makes its own brand of spice rubs. This recipe was created with Mesa Rosa Rub in mind, but McCormick's Grill Mates Montreal Chicken works just fine.

At the restaurant, this dish is made with the French cheese Brillant-Savarin, a wonderful triple-cream cow's milk cheese. You can substitute Boursin, Camembert, chèvre, or Brie, depending on what's available to you.

A bain-marie is a water bath used to cook foods gently by surrounding the cooking vessel with simmering water. This is a good technique for delicate dishes like savory mousses, custards, and sauces.

Clarified butter is simply melted unsalted butter that has been strained of any milk solids. To make clarified butter, melt butter in a small saucepan over moderate heat, stirring but not letting it come to a boil; this allows the milk solids to separate from the liquid butter. Upon heating, butter will separate into three distinct layers: foamy milk solids on top, clarified butter in the middle, and milk solids on the bottom. As the butter continues to warm, skim the froth from the surface and discard. When the froth is eliminated, carefully pour off the clear, melted clarified butter into another container, leaving the milk solids at the bottom of the saucepan. Discard the milk solids. Clarified butter can be used immediately or kept in an airtight container in the refrigerator for up to four weeks.

and to drink
$ 2000 Arrowood Chardonnay, California
$$ 2000 Olivier Leflaive, Chassagne-Montrachet White, Burgundy, France

fountain restaurant

FOUR SEASONS HOTEL   1 LOGAN SQUARE   PHILADELPHIA, PA 19103

215-963-1500   WWW.FOURSEASONS.COM/PHILADELPHIA

The Fountain Restaurant is easily one of Philadelphia's most beautiful formal dining rooms, acclaimed both for its elegant ambiance and exquisite cuisine. Rated number one in Philadelphia by the *Zagat Survey*, this gourmet oasis has special occasion written all over it. With executive chef Martin Hamann at the helm, the Fountain Restaurant is a marriage between classic French technique and bold global flavors. Every note rings true, from the exquisite wine list to the unpretentious fine service. Try the Spontaneous Taste menu, six inspired courses best enjoyed with a wine pairing. Ask for a table facing the Swann Fountain, one of Philadelphia's most beautiful outdoor landmarks.

Chef Hamann substituted chicken breast for muscovy duck and mandarin orange segments for blood oranges in this straightforward main dish, which is pretty enough to serve at a dinner party.

roasted orange chicken breast
with wild rice pancakes

SERVES 4

½ cup pecans, chopped

1 cup chicken stock

1 cup orange juice

Zest of 1 orange

2 tablespoons cornstarch

2 tablespoons water

Coarse salt and freshly ground black pepper, to taste

One 6.2-ounce package wild rice mix (Uncle Ben's long-grain and wild rice works well)

2 large eggs, lightly beaten

½ cup bread crumbs

2 tablespoons olive oil

2 tablespoons unsalted butter

4 boneless, skinless chicken breast halves

One 12-ounce can mandarin orange segments, drained

1. Preheat the oven to 350°F. Place the pecans on a sheet pan and bake, stirring once or twice, until they are lightly toasted and fragrant, 3 to 4 minutes. Set aside.

2. In a small saucepan, combine the chicken stock, orange juice, and orange zest. Bring to a boil over high heat, lower the heat, and simmer until reduced by half, about 10 minutes.

3. In a cup, combine the cornstarch and water and stir until smooth. Whisk the cornstarch into the boiling stock and orange juice and cook, stirring, until thickened, about 2 minutes. Season with salt and pepper and set aside.

4. Meanwhile, prepare the wild rice mix according to package directions; transfer to a large bowl and allow to cool slightly. Stir in the eggs and bread crumbs. Form into 8 pancakes.

5. In a large sauté pan, combine 1 tablespoon of the oil and 1 tablespoon of the butter over medium-high heat. When the butter melts, working in two batches, cook the pancakes until golden on each side, about 4 minutes per batch. Keep warm.

6. Wipe out the pancake skillet and return it to medium heat. Add the remaining 1 tablespoon olive oil and 1 tablespoon butter. Season the chicken with salt and pepper. Cook the chicken over medium-high heat until the breasts just start to brown and are cooked through, about 10 minutes.

7. To serve, reheat the sauce if necessary. Slice the cooked chicken breasts on the bias into 6 to 8 slices each. Place 2 pancakes on each of 4 plates. Arrange the chicken on the pancakes. Ladle sauce over each serving, place a few mandarin orange segments on each plate, and scatter with pecans.

chef's notes   Although we substituted chicken for the chef's original muscovy duck in this recipe, duck is favored by chefs for its depth of flavor and juicy richness. What most people don't realize about duck is that it's not high in fat, especially if you don't eat the skin. According to the USDA., boneless, skinless duck breast has slightly less fat and calories than boneless, skinless chicken breast. A 3.5-ounce serving of skinless duck breast has 2.5 grams of fat and 140 calories, compared with chicken breast's 3.6 grams of fat and 165 calories. And as far as flavor and moistness goes, duck wins over chicken every time. Chef Hamann prefers muscovy duck, a nonmigrating duck originally from South America.

WHERE TO BUY

Duck:

D'Artagnan, Inc., 800-327-8246, www.dartagnan.com

Prawn Corporation of America, 866-772-9626, www.prawnco.com

lacroix at the rittenhouse

210 W. RITTENHOUSE SQUARE   PHILADELPHIA, PA 19103

215-735-2533   WWW.LACROIXRESTAURANT.COM

Chef Jean-Marie Lacroix, a culinary guru long synonymous with the Four Seasons Hotel, has made a new home for himself in this drop-dead gorgeous restaurant overlooking leafy Rittenhouse Square. The James Beard Award–winning chef's invigorated classic French dishes are offered in three-, four-, and five-course groupings. Named by *Esquire* magazine as Restaurant of the Year when in opened in 2003, Lacroix (pronounced la-KWA) is an extraordinary culinary experience. If you visit on Monday through Thursday, the chef welcomes guests into his kitchen for an interactive dinner experience that allows diners to sample dishes, chat with the chef, and take a tour of the kitchen.

Chef Lacroix's Eggs on Eggs recipe makes an elegant brunch or summer supper entrée. If you want to splurge with osetra caviar, please do. But the salmon roe available in the grocery store makes a less pricey substitution.

Chef Lacroix uses an egg topper to cut the top off each egg, saving the shell for later presentation. If you don't have an egg topper handy, you can simply serve the eggs in a small bowl. But consider getting one—it's an inexpensive way to add elegance to the presentation of this dish. Another option is to very gently saw the tops off the eggs with a large serrated knife, which also works well once you get the hang of it.

eggs
on eggs

SERVES 4

4 large eggs

1 tablespoon cold water

½ cup heavy cream

4 teaspoons finely chopped smoked salmon

Coarse salt and freshly ground white pepper, to taste

4 teaspoons salmon caviar

4 sprigs fresh chervil or parsley

Toast, for serving

1. If using an egg topper, cut the top of the eggshells off, carefully rinse out the shell, and reserve for later.

2. Bring an inch of water to a boil in the bottom of a double boiler or in a medium saucepan. Whisk the eggs and cold water together in the top of a double boiler or in a medium stainless-steel bowl that will fit over your saucepan. Place the eggs over the boiling water and whisk constantly until the eggs are soft and have begun to set. Gently whisk in the cream, smoked salmon, and salt and pepper to taste. Remove from the heat.

3. Divide the cooked eggs between the eggshells or 4 small serving bowls. Top each with 1 teaspoon of the caviar and a sprig of chervil or parsley. Serve with toast.

chef's notes   Since salmon caviar is a lesser grade than the chef's original choice—the more expensive sturgeon caviar—consider perking it up with a splash of fresh lemon juice.

For a final wow, use soldier's toast to garnish the top of the egg. Soldier's toast is a ½- by 3-inch crouton made of brioche or challah bread.

and to drink

$ Korbel Brut Champagne

$$ 1987 Veuve Clicquot La Grande Dame Rosé

WHERE TO BUY

Caviar:

Browne Trading Company, 800-944-7848, www.brownetrading.com

Caviar Assouline, 800-521-4491, www.icaviar.com

Egg topper: Fante's, 800-443-2683, www.fantes.com

le bec-fin

1523 WALNUT STREET   PHILADELPHIA, PA 19102

215- 567-1000   WWW.LEBECFIN.COM

No doubt about it, Le Bec-Fin is five-star French dining at its finest. Chef-owner Georges Perrier and his team match the sumptuous surroundings (love that salmon Scalamandre silk!) with seasonally changing menus featuring indulgences like the best foie gras and Perigord truffles money can buy. (Last time we checked dinner was $135 per person, before wine and service, but worth every penny.) Chef Perrier has added global touches to his menu—roasted salmon, cauliflower, grape, and grapefruit fricassee with curry emulsion is one example—but his classic French dishes will always be his forte. A highlight is always the all-you-can-eat daily dessert cart, groaning with forty different tempting desserts. The cheese cart is just as impressive, and the wine list is downright memorable.

For this dish, chef Perrier swaps four squabs for one chicken, substitutes chicken broth for squab stock, and provides a terrific low-cost alternative to port: red wine with the addition of sugar.

While your chicken cooks, you can prepare the plum sauce and Swiss chard, making this a surprisingly quick meal that's elegant enough for company.

roast chicken
with poached plums and swiss chard

SERVES 4

One 3$\frac{1}{2}$- to 4-pound chicken

Coarse salt and freshly ground black pepper, to taste

$\frac{1}{2}$ cup dried plums or prunes

4 cups light, inexpensive red wine (such as Beaujolais)

1 cup sugar

1 tablespoon breakfast tea (the tea from 1 or 2 tea bags will do)

Zest from $\frac{1}{2}$ orange

1 cinnamon stick (or $\frac{1}{2}$ teaspoon ground cinnamon)

2 pink, black, or white peppercorns

Leaves from 1 bunch Swiss chard, tough stems and ribs discarded

1 cup apple-cider vinegar

4 cups chicken broth

2 tablespoons unsalted butter, cut into chunks

1 tablespoon olive oil

2 shallots, minced

1 clove garlic, minced

1. Preheat the oven to 350°F. Pat the chicken dry with paper towels and season with salt and pepper. Place the chicken in a roasting pan fitted with a rack and bake until the juices run clear when the thickest part of the thigh is poked with a knife, about 1 hour.

2. While the chicken roasts, combine the plums, wine, sugar, tea, zest, cinnamon, and peppercorns in a medium saucepan and bring to a boil. Let simmer for 15 minutes to soften the fruit. Strain the liquid; reserve the liquid and plums (discard the seasonings). Wipe out the saucepan and return the liquid to it. Continue to cook over medium heat until the liquid becomes syrupy, about 7 minutes. Return the plums to the sauce and set aside.

3. Bring a large pot of salted water to a boil over high heat. Add the Swiss chard and cook 1 minute. Drain and cool in a bowl of ice water. Drain again and pat dry with paper towels. Set aside.

4. Place the chicken on a platter and cover loosely with foil. Pour off all but 1 tablespoon of the fat from the roasting pan. Add the vinegar to the pan, stirring and scraping the bottom of the pan with a wooden spoon. Add the chicken broth, place the roasting pan over high heat, and simmer until reduced by one third, about 10 minutes. Remove from the heat and swirl in the butter one chunk at a time. Season with salt and pepper and keep warm.

5. Right before serving, slice the Swiss chard leaves into bite-size pieces. Heat the oil in a medium sauté pan over medium heat and add the shallots and garlic. Cook, stirring, 1 minute, then add the chard and cook until warmed through, about 3 minutes. Season with salt and pepper to taste.

6. Reheat the plums and sauce. Spoon the poached plums around the plate. Place a quarter of the chard on each. Cut the chicken into 8

pieces and place a piece on top of the Swiss chard. Spoon some of the chicken broth and butter sauce over the chicken. Finally, drizzle some of the red wine sauce over all.

and to drink
$ 2001 Charles Audoin
Marsannay Longeroies, France
$$ 1999 Denis Mortet
Chambertin, France

chef's notes Chef Perrier loves to use squab in this recipe. If you have never eaten squab, you're missing out on the king of birds! A squab is not your average pigeon. These month-old young birds are domesticated and extremely tender, since they have never flown. Squabs typically weigh a pound or less and are prized for their delicately flavored dark meat. Ideal for grilling and quick sautéing, their full flavor stands up to strong marinades. They are best served rare to medium rare.

WHERE TO BUY
Squab: D'Artagnan, Inc., 800-327-8246, www.dartagnan.com

¡pasion!

211 SOUTH 15TH STREET   PHILADELPHIA, PA 19102

215-875-9895   WWW.PASIONRESTAURANT.COM

Award-winning chef Guillermo Pernot, named 2002 Mid-Atlantic chef of the year by the James Beard Foundation, brings his native Latin American passion for food, an electrifying atmosphere, and exotic presentation to ¡Pasion! in downtown Philadelphia. Pernot connects to his Argentine roots with dishes like ceviche, smoked rib eye served with Moros y Cristianos (black beans and rice), and Parrillada, an Argentinean mixed grill for two served on an ox-shaped hibachi. His book, *¡Ceviche!*, won the World Gourmand Award for Best Latino Cook-book. Partner Michael Dombkoski brings an expertise in wine to the carefully stocked wine cellar, with an emphasis on wines from the Americas to complement Pernot's flair for the exotic. The bar also offers an array of sultry Caribbean- and South American–inspired libations including Caipirinha, Sangría, and Mojitos.

Although chef Pernot smokes his steaks on the stovetop, this isn't as easy as he makes it sound—especially if you don't have a restaurant-size exhaust fan and a super-hot commercial stove at your fingertips. But adapted for the grill, this is one of the best steaks you'll ever eat. Plan to marinate the steaks for at least a few hours, or better yet, overnight. Chips of mesquite, oak, or hickory wood give the meat its tantalizing smoke—wood chips are sold seasonally in the supermarket with other barbecue items.

chile-rubbed
rib eye steaks

SERVES 4

1 cup vegetable oil

2 tablespoons chipotle chile powder

1/2 cup ancho chile powder, or another 1/2 cup chipotle chile powder

1/2 cup paprika

1/4 cup garlic powder

2 tablespoons sugar

1 tablespoon dried oregano

Four 12-ounce rib eye steaks

Coarse salt, to taste

1 cup mesquite or hickory wood chips, soaked in water for 15 minutes

1. In a medium bowl, whisk together the oil, chipotle chile powder, ancho chile powder, paprika, garlic powder, sugar, and oregano. The mixture should be pasty.

2. Rub each steak with the spice mixture, place the steaks in a nonreactive container or a large resealable plastic bag, and refrigerate at least 4 hours, or overnight.

3. When you're ready to cook, start a charcoal fire or preheat a gas grill; the fire should be hot, and the rack should be at least 4 inches from the heat source. If you're using a charcoal grill, sprinkle the drained chips over the charcoal; for a gas grill, place the drained chips on a piece of aluminum foil. Place the foil directly on the source of heat.

4. Scrape most of the marinade off of the steaks. Season with salt. Place them on the grill and cook, turning once, until they reach the desired doneness, 8 to 10 minutes for medium rare.

WHERE TO BUY

Chipotle powder: PepperFool, 10153 1/2 Riverside Drive, #459, Toluca Lake, CA, 323-578-5603, www.pepperfool.com

Rib eye steaks: Lobel's, 877-783-4512, www.lobels.com

chef's notes This recipe works great with other meats, including filet and pork tenderloin. Set off the slight smokiness of the rib eye with a watercress salad with tomatoes and blue cheese.

Testing steaks for doneness will take some practice. For beginners, there's nothing wrong with using a small knife to make a little cut in the steak to peek inside. You can also use an instant-read food thermometer. Insert the thermometer sideways into the deepest part of the steak. Rare beef is about 115 to 120°F, medium rare is 125°F, and medium is 135 to 140°F.

Mainstream spice companies like McCormick have moved beyond generic chili powder to feature specialty chiles in their gourmet collection, like chipotle and ancho. Ancho, or dried poblano peppers, are mild peppers commonly used to infuse Mexican cuisine with a dark, earthy flavor. Chipotle peppers, or smoked jalapeños, are much spicier, and lend a wonderful smoky flavor to sauces and marinades.

and to drink
$ 2003 Alamos Cabernet Sauvignon Mendoza, Argentina
$$ 2002 Montes Alpha Cabernet, Chile

the grill at the ritz-carlton

10 AVENUE OF THE ARTS   PHILADELPHIA, PA 19102

215-523-8000   WWW.RITZCARLTON.COM/HOTELS/PHILADELPHIA/

Located in the former Girard Trust Company and Mellon Bank, a marble temple at the corner of Broad and Chestnut Streets fashioned after the Roman Pantheon, Philadelphia's Ritz-Carlton is ritzy indeed. A striking example of neoclassical architecture, the hotel offers first-class dining in the Grill, powered by culinary luminary Terence Feury, whose pedigree includes Striped Bass and Manhattan's Le Bernardin. Working from an open exhibition kitchen, chef Feury produces uncluttered new American classics, using seasonal and locally sourced ingredients. Known for his keen creative eye and relentless attention to detail, Feury's specialties include grilled bigeye tuna with chorizo, roasted tomatoes, and peas and wild sea bass with crispy red lentils and lemon-coriander sauce.

Chef Feury replaces black bass with the always available salmon in this recipe for Thai curried fish. He recommends buying wild salmon over farmed if at all possible. You'll find both the coconut milk and the red curry paste in the Asian foods section of the supermarket.

salmon with steamed mussels
in thai curry broth

SERVES 4

1 tablespoon unsalted butter

4 shallots, sliced

Coarse salt and freshly ground white pepper, to taste

1 tomato, chopped

1 teaspoon Thai red curry paste

2 pounds mussels, scrubbed (discard any mussels that do not close)

2 tablespoons white wine

One 13.5-ounce can unsweetened coconut milk

½ cucumber, peeled and sliced

¼ cup Thai or regular basil leaves, left whole if small and torn into pieces if large

1 tablespoon canola oil

Four 6-ounce pieces salmon fillet

1 lime

1. In a large saucepan, melt the butter over medium heat. Add the shallots and sprinkle with salt and pepper. Cook, stirring, 2 minutes. Stir in the tomato and curry paste and cook 1 more minute.

2. Add the mussels and white wine. Cover the pot and steam until the mussels open, about 3 minutes.

3. Add the coconut milk to the mussels and bring to a boil. Toss in the cucumber and basil leaves and heat through. Discard any mussels that do not open.

4. Meanwhile, in a large nonstick sauté pan, heat the oil over high heat. Salt the salmon fillets and place them in the pan, skin side down, and cook until the skin is browned, about 3 minutes. Lower the heat to medium, turn the fillets, and continue cooking until the fillets are nicely browned and the flesh is firm to the touch, about 2 more minutes. Remove from the heat and keep warm.

5. To serve, divide the mussels among 4 bowls and pour their cooking liquid over them. Place a salmon fillet on top of each and drizzle with lime juice.

chef's notes Mussels from the cold waters of Prince Edward Island in Canada are prized by chefs for their clean taste and tender sweet meat. Just before cooking, rinse and scrub the mussels well under cold water and use a small sharp paring knife to remove any beardlike strands along the outer edge of the shell. Mussel shells may gape open; this doesn't necessarily mean the animal is spoiled or dead. A gentle tap on the shell will usually cause the mussel to close. If it doesn't, discard it to be on the safe side.

and to drink

$ 2003 Frey Organic Gewürztraminer, California

$$ 2001 Hugel Gewürztraminer Cuvée Jubilee, Alsace, France

WHERE TO BUY

Prince Edward Island mussels: Gorton's of Gloucester, 800-335-3674, www.gortonsfreshseafood.com

striped bass

1500 WALNUT STREET   PHILADELPHIA, PA 19102

215-732-4444   WWW.STRIPEDBASSRESTAURANT.COM

One of Philadelphia's defining restaurants for more than a decade, Striped Bass was reborn in 2004, rejuvenated under the new ownership of noted Philadelphia restaurateur Stephen Starr. Besides dramatically enhancing the restaurant's stunning interior with decadent chandeliers, chocolate brown velvet seating, and calf brown leather banquettes, Starr brought in heavy hitter Alfred Portale (Gotham Bar and Grill) as consulting chef and Christopher Lee (Oceana Restaurant, Jean Georges) as chef de cuisine. Lee earned the prestigious Rising Star Chef of the Year Award from the James Beard Foundation in 2005. The restaurant's imaginative menu is swimming in seafood, with creations like wild striped bass ceviche and smoked eel with micro arugula and quail eggs. But Portale's signature grilled Gotham steak—a 13-ounce New York strip cut with bone marrow and Dijon custard, Vidalia onion rings, and bordelaise sauce—is also a favorite.

Chef Lee usually pairs the wild striped bass in this recipe with black beluga lentils, but regular lentils will suffice. He recommends wild bass over farmed, if at all possible.

You'll need plastic wrap and kitchen twine or string handy for this recipe. Although this dish has multiple steps, none of them are difficult. Be sure to assemble all of your ingredients in advance to make things easier.

steamed stuffed striped bass
with cabbage and prosciutto

SERVES 4

1 head Savoy cabbage

1 tablespoon canola oil

½ pound fresh porcini or shiitake mushrooms, coarsely chopped

2 shallots, minced

¼ pound prosciutto di Parma, finely diced

Leaves from 2 sprigs fresh thyme, or ¼ teaspoon dried

Coarse salt and freshly ground black pepper, to taste

Four 6-ounce pieces skinless wild striped bass fillet

¼ pound smoked bacon, cut into chunks

1 onion, halved

1 cup black beluga lentils, rinsed

5 cups chicken broth

3 carrots, chopped

1 onion, chopped

One 750-milliliter bottle white wine

8 tablespoons (1 stick) cold unsalted butter, cut into chunks

4 sprigs parsley or chervil, for garnish

1. Remove all the leaves from the Savoy cabbage. Bring a large pot of salted water to a boil. Once the water is at a rolling boil, add the leaves and cook for 2 minutes. Drain the leaves and immediately cool them in a large bowl of ice water. Once the leaves are cool, drain again and lay them flat on a sheet pan between paper towels. Refrigerate the leaves for about ½ hour to allow them to dry.

2. Meanwhile, heat a medium sauté pan over high heat. When the pan is hot, add the oil, mushrooms, and shallots. Cook, stirring, until the mushrooms start to soften, about 5 minutes. Stir in the prosciutto and thyme leaves, cooking just until heated through. Season with salt and pepper and set aside.

3. Slice each fish fillet horizontally, leaving the two halves attached on one side so that you can open each fillet like a book. Season the fillets all over with salt and pepper and divide the filling among the fillets. Fold the bass over the filling.

4. Lay 2 to 3 leaves of cabbage on your cutting board. Wrap a fillet with the cabbage. Lay the fish on a 12 x 12-inch piece of plastic wrap. Wrap up the fish package firmly in the plastic and twist both ends to form a tight cylinder. Tie the loose ends tightly with string to prevent the package from opening. Refrigerate until needed.

5. Place a large, heavy-bottomed saucepan over high heat. Add the bacon and halved onion and cook for 1 minute. Add the lentils and 3 cups of the chicken stock and bring to a boil. Lower the heat and simmer until the lentils are tender but not mushy, 20 to 30 minutes. Strain the lentils, discard the liquid, and pick out and discard the onion halves and bacon chunks. Set the lentils aside to cool.

6. In a heavy, medium saucepan, combine the carrots, chopped onion, and remaining 2 cups chicken broth. Bring to a boil over high heat, lower the heat, and simmer until almost all the liquid has evaporated, about 15 minutes.

7. Reserve 2 tablespoons of the wine. Add the remaining wine to the pan and simmer until only about a ¼ cup of liquid remains, 20 to 25 minutes. Strain the contents of the saucepan, discard the solids, and return the liquid to the pan. Place over very low heat. Whisk in one chunk of the butter at a time, whisking constantly and only adding another chunk of butter when the last has been incorporated. Whisk in the reserved 2 tablespoons wine. Season with salt and pepper. Cover the pan and set the butter sauce aside.

8. To steam the fish, prepare a steamer or large pot of water with a steamer inset that will suspend the fish about 2 inches over boiling water and add water as needed. Place over high heat. When the water begins to boil, add the fish packages, cover the pot, and steam for 12 minutes.

9. Meanwhile, reheat the lentils and the butter sauce. (Do not allow the sauce to boil or it will separate; reheat it over low heat, stirring constantly until just warmed.) Unwrap each package of bass and slice each into 3 rounds. Place the rounds on top of the lentils, drizzle with sauce, and garnish with a parsley or chervil sprig.

and to drink
$ 2001 Whitehall Lane Sauvignon Blanc, California
$$ 2001 Chalk Hill Sauvignon Blanc, California

chef's notes Black beluga lentils are truly the caviar of lentils: glistening black legumes that are packed with protein. Originally a wild lentil native to the area around Syria, this lentil is very quick cooking, so it's a perfect side dish or bed for fish or poultry. Peppery French green lentils are a fine substitute. If you use common brown lentils, be careful not to overcook them or they'll get mushy. Before cooking, always rinse lentils and pick out stones and other debris. Unlike dried beans and peas, there's no need to soak them. Dried lentils can be stored for up to a year in a cool, dry place.

WHERE TO BUY
Black beluga lentils: Whole Foods, multiple locations, www.wholefoods.com
Prosciutto di Parma: Gourmet Pasta Cheese, 800-386-9198,
www.pastacheese.com

zanzibar blue at the bellevue

200 SOUTH BROAD STREET   PHILADELPHIA, PA 19102

215-732-4500   WWW.ZANZIBARBLUE.COM

One of Philadelphia's premier jazz destinations, Zanzibar Blue is also a world-class restaurant, thanks to the collaboration between sibling owners Robert and Benjamin Bynum and executive chef Albert Paris. Paris, a native Philadelphian and a fixture on the local dining scene since the 1990s, improvises impressive global fare against a palate of black and white, accented with splashes of red and vintage jazz portraits. A few of Paris's swoon-worthy appetizers include plump seared scallops finished in a peppery orange butter glaze and Louisiana mussels over pasta in a smoky tasso ham and tomato cream sauce. Paris puts a Southern spin on sushi-quality tuna, topping it with lump crabmeat and crawfish finished with cream, seared greens, and corn-scallion hushpuppies, and the braised short ribs over creamy cheddar polenta and collard greens showcase new Southern cooking at its best.

For this boldly flavored Asian seafood salad, virtually anything fresh goes. Just buy a total of about four pounds of seafood. At the restaurant, Paris uses fresh baby squid—not typical of most supermarket seafood departments but available at Asian supermarkets and seafood markets. If you feel like splurging on lobster, go ahead, but you'll do just fine using fish, scallops, and shrimp. This dish is an excellent summer main course, but can also work as a tasty appetizer.

hong kong
seafood salad

1 tablespoon canola oil

1 medium red onion, cut into rings

1 medium white onion, cut into rings

1 pound sea scallops

½ cup sake or white wine

2 teaspoons coarse salt, plus more for seasoning the fish

1 teaspoon freshly ground black pepper, plus more for seasoning the fish

2 pounds medium shrimp, peeled and deveined

½ pound vermicelli

Juice of 2 limes

1 tablespoon rice vinegar

2 tablespoons sesame oil

2 teaspoons peeled, chopped fresh ginger

½ teaspoon ground coriander

1 bunch fresh cilantro, finely chopped (leaves and stems)

4 minced red Thai bird chiles (or 1 teaspoon dried red chile pepper)

4 tablespoons peanut oil

Four 3-ounce pieces red snapper fillet, skin on

Fresh lime, for serving

1. In a large sauté pan set over medium heat, heat the canola oil. Add the onion and cook, stirring, until it starts to soften, about 3 minutes.

2. Stir in the scallops, sake, 1 teaspoon of the salt, and ½ teaspoon of the black pepper. Cover the pan and continue cooking, stirring occasionally, until the scallops are cooked through and no longer translucent, about 8 minutes.

3. With a slotted spoon, remove the scallops and onion to a plate and reserve. Return the pan with the liquid in it to medium-high heat and bring to a boil. Add the shrimp and cook, covered, until the shrimp are just cooked through, about 6 minutes. (Add a little more sake to the pan if you don't have enough liquid.) Set aside the pan with the shrimp in it.

4. Bring a large pot of salted water to a boil. Add the vermicelli and cook until almost tender, about 5 minutes. Drain in a colander, rinse with cold water, and set aside.

5. In a large bowl, whisk together the lime juice, vinegar, sesame oil, ginger, coriander, cilantro, chiles, and 3 tablespoons of the peanut oil. Whisk in the remaining teaspoon salt, remaining ½ teaspoon black pepper, and 3 tablespoons of the liquid the shrimp cooked in. Add the scallops, onion, and noodles. Drain the shrimp, discard the liquid, and add the shrimp to the bowl. Toss well and refrigerate just until chilled, about 15 minutes.

6. Sprinkle the snapper fillets with salt and pepper. Heat the remaining tablespoon peanut oil in a large sauté pan and cook the snapper until browned, about 3 minutes per side. Cut each fillet into 3 pieces and cool.

7. To serve, divide the noodle and seafood mixture among 6 plates and place the fish on top. Serve with fresh lime and chopsticks.

chef's notes All seafood should be as fresh as possible, but if you want to save time you can substitute cleaned, frozen shrimp for fresh.

To turn down this salad's heat, remove the seeds from the chile peppers. Remember that the chile oil stays on your fingers for a while, so consider wearing disposable gloves when handling chiles.

Make it easy on yourself by premeasuring your ingredients into small bowls before you get started. Once that's done, this salad comes together in about the time it takes to cook the pasta and chill the salad a bit.

WHERE TO BUY

Fresh seafood:
Anastasi Seafood, 215-462-0550
Legal Sea Foods, 800-343-5804, www.legalseafoods.com

vetri

1312 SPRUCE STREET   PHILADELPHIA, PA 19107

215-732-3478   WWW.VETRIRISTORANTE.COM

When Marc Vetri was named best chef in the Mid-Atlantic at the 2005 James Beard awards, the accolade didn't surprise any of his Philadelphia fans. Vetri is well known for creating rustic, regional Italian cuisine, not unlike what Mario Batali is doing at Babbo in New York's Greenwich Village. Situated in Georges Perrier's original digs on Spruce Street, Vetri is an intimate and elegantly simple restaurant of just thirty-five coveted seats. On a typical evening, Vetri is in and out of the dining room often, usually to slice prosciutto for the antipasti on his gleaming antique meat slicer. While his specialties are many, the chestnut fettuccine with wild boar ragu and cocoa and the spinach gnocchi with smoked ricotta and brown butter are two dishes at the top of the list. Expect interesting ingredients, unusual pairings, and attentive service; it's an expensive night out, but worth every penny. Saturday nights are limited to a five- or seven-course tasting menu.

wilted tuscan salad
with egg and pancetta

SERVES 4

¼ cup thinly sliced pancetta or bacon

2 tablespoons unsalted butter

4 cups mixed lettuces

1 tablespoon sherry vinegar

1 tablespoon balsamic vinegar

2 tablespoons extra-virgin olive oil

Coarse salt and freshly ground black pepper, to taste

3 large eggs, lightly beaten

1. In a small saucepan over medium heat, cook the pancetta and butter until the pancetta is crispy, about 10 minutes.

2. Meanwhile, in a large bowl, toss the lettuces, sherry vinegar, balsamic vinegar, oil, and salt and pepper to taste.

3. When the pancetta is crispy, add the eggs to the pan and stir until softly scrambled but still a bit runny, then scrape into the bowl with the salad mixture. Toss and serve immediately.

and to drink

$ 2003 Tocai Friulano Bastianich, Italy

$$ 2001 Tocai Plus, Bastianich, Italy

chef's notes For this dish, it's important not to cook the eggs too much. They must be very runny so they almost emulsify with the oil and the vinegar. This dish is very messy, but very tasty!

Pancetta, or Italian bacon, is cured but not smoked. Often used to impart a subtle saltiness to sauces, pancetta can be found in Italian specialty stores. If you substitute American bacon, be sure to blanch it first in boiling water for a minute or two to cut down on the smoky flavor. You can also use prosciutto.

You can use almost any combination of vinegars for this recipe, but sherry and balsamic work best.

WHERE TO BUY
Pancetta: Di Bruno Brothers, 888-322-4337, www.dibruno.com

phoenix

dining defined in the valley of the sun

It's no surprise that the dining scene in Greater Phoenix is as bold as the chile-spiked Southwestern cuisine that is synonymous with this grown-up cowboy town. But don't make the mistake of thinking that ancho chiles, cowboy steaks, and homemade tortillas define restaurants in Phoenix. In Phoenix, you'll find the best sushi you may taste anywhere, an Italian sandwich shop distilled to its purest form, and, at a funky downtown diner, a plate of fritters doused in maple syrup that will transport you to a county fair state of mind.

As Phoenix grows in population, its table keeps expanding. Chefs like Douglas Rodriguez and Mark Dow at Deseo in the Westin Kierland Resort, Chris Bianco of Pizzeria Bianco and Panne Bianco, and Michael White and Patrick Fegan of Fiamma Osteria in the spunky new James Hotel in Scottsdale are raising the bar on what tastes good, not just in Phoenix but in any American city.

Naturally, there's always room for the French grandeur of Mary Elaine's, the city's lone five-star Mobil-rated experience at the Phoenician Resort.

And you don't want to miss the Western kitsch of old standbys like Pinnacle Peak Patio, where greenhorns who make the mistake of ordering their steak well done are served a charred cowboy boot instead, and any city slicker sporting a tie has it cut in half and hung from the rafters. It is just this kind of gastronomic range that provides the comfortable under-pinnings of what has become a great food town. But it's the for-ward thinkers, the trailblazers, the chefs who are passionate about everything from serving line-caught fish to making their own fresh mozzarella cheese; these are the chefs who inspire.

You'll be inspired by these ten recipes from a short list of some of the finest restaurants in Phoenix.

eddie matney's restaurant

2398 EAST CAMELBACK ROAD   PHOENIX, AZ 85016

602-957-3214   WWW.EDDIEMATNEYS.COM

Located in the heart of the Biltmore district at 24th Street and Camelback Road, Eddie Matney's Restaurant is home to one of the most colorful chefs in town. Matney, who hosts a local television cooking show, creates multicultural comfort cuisine that includes strong influences from his own Lebanese heritage. A few of his specialties include Matney meatloaf, served with bacon, basil, and tomatoes over country mashed potatoes with wild mushroom gravy; mo-rockin' shrimp, a bold casserole of cumin-spiced shrimp and honey dumplings; garlic mashed potato–encased filet mignon, served with Cabernet Sauvignon demi-glace; and East Meets West, a combo of sesame-seared ahi over Japanese vegetables and Parmesan-encrusted sea bass over asparagus risotto. Top off your meal with Eddie's peanut buttery Boston cream pie or the cappuccino bread pudding.

Fetoosh salad is a typical chopped salad served in many types of Middle Eastern cuisine, including chef Matney's native Lebanese. Toasted pita triangles stand in for croutons. You can substitute boneless leg of lamb for the lamb chops, grilling or roasting until the meat registers 130ºF on a meat thermometer for medium rare.

fetoosh salad

with minted lamb chops

SERVES 4

Lamb Chops

1 cup olive oil

1 cup fresh lemon juice

4 cloves garlic

1 shallot

2 tablespoons chopped fresh mint

1 teaspoon salt, plus more to taste

1 teaspoon freshly ground black pepper, plus more to taste

8 to 12 small lamb chops

Salad

Six 8-inch pitas

4 tablespoons olive oil

3 tablespoons sumac or freshly grated lemon zest

Coarse salt and freshly ground black pepper, to taste

½ pound baby field greens

1 head romaine lettuce, chopped

3 scallions, chopped

1 cucumber, peeled, seeded, and thinly sliced

1 bunch radishes, sliced

1 cup chopped fresh parsley leaves

1 cup chopped fresh mint leaves

3 plum tomatoes, chopped

Juice of 1 lemon

1. To make the lamb chops, in a blender, combine the oil, lemon juice, garlic, shallot, mint, 1 teaspoon of the salt, and 1 teaspoon of the pepper. Blend until smooth. Place in a nonreactive dish, add the lamb chops, turn to coat, and marinate, refrigerated, at least 1 hour and up to 6 hours.

2. Meanwhile, make the salad. Preheat the oven to 350ºF.

3. Brush the pitas with 1 tablespoon of the olive oil and sprinkle with 2 tablespoons sumac and salt and pepper to taste. Lay the pitas on a baking sheet. Bake until golden brown, about 5 minutes. Cut each pita into 8 triangles and let cool.

4. In a large bowl, combine the field greens, romaine, scallions, cucumber, radishes, parsley, mint, and tomatoes and toss.

5. Just before serving, add the cooled pita wedges to the bowl. Drizzle the remaining 3 tablespoons olive oil over the salad and sprinkle with the remaining tablespoon sumac and the lemon juice. Toss and season to taste with salt and pepper.

6. Prepare a charcoal or gas grill for high-heat cooking. Remove the lamb from the marinade. Grill the chops until they reach the desired doneness, about 2 minutes per side for medium rare.

7. Divide the salad among 4 plates, place 2 or 3 lamb chops on top of the salad, and serve.

WHERE TO BUY

Sumac:

Middle Eastern Bakery, 602-277-4927

Wild Oats Natural Marketplace, multiple locations, 800-494-WILD (9453), www.wildoats.com

Fetoosh Salad (*continued*)

and to drink

$ 2004 Frogs Leap Sauvignon
Blanc, California

$$ 2002 Saintsbury Pinot Noir
Carneros, California

chef's notes Sumac is a burgundy-colored, tart spice used widely in cookery in Saudi Arabia, Turkey, the Eastern Mediterranean, and especially in Lebanese cuisine. In addition to using lemon, Middle Eastern cooks turn to sumac as a souring agent. It is rubbed on kebabs before grilling and may be used in this way with fish or chicken. The juice extracted from sumac is popular in salad dressings and marinades, and the powdered form is used in stews and vegetable and chicken casseroles.

alchemy restaurant at copperwynd resort

13225 N EAGLE RIDGE DRIVE   FOUNTAIN HILLS, AZ 85268

480-333-1880   WWW.COPPERWYND.COM

Follow a long and winding road into the foothills of the McDowell Mountains and you'll be rewarded with the stunning Copperwynd Resort and Alchemy restaurant. The restaurant's setting is sheer drama, with its floor-to-ceiling glass panels that slide open to reveal incredible views of Four Peaks, Red Mountain, the Mazatzals, and the Superstitions. With Valley chef Paul O'Connor in the executive spot (as of June 2005), the restaurant's menu reflects its name— an alchemy of Southwestern, French, Italian, and Middle Eastern flavors. Try the avocado-cremini wonton with shaved napa cabbage and a lemongrass-scallion emulsion and Moroccan swordfish with bronzed citrus-glazed fennel. At the restaurant, chef O'Connor pairs this satisfying crusted sea bass with a wheat berry basmati and toasted orzo medley.

Halibut, grouper, or any white, flaky fish can be substituted for the Chilean sea bass. The fish is served with an easy-to-make coulis (KOO-lee), a thick puree or sauce often made with fruit.

chutney and pistachio-crusted
chilean sea bass
with mango coulis

SERVES 4

¾ cup plus 2 tablespoons Major Grey's mango chutney

½ cup water

¼ cup Cointreau or Triple Sec

Coarse salt and freshly ground white pepper, to taste

1 cup roasted and shelled pistachio nuts

½ cup plain bread crumbs

Vegetable oil, as needed

Four 6-ounce pieces Chilean sea bass or other firm, white fish fillet

Cooked basmati rice or basmati rice blend, for serving

1. In a blender, combine 2 tablespoons of the chutney, the water, and Cointreau. Blend until smooth. Season the coulis to taste with salt and white pepper and refrigerate until needed.

2. Preheat the oven to 350°F.

3. Combine the pistachios and bread crumbs in a food processor and pulse until the nuts are finely chopped. (If a food processor is not available, place in a resealable plastic bag and gently crush with the bottom of a small sauté pan.) Season with salt and pepper and set aside.

4. Heat a large sauté pan over medium-high heat. When the pan is hot, add just enough oil to film the bottom of the pan. Place the fish pieces in the pan and season lightly with salt and pepper. Cook for 2 minutes on one side, then gently flip the fish, season with salt and pepper, and cook for another 2 minutes. Remove from the sauté pan and place in a nonstick baking dish or glass casserole dish sprayed with cooking spray. Allow the fish to cool.

5. Preheat the oven to 350°F. Spread the remaining ¾ cup mango chutney on top of the fish. Spread a generous layer of the pistachio crust on the chutney-covered fish. Bake until the fish is cooked through and the crust begins to crisp, about 10 minutes. Serve immediately with basmati rice drizzled with the mango coulis.

WHERE TO BUY

Basmati rice blend: Mount Hope Foods, 928-634-2498, www.mounthopefoods.com

and to drink

$ 2001 Deloach Chardonnay,
California

$$ 2002 Amici Napa
Chardonnay, California

chef's notes   There are many basmati rice blends available. The one that chef O'Connor prefers is a blend of 75 percent basmati rice, 15 percent toasted orzo pasta, and 10 percent wheat berries. It is available through Mount Hope Foods. Near East brand also makes several basmati blends that are available at most supermarkets. Pick the one that most appeals to your tastes and follow the cooking directions on the package.

vu at the hyatt regency scottsdale resort

7500 E. DOUBLETREE RANCH ROAD   SCOTTSDALE, AZ 85258

480-991-3388   WWW.SCOTTSDALE.HYATT.COM

Wonderfully talented chef William Bradley is putting out world market cuisine at Vu (pronounced "view") in the stunning Hyatt Regency set amidst flowering cactus, breathtaking sunsets, and the backdrop of the majestic McDowell Mountains. Bradley works with artisanal purveyors and farmers to create such memorable dishes as gnocchi with pancetta; cauliflower with currants in a curry sauce; tender braised Kobe beef short ribs; briny sweet Taylor Bay scallops; and a brilliant parade of vegetables including beets with goat cheese, pistachios, and cranberries; baby carrots glazed with honey, citrus, and cumin; and fennel with olives, gooseberries, and Meyer lemon. Bradley, who came to the Hyatt in 2002 after a stint as sous chef at Mary Elaine's, is in top form at the reconceived contemporary Vu, formerly the more traditional Golden Swan. Try the Perfect Vu, Bradley's signature four-course tasting menu.

Brussels sprouts have never been so delicious as in this flavorful pairing with bacon, blue cheese, and tart green apples. You can use regular brandy if there's no Calvados in the liquor cabinet.

brussels sprouts with bacon,
blue cheese, and green apples

SERVES 4

1 tablespoon grapeseed oil or light olive oil

1 cup peeled, diced Granny Smith apples

8 tablespoons (1 stick) unsalted butter

2 tablespoons sugar

1 tablespoon cinnamon

½ cup apple juice

½ cup Calvados (apple brandy) or regular brandy

Coarse salt and freshly ground black pepper, to taste

4 slices smoked bacon

3 cups baby brussels sprouts, trimmed and halved

½ cup chicken broth

¼ cup crumbled blue cheese

Extra-virgin olive oil

1. Preheat the oven to 300ºF.

2. In a large nonstick sauté pan over medium-high heat, heat the grapeseed oil. When the oil just begins to smoke, add the apples and cook for 45 seconds. Add 4 tablespoons of the butter. When the butter begins to brown, add the sugar and cinnamon. As soon as the sugar begins to caramelize, pour in the apple juice and cook, stirring, until the sugar has melted. Simmer until the liquid has completely evaporated, 8 to 10 minutes. Remove the pan from the heat and add the Calvados. Return the pan to the heat and cook until the liquid has evaporated. Season with salt and pepper. Set aside.

3. Preheat the oven to 300ºF. Slice the bacon into 2-inch pieces, place on a baking sheet, and bake until the bacon is completely cooked through, about 10 minutes. Transfer the bacon to paper towels to drain. Pour the bacon fat on the baking sheet into a large nonstick pan.

4. Place the pan with the fat in it over medium heat. Add the brussels sprouts, placing each one cut side down. When the brussels sprouts begin to brown, add the remaining 4 tablespoons butter and let cook until the butter begins to brown. Add about two thirds of the chicken broth. Simmer until the broth is completely absorbed. Transfer the brussels sprouts to paper towels to drain. Sprinkle with salt and pepper.

5. Wipe out the pan and place over medium heat. Return the sprouts to the pan and add the apples and bacon and cook, stirring gently, until warmed. Pour in the remaining broth. Divide the mixture among 4 small serving dishes. Top each with blue cheese, a pinch of coarse salt, and a drizzle of extra-virgin olive oil.

and to drink

$ 2001 Erath Pinot Blanc, Oregon

$$ 2001 Rudi Pichler Gruner Veltliner Smaragd Hochrain, Austria

chef's notes Brussels sprouts are the most maligned of vegetables. Loathed by many grown-ups who were forced to eat boiled-to-death sprouts as kids, brussels sprouts really don't get the respect they deserve. Prepared fresh and cooked to barely tender perfection, these mini cabbages are tasty and loaded with antioxidants, along with a healthy dose of fiber, potassium, vitamin C, and iron. To prepare, first soak brussels sprouts in cold water for a few minutes, then drain. Trim the bottom of the stem and remove the tough outermost leaves. Versatile little veggies, sprouts can be braised, boiled, steamed, or blanched and then quickly infused with flavor by roasting or sautéing. The key is to cook until barely tender—err on the side of crunchiness, and your reward will be a mild flavor.

WHERE TO BUY

Organic vegetables: Wild Oats Natural Marketplace, multiple locations, 800-494-WILD (9453), www.wildoats.com

deseo

WESTIN KIERLAND RESORT   6902 EAST GREENWAY PARKWAY   SCOTTSDALE, AZ 85254

480-624-1030   WWW.KIERLANDRESORT.COM

One of the most exciting restaurants in town is definitely Deseo in the Westin Kierland Resort. Created by Nuevo Latino chef Douglas Rodriguez (Ola, New York; Alma de Cuba, Philadelphia) and chef de cuisine Mark Dow, this sexy restaurant earns its name—which means "desire" in Spanish. The menu's vibrant Latin fusion places ingredients and preparations from Mexico, Central and South America, and the Caribbean in a contemporary context. Sit at the open kitchen and feel a part of the action, as an army of good-looking chefs prepare bold ceviches, Kobe beef three ways, adobo-spiced seafood, and outstanding desserts, especially the Café y Tabaco, a white mousse "cigar" dipped in dark chocolate and served with dulce de leche, coffee ice cream, and chocolate espuma.

This is chef Dow's version of the traditional enchilada. You'll notice there isn't a corn tortilla or a layer of melted cheese in sight.

sea bass
enchilada

Verde Sauce

Leaves from
⅔ bunch cilantro

Leaves from
⅔ bunch parsley

⅓ pound spinach leaves

3 jalapeños, seeded,
or ½ green bell pepper

½ cup clam juice

⅔ cup olive oil

**Sea Bass and
Enchilada Sauce**

⅓ cup plus
2 tablespoons olive oil

1 cup diced onion

4 tablespoons minced garlic

3 to 4 jalapeños, seeded and
minced (optional)

2 red bell peppers,
finely diced

2 green bell peppers,
finely diced

Coarse salt and freshly
ground black pepper,
to taste

2 cups white wine

One 15-ounce can
tomato juice

One 14.5-ounce can
diced tomatoes

2 tablespoons tomato paste

1 cube vegetable bouillon,
dissolved in ½ cup hot water

2 tablespoons fresh
or frozen peas

1. To make the verde sauce, combine all the ingredients in a food processor or blender and puree. Set aside.

2. To make the sea bass and enchilada sauce, in a large sauté pan over medium heat, heat ⅓ cup of the oil. Add the onion and cook, stirring, until translucent, 3 to 5 minutes. Add 2 tablespoons of the garlic, the jalapeños, and bell peppers and cook until the peppers are just softened, about 4 minutes. Season with salt and pepper and add the white wine. Simmer, stirring occasionally, until the liquid is reduced by half, about 15 minutes. Add the tomato juice, diced tomatoes, tomato paste, and bouillon cube dissolved in water. Bring to a boil over high heat, lower the heat, and simmer for 10 minutes more.

3. Remove from the heat, season with salt and pepper, and cool. This is the enchilada sauce.

4. In a medium sauté pan over medium heat, heat 1 tablespoon of the remaining oil. Add the peas and 1 tablespoon of the remaining garlic and cook, stirring, until the peas are just tender, about 3 minutes. Add the cooked rice and ½ cup of the verde sauce. Season with salt and pepper and cook until warmed through. Stir in the scallions and keep warm.

5. Season the fish on both sides with salt and pepper. In a very large sauté pan, heat the remaining tablespoon olive oil over high heat. Add the fish and cook on both sides until golden brown and just cooked through, about 4 minutes. Remove the fish and set aside.

6. Return the pan the fish cooked in to high heat and add the shrimp and remaining tablespoon of garlic. Stir in the wine, scraping up any browned bits from the bottom of the pan. Return the fish to the pan. Add ½ cup of enchilada sauce to the pan and hot pepper sauce to taste. Allow the fish to cook through in the sauce. Serve the fish over the rice, topped with more of the verde and enchilada sauces.

2 cups cooked white rice

2 tablespoons thinly
sliced scallions

Six 8-ounce pieces sea bass
or other firm, white fish fillet

½ pound cooked,
peeled shrimp

¼ cup red wine

Hot pepper sauce, to taste

and to drink

$ 2003 Grgich Hills Estate
Fumé Blanc, California

$$ 2002 Chalone Pinot Blanc,
California

chef's notes Deglazing is a technique used just about every time you make a pan sauce. After food has been sautéed and removed from the pan, add a small amount of liquid to the pan and stir to loosen browned bits of food from the bottom of the pan. This goodness becomes the flavor base for a sauce or stock.

WHERE TO BUY

Fresh and organic seafood: The Fish Market, 602-277-3474,
www.thefishmarket.com/phoenix.htm

Sea bass: Browne Trading Company, 800-944-7848,
www.brownetrading.com

kai restaurant

SHERATON WILD HORSE PASS   5594 WEST WILD HORSE PASS BOULEVARD   PHOENIX, AZ 85070

602-225-0100   WWW.WILDHORSEPASSRESORT.COM

Kai is the signature restaurant in the Sheraton Wild Horse Pass, a hotel wholly owned by the Pima and Maricopa Native American tribes and located twenty minutes south of the airport. Meaning "seed" in the Pima language, Kai features a menu rich in creativity, history, and Native American culture. Native American chef Sandy Garcia incorporates the essence of the Pima and Maricopa tribes and locally farmed ingredients from the Gila River Indian Community to create dishes as unique as the Sonaran landscape. James Beard Award–winning chef Janos Wilder, known for creating indigenous menu experiences, is consulting chef. Garcia, long a proponent of cooking with regional ingredients, is a graduate of the CIA. Kai specialties include braised lobster tail, avocado mousse, and teardrop tomato salsa on third-generation fry bread; tenderloin of buffalo from the Cheyenne River tribe with smoked corn puree and saguaro blossom syrup; and smoked veal chop rubbed with toasted ground Fair Trade coffee and desert cactus. Kai was awarded the AAA four-diamond rating and was featured in *Food & Wine* magazine as one of Phoenix's top new restaurants in its first year of operation.

Chef Garcia usually makes this dish with duck breast, a delicious alternative to chicken breast that is now available at most supermarkets and wholesale clubs.

pan-seared duck

with cherry and ancho chile essence

SERVES 4

Two 8-ounce jars Ortega's or Baca's red chili sauce

4 tablespoons dried ancho chile powder

1 cup sun-dried tart cherries

8 cups chicken broth

Four 6-ounce duck breasts

1 tablespoon olive oil

Coarse salt and freshly ground black pepper, to taste

½ cup water

Leaves from 1 small bunch fresh spinach

1. In a medium saucepan, combine the chili sauce, chile powder, cherries, and broth. Bring to a boil over high heat, lower the heat, and simmer, uncovered, until reduced by half, about 30 minutes. Let cool to room temperature. Transfer to a blender and puree. Strain through a fine-mesh sieve; reserve the liquid and discard the solids.

2. Preheat the oven to 350°F.

3. Score the duck breasts by cutting through the skin—but not the meat—at ¼-inch intervals. Rotate and repeat, making a cross-hatch pattern. In a large, ovenproof sauté pan, heat the oil over high heat. Season the duck with salt and pepper, add it to the pan, and reduce the heat to medium. Cook, uncovered, until the skin is browned and crispy, about 15 minutes. Turn over and brown the other side for 1 minute, pouring off the excess fat. Transfer the pan to the oven and cook until the duck reaches the desired doneness, about 5 minutes for medium rare, 8 minutes for medium. Remove from the oven and let rest for 5 minutes.

4. In a small saucepan, bring the water to a boil. Add the spinach and cook until just wilted, about 30 seconds. Drain.

5. To serve, divide the spinach among 4 plates. Slice the duck breasts thinly and top the spinach with the slices. Spoon about 2 tablespoons cherry–ancho chili sauce over each plate.

and to drink

$ 2003 Alexander Valley Vineyards "Sin Zin" Zinfandel, California

$$ 2001 Zinfandel Beaulieu Vineyards "BV," Napa Valley, California

chef's notes Ancho chiles are dried poblano peppers commonly used in Mexican cuisine and available in many specialty markets. McCormick's Gourmet Collection® line, available in most supermarkets, includes ancho chile powder.

WHERE TO BUY

Dried ancho peppers and ground ancho chiles: Chile Shop, 505-983-6080, www.thechileshop.com

lon's at the hermosa

5532 NORTH PALO CRISTI   PARADISE VALLEY, AZ 85253

602-955-7878   WWW.LONS.COM

The Hermosa Inn, a Spanish hacienda built by cowboy artist Lon Megargee as his home and studio in 1930, is tucked away in Paradise Valley, a residential area with zoning laws that protect the darkness of the vast desert sky. Step inside and the Old West comes to life at Lon's at the Hermosa, a romantic setting that oozes old-time Arizona charm.

With a nod to both past and present, chef Michael Rusconi salutes the robust era of Lon Megargee while still honoring classic culinary techniques. Rusconi grows a wide selection of herbs and heirloom fruits, vegetables, and grains on the inn grounds. Harvested at the peak of their flavor and combined with other locally grown produce, the ingredients are incorporated into dishes that are brilliantly creative, yet direct and approachable. Menus are designed for maximum culinary impact, with dishes that range from the pecan-roasted pork chop to the cactus pear–lacquered breast of duck. The pecan-roasted pork chop with prickly pear–braised red cabbage, green beans, and garlic mashed potatoes is the definition of cowboy comfort food. With its comfortable retro-Western chic and satisfying ranch-house cuisine, Lon's is a locals' favorite.

Chef Rusconi makes this salad with farm-raised Arizona Desert Sweet Shrimp (see Where to Buy), but any medium-sized shrimp will work.

arizona shrimp salad

SERVES 4

Dressing

6 tablespoons olive oil

½ cup chopped fennel

1 small shallot, chopped

1 cup fresh orange juice

1 tablespoon honey

4 tablespoons rice vinegar

Coarse salt and freshly ground white pepper, to taste

Shrimp Salad

1 pound Arizona Desert Sweet Shrimp or other medium shrimp

2 tablespoons olive oil

1 tablespoon chopped garlic

Pinch red pepper flakes

¼ cup fresh orange juice

¼ cup white wine

1 tablespoon unsalted butter

1 tablespoon chopped fresh parsley

Coarse salt, to taste

2 oranges, peeled and cut into segments

1 pink grapefruit, peeled and cut into segments

1 avocado, peeled, pitted, and diced

2 heads cleaned Bibb or Boston lettuce

1. To make the dressing, in a small sauté pan over low heat, heat 1 tablespoon of the oil. Add the fennel and shallot and cook, stirring, until softened, about 6 minutes. Add the orange juice and honey and simmer until the liquid is reduced by two thirds, about 5 minutes. Allow to cool, then transfer the mixture to a blender and puree. Blend in the vinegar. With the motor running, slowly pour in the remaining olive oil. Season to taste with salt and white pepper. Chill the dressing.

2. To make the shrimp salad, toss the shrimp with 2 tablespoons of the olive oil, the garlic, and red pepper flakes. Marinate for 10 minutes.

3. In a large sauté pan over high heat, add the shrimp and cook, stirring, until the shrimp are just pink. This should take only about a minute. Add the orange juice and white wine and simmer until the liquid has almost evaporated, about another minute. Toss with the butter and parsley. Season to taste with salt and set aside to cool.

4. Place the shrimp, oranges, grapefruit, avocado, and lettuce in a large bowl. Toss with the dressing. Season to taste with salt if necessary and serve in bowls.

chef's notes Boston and Bibb are types of butterhead lettuce, loose heads of tender, pale green leaves that are wonderful in salads, on sandwiches, and as lettuce leaf "dishes" for dips and spreads.

To segment a citrus fruit, see Chef's Notes, page 186.

and to drink

$ 2003 Kendall Jackson Chardonnay, California

$$ 1998 Sonoma Cutrer Le Pierre Chardonnay, California

WHERE TO BUY

Arizona Desert Sweet Shrimp: Desert Sweet Shrimp, 623-393-0136, www.desertsweetshrimp.com

mary elaine's at the phoenician

6000 EAST CAMELBACK ROAD   SCOTTSDALE, AZ 85251

480-423-2444   WWW.THEPHOENICIAN.COM

You'll see plenty of stars at Mary Elaine's, the gourmet restaurant located in the ultra-luxe Phoenician resort in Scottsdale. The restaurant's floor-to-ceiling windows offer a nighttime view of the city lights and starry skies, but inside Mary Elaine's five-star and five-diamond ratings command plenty of sparkle. Upscale dining at its best, Mary Elaine's offers polished service, an elegantly appointed dining room (Italian Frette linens, Austrian Riedel crystal, French Ercuis silver, and Wedgwood bone china adorn every table) and an extraordinary $3 million wine collection. But it's the cuisine of chef Bradford Thompson, named one of the top ten best new chefs in America by *Food & Wine* magazine, that truly glitters. His take on modern French cuisine, certainly influenced by the five years he spent working under Daniel Boulud in New York, is clearly evident in dishes like sole meunière napped with sauce Bercy (fish sauce with wine and shallots) and paired with aromatic basmati rice and a trio of colorful baby beets, and delicate John Dory, served with crisp, French-style bacon, artichokes, and fresh salsify. Tenderloin Rossini features buffalo instead of beef and is topped with buttery foie gras and reduced truffle sauce. The menu also includes full-course vegetarian meals. Better yet, ask one of the knowledgeable sommeliers to pair the seven-course tasting feast with wine, truly a memorable experience. One of the few restaurants in resort-casual Phoenix where you dress to impress, gentlemen need jackets to get in the door.

Turnips or potatoes can stand in for the Jerusalem artichokes (also called sunchokes) in this tasty soup, but you shouldn't have any problem locating this interesting vegetable.

jerusalem artichoke
soup

⅓ pound lightly smoked or unsmoked slab bacon, cut into 1-inch cubes

4 tablespoons (½ stick) unsalted butter

1 medium onion, diced

1 head fennel, diced

1 stalk celery, diced

1 leek, diced and well rinsed

3 cloves garlic, chopped

3 pounds Jerusalem artichokes, peeled and quartered

4 cups chicken broth

1 cup heavy cream

1 Idaho potato, peeled and diced

2 sprigs fresh thyme, or ½ teaspoon dried

12 whole black peppercorns

2 bay leaves

Coarse salt and freshly ground black pepper, to taste

2 tablespoons minced fresh chives

1. In a large, heavy stockpot, combine the bacon with the butter and place over medium heat. Cook, stirring frequently, until the bacon is browned, about 5 minutes. Add the onion, fennel, celery, leek, and garlic and cook, stirring frequently, until the vegetables are very soft, about 10 minutes.

2. Add the Jerusalem artichokes and turn the heat to medium-high. Cook until the vegetables begin to brown, about 10 minutes.

3. Add the chicken broth, cream, potato, thyme, peppercorns, and bay leaves. Bring to a boil, lower the heat to medium, and cook until the Jerusalem artichokes are fork-tender, about 30 minutes.

4. Discard the bay leaf and the thyme sprigs. In a food processor or blender, puree the soup in small batches. Strain the soup through a fine-mesh sieve. Return the soup to the pot, reheat if necessary, and season to taste with salt and pepper. Serve sprinkled with chives.

chef's notes Jerusalem artichokes aren't artichokes at all, but tubers that look like small, knobby potatoes. A member of the sunflower family, Jerusalem artichokes are native to North America, where they grew along the eastern seaboard from Georgia to Nova Scotia. Explorer Samuel de Champlain thought they tasted like artichokes, and carried that name back with him to France. They are widely available in produce departments, but if you're not familiar with their rather homely appearance, ask for assistance in hunting them down. Available year-round, they are most plentiful (and at their best) from late fall through early spring.

and to drink

$ 2003 Craneford Riesling Eden Valley, Australia

$$ 2001 Domaine Weinbach "St. Catherine" Riesling, Alsace, France

WHERE TO BUY

Jerusalem artichokes (sunchokes): Whole Foods, multiple locations, www.wholefoods.com

roaring fork

4800 NORTH SCOTTSDALE ROAD   SCOTTSDALE, AZ 85251

480-947-0795   WWW.ROARINGFORK.COM

Brawny chef Robert McGrath's brainy interpretation of western cuisine is the main reason to visit Roaring Fork, a comfortable American bistro and saloon named for a river in Aspen, Colorado. Boasting a ranch house–meets–fishing lodge decor, the restaurant's handsome accents include hammered copper, rough-hewn wood, barbed wire–etched glass, and antler chandeliers. A patio fire pit makes outdoor dining cozy and inviting. The sometimes-rowdy saloon hits its stride during happy hour. Mustard-crusted trout, Dr. Pepper barbecue braised beef short ribs, and pork porterhouse steak are a few popular dishes, but don't miss the green chile macaroni and the New Mexican fondue pot, and if you're in the mood for a "Big Ass Burger" (as it's described on the menu), this is the place to come. More than a dozen wines are featured by the glass, along with a respectable selection of single malts, barrel-aged bourbons, and reserve tequilas. McGrath, who earned the 2001 James Beard Foundation award for best chef in the Southwest, opened a second Roaring Fork in Austin, Texas, in 2004.

Chef McGrath's version of a savory cheesecake includes smoked salmon and a topping of tobiko caviar, or flying fish roe. You can omit these crunchy little eggs altogether if you like. Since you make the cheesecake the day before you serve it and refrigerate it overnight, this is a terrific make-ahead party appetizer.

smoked salmon cheesecake
with watercress salad

1 tablespoon vegetable shortening

2 cups Ritz cracker crumbs

6 tablespoons (¾ stick) unsalted butter, melted

1 pound cream cheese

2 tablespoons cornstarch

2 large eggs

½ cup heavy cream

2 tablespoons chopped fresh chives

1 cup coarsely chopped smoked salmon

¼ cup champagne vinegar

2 tablespoons extra-virgin olive oil

1 tablespoon finely chopped shallots

2 tablespoons chopped fresh dill

Coarse salt and freshly ground black pepper, to taste

4 cups watercress sprigs

8 thin slices smoked salmon

2 tablespoons tobiko (red flying fish roe; optional)

and to drink
$ 2003 Snoqualmie, Sauvignon Blanc, Columbia Valley, Washington
$$ 2003 Civello, Pinot Gris, Oregon

SERVES 8

1. Position a rack in the center of the oven and preheat the oven to 350°F. Using a paper towel, grease a 9-inch springform pan with the shortening.

2. To make the crust, combine the cracker crumbs and the melted butter. Scrape the mixture into the prepared pan and use your fingers to press it over the bottom and 1 inch up the sides of the pan. Bake the crust in the center of the oven for 5 minutes. Remove from the oven and cool to room temperature on a rack.

3. To make the filling, in the bowl of an electric mixer on medium speed, beat the cream cheese and cornstarch together until smooth. Beat in the eggs one at a time. Reduce the speed to low and beat in the cream, chives, and chopped smoked salmon.

4. Spoon the filling into the cooled crust. Bake until the tip of a paring knife comes out clean, about 50 minutes. Cool to room temperature and refrigerate overnight, covered.

5. When ready to serve, in a small bowl, whisk together the vinegar, olive oil, shallots, and dill. Season to taste with salt and pepper and set aside. Slice the cheesecake into 8 wedges and place one slice on the side of each of 8 serving plates. Place a small mound of the watercress next to the cheesecake, and spoon the vinaigrette over the salad. Place a slice of smoked salmon on top of each cheesecake wedge, top each with a ¾-teaspoon dollop of the tobiko, and serve.

chefs notes Japanese tobiko is popular for its crunchy texture and brilliant, glittering orangey-red color. It is commonly used in sushi and maki rolls.

WHERE TO BUY
Tobiko (flying fish roe): Earthy Delights, 800-367-4709, www.earthy.com

t. cook's at the royal palms

5200 EAST CAMELBACK ROAD   PHOENIX, AZ 85018

866-579-3636   WWW.ROYALPALMSHOTEL.COM

Nestled within a Moorish den of rich earthen colors, high-vaulted ceilings, and panoramic views, T. Cook's is undoubtedly one of the finest restaurants in the Valley of the Sun. Executive chef Gregory Casale (formerly of Gregory's World Bistro) creates *à la minute* Mediterranean cuisine with select seasonal dishes from Barcelona, Spain, and the Tuscan region of Italy. For lunch, there's seafood lasagna with grilled asparagus, spinach, and tomato coulis. The signature mussels, sautéed in Chardonnay-thyme broth, are just right, as is the antipasto platter with roasted duck breast and the grilled loin of lamb with artichokes, red wine leeks, and potato goat cheese custard. Don't miss the architectural desserts, almost too pretty to eat. The Cigar Room by the bar, all red leather and antiques, is the perfect setting for savoring a brandy and a Cohiba Churchill. More than twenty-five wines plus sherries and ports are available by the glass, with wine flights offered in the restaurant and the bar.

Chef Casale pairs monkfish with prosciutto in this easy-to-make recipe, but mahi mahi, mako, or red snapper will substitute perfectly. Canned cannellini, navy, or other white beans work just fine for this recipe. Just be sure to drain the beans and rinse well.

prosciutto-wrapped monkfish
with sautéed escarole, cannellini beans, and roasted fingerling potatoes

SERVES 4

12 fingerling potatoes, peeled

8 slices prosciutto

Four 6-ounce pieces monkfish fillet

Coarse salt and freshly ground black pepper, to taste

4 tablespoons extra-virgin olive oil

4 cloves garlic, sliced

Leaves from 1 large head of escarole, well rinsed, tough stems discarded

1 cup cooked, drained cannellini beans, or other white beans such as navy

4 sprigs fresh parsley

1. Preheat the oven to 400°F.

2. On a baking sheet, roast the potatoes until just tender, about 20 minutes. When cool enough to handle, slice into thin disks. Set aside.

3. Lay out 2 slices of the prosciutto next to each other on a work surface. Season the fish with salt and pepper, place the fish at the bottom edge of the prosciutto, and roll the fish up in the prosciutto, cutting away any excess prosciutto. Repeat with the remaining fillets.

4. In a large, ovenproof sauté pan, heat 2 tablespoons of the oil over high heat. Add the fish and bake, turning, until the prosciutto is crisp, about 7 minutes. Transfer the pan to the oven and cook until the fish is just opaque in the center, about 5 minutes.

5. Meanwhile, in another large sauté pan, heat the remaining 2 tablespoons oil over medium-high heat. Add the garlic and cook, stirring, just until tender, about 3 minutes. Add the escarole, beans, and sliced potatoes to the pan. Cook until the escarole is wilted and tender, about 3 minutes. Season with salt and pepper.

6. Slice each fish fillet in half. Divide the escarole mixture among 4 plates. Stack the 2 pieces of fish next to each other on top of the escarole on each plate. Garnish with a sprig of fresh parsley and serve.

and to drink

$ Amity Gamay Noir, Oregon

$$ Brick House Vineyards Gamay Noir, Oregon

chef's notes Monkfish is a very forgiving fish to cook—it just about always tastes good, no matter what you do to it.

WHERE TO BUY

Monkfish:

Fresh Seafood, 800-392-3474, www.freshseafood.com

Whole Foods, multiple locations, www.wholefoods.com

vincent guerithault on camelback

3930 EAST CAMELBACK ROAD   PHOENIX, AZ 85018

602-224-0225   WWW.VINCENTSONCAMELBACK.COM

French cuisine meets Southwestern style at chef Vincent Guerithault's eponymous restaurant in the shadow of Camelback Mountain. Guerithault, who worked at Maxim's and Fauchon in Paris before leaving for Chicago's Le Français and then Phoenix, re-creates the charm of his homeland in the restaurant's decor, which conjures up visions of the romantic south of France. The restaurant's menu is an eclectic mix, including duck tamale with Anaheim chile and raisins, lavender beignets, wild mushroom tarts, and duck confit with green olive sauce. A native of France, Guerithault has received numerous awards, including the first Citation of Excellence from the International Food and Wine Society, the James Beard Foundation award for Best Chef in the Southwest in 2002, and the French Chevalier de L'Ordre du Merite Agricole. On Saturdays from mid-October through April, Guerithault runs the Camelback Market in his parking lot, featuring the freshest produce, cooked-to-order crepes and pastas, breads, cheeses, pizzas, and more.

Any mild white fish can stand in for the John Dory.

baked john dory
with cilantro cream

SERVES 4

Four 6-ounce John Dory, halibut, or other firm white-fleshed fish fillets

Coarse salt and freshly ground black pepper, to taste

½ cup dry white wine

½ cup chopped shallots

1 cup heavy cream

1 cup chopped fresh cilantro, plus extra leaves for garnish

½ cup diced tomato

1. Preheat the oven to 475°F.

2. Season the fish fillets with salt and pepper and place in a deep baking dish large enough to hold them in a single layer. Combine the white wine, shallots, cream, and chopped cilantro and pour the mixture over the fish. Bake, uncovered, until opaque in the center, about 7 minutes. Remove the dish from the oven and transfer the fish to serving plates.

3. Pour the liquid from the baking dish into a blender and blend until creamy. Strain the liquid through a fine-mesh sieve into a bowl. Discard the solids. Season the sauce with salt and pepper. Pour the sauce over the fish and garnish with diced tomato and cilantro leaves.

and to drink

$ 2002 Eagle Vale Margaret River Semillon/Sauvignon Blanc, Washington

$$ 2001 Robert Mondavi, Sauvignon Blanc, "Unfiltered" Stag's Leap, California

chef's notes   Native to Southern Australia, John Dory, formerly known as St. Peter's fish, is a mild white fish with a delicate flavor.

Cilantro, once considered an exotic herb, is now as common as parsley in the supermarket produce section. An important ingredient in the global larder, cilantro is used by Hispanic cooks in salsas, by Asian chefs in stir-fries, and by Indian cooks in curries. Its distinctive, flowery flavor can dominate a recipe if not used judiciously. When adding cilantro to a hot dish, preserve its fresh flavor by adding it at the last minute.

WHERE TO BUY

John Dory: AJ's Fine Foods, multiple locations, 602-522-0956, www.ajsfinefoods.com

san francisco

savor the city by the bay

It seems hard to believe, but there was a time, not all that long ago, that organic, free-range, line-caught, and grass-fed meant nothing to the average diner. These phrases, now as common as shaved truffles on every serious chef's menu, simply weren't in our gastronomic lexicon. We were a nation brought up on canned peas and meatloaf. Our only flavor of lettuce was iceberg. It took a food revolution on both sides of the San Francisco Bay Bridge to change forever how we think about food and how we eat.

In 1971 California cuisine was introduced in Berkeley by chef Alice Waters at the now-legendary Chez Panisse restaurant. America's high priestess of sustainable agriculture just said no to the overwrought, rich "gourmet" food that lived in four-star kitchens across the country at the time. Waters, along with a cavalcade of Bay Area chefs, including Jeremiah Towers and later Thomas Keller, Gary Danko, and Ron Siegel, banished pretentious eats in favor of elegant unadorned, natural fare. As San Francisco food critic Patricia Unterman noted, "Julia [Child] set the stage for the culinary boom in America by teaching people how to cook, and then Alice Waters took everyone to the next step by teaching about ingredients."

Fast forward 3½ decades later, and San Francisco chefs have learned their lesson well. Fresh, seasonal, and locally sourced ingredients are at the beating heart of the city's formidable restaurant community. Blessed by nearly year-round farm-fresh produce and the country's richest wine region at its back door, the City by the Bay is home to a restaurant community that creates dining trends other chefs can only follow.

In this chapter, we visit icons like Fleur de Lys and trendsetters like Farallon, just two of the ten restaurants that continue to give San Francisco a respected spot at the world's table.

farallon restaurant

450 POST STREET   SAN FRANCISCO, CA 94102

415-956-6969   WWW.FARALLONRESTAURANT.COM

Step into the underwater dream world of Farallon and you've entered one of San Francisco's finest seafood restaurants. With its famous blown-glass jellyfish chandeliers, curvaceous lines, and whimsical aquatic motif, Farallon is the creation of famed restaurant designer and co-owner Pat Kuleto. But it's his partner, chef Mark Franz, who breathes life into the menu of coastal cuisine. Franz's menu changes daily, allowing him to highlight the freshest fish and shellfish available, as well as seasonal meat and game dishes. Hamachi tartare arrives in a tangle of pea sprouts and quail eggs. For the main course, options might include roasted wild Maryland striped bass with English pea ravioli, braised endive and mint pesto, seared Louisiana Gulf prawns, and Atlantic skate. A Bay Area native, Franz spent more than a decade as executive chef at Jeremiah Tower's Stars and is credited with making major contributions to other Tower restaurants. Nominated by the James Beard Foundation as one of the best restaurants in the nation, Farallon was also chosen as one of the best newcomers in the country by national magazines such as *Esquire, Bon Appétit,* and *Food & Wine*. Recognized for its cuisine, decor, and service, Farallon was the highest-rated newcomer in the 1999 *Zagat Survey*.

This recipe for crab gratin is adapted from *The Farallon Cookbook* (Chronicle Books, 2001).

crab gratin
with corn, potatoes, and tarragon

SERVES 4

3 red potatoes, peeled and cut into ¼-inch dice

2½ tablespoons plus 1 teaspoon unsalted butter

½ cup corn, fresh or frozen

½ pound Dungeness crabmeat (or one 6-ounce can pasteurized crabmeat, picked through to remove any bits of cartilage or shell)

½ cup crème fraîche or sour cream

1 tablespoon grated fresh lemon zest

1 teaspoon chopped fresh tarragon

1 teaspoon olive oil

Coarse salt and freshly ground black pepper, to taste

½ cup dried bread crumbs

½ teaspoon chopped fresh thyme, or ¼ teaspoon dried thyme

1. Bring a medium saucepan of salted water to a boil. Add the potatoes and cook until they are barely tender, about 5 minutes. Drain.

2. In a small sauté pan, melt 1½ tablespoons of the butter over low heat. Add the corn and cook until soft, about 3 minutes. Scrape the corn into a medium bowl and add the potatoes, crabmeat, crème fraîche, lemon zest, tarragon, and oil and stir thoroughly to combine. Season with salt and pepper. Refrigerate, covered, for up to 1 day.

3. Preheat the oven to 400°F and place a baking rack in the top third of the oven.

4. In a small sauté pan, melt 1 tablespoon of the remaining butter over medium heat. Add the bread crumbs and thyme and cook, stirring, until the crumbs are golden and crunchy, 2 to 3 minutes. Season with salt and pepper to taste.

5. Butter four 6-ounce individual baking dishes or ramekins with the remaining teaspoon butter. Divide the crab mixture among the baking dishes and top with the bread crumbs. Put the dishes on a baking sheet and bake until golden and bubbling, about 10 minutes. Transfer the hot gratins to serving plates lined with folded napkins and serve.

and to drink

$ 2002 Michel Thomas Sancerre, France

$$ 2003 Lucien Crochet Sancerre Le Chene, France

chef's notes Dungeness crab is a sweet-tasting, oversized crab from the Pacific coast. Frozen or canned crab can be used with good results, or you can even use cooked, chopped shrimp.

What makes this dish really terrific is that it can be assembled a day ahead, refrigerated, and baked right before serving, making it ideal for an elegant dinner party appetizer.

WHERE TO BUY

Dungeness crab: Fresh-Fish-Fast.com, 888-753-2154, www.fresh-fish-fast.com

fleur de lys restaurant

777 SUTTER STREET   SAN FRANCISCO, CA 94109

415-673-7779   WWW.FLEURDELYSSF.COM

Fleur de Lys has been a San Francisco icon of haute French cuisine for close to five decades, proudly surviving the city's changing restaurant landscape and even a devastating fire. But in the hands of chef Hubert Keller, in the kitchen since 1986, Fleur de Lys has really come into its golden age. Dripping in glamour and romance, the tented main dining room is awash in deep reds and golds, with a dramatic, ceiling-high floral centerpiece the focal point in the center of the room. But it's Keller's innovative French-California cuisine, available in three- or five-course menus, that really steals the show. His enlightened approach includes dishes like Hudson Valley foie gras and smoked duck breast in Gewürztraminer gelée; tender day boat scallops paired with melted leeks, lobster, and caviar; and lamb loin with spiced honey, caramelized cumin-seed sauce, and mint oil. The selection of some 700 French and California wines is also impressive. Chef Keller opened a handsome new Fleur de Lys in the Mandalay Bay in Las Vegas a few years ago.

Chef Keller makes this dish with roasted lobster and artichoke puree, but the salmon and potato pairing works equally well, and is both less expensive and quicker to prepare.

roasted salmon
with potato puree and citrus salad

SERVES 4

4 russet potatoes, peeled and quartered

¼ cup heavy cream, plus more as needed

Coarse salt and freshly ground black pepper, to taste

1 orange, peeled, cut into sections, and diced

1 lime, peeled, cut into sections, and diced

1 scallion (white part only), minced

½ teaspoon olive oil

1 cup fresh orange juice

4 tablespoons (½ stick) unsalted butter, cut into chunks

1 tablespoon vegetable oil

Four 6-ounce pieces salmon fillet

4 sprigs chervil

1. Bring a large pot of salted water to a boil. Add the potatoes and cook until tender when pierced with a fork, about 10 minutes. Drain.

2. In a medium saucepan, bring the cream to a boil over medium heat. Add the potatoes and cook, stirring, for 3 minutes. Transfer the mixture to a blender and puree until very smooth, adding more cream if necessary. Season to taste with salt and pepper and return to the saucepan.

3. Preheat the oven to 400ºF.

4. In a small bowl, combine the orange, lime, scallion, olive oil, and salt and pepper to taste and toss gently.

5. In a small saucepan set over medium heat, bring the orange juice to a boil. Adjust the heat and simmer until the juice is reduced by half, about 15 minutes. Lower the heat to low and whisk in the butter a chunk at a time. Season with salt and pepper and keep warm.

6. Heat the vegetable oil in a large, ovenproof skillet over high heat. Sprinkle the salmon with salt and pepper and cook, turning once, until just browned, about 2 minutes per side. Transfer the skillet to the oven and bake until the salmon is just opaque in the center, about 6 minutes. Keep warm.

7. To serve, reheat the potato puree and spoon a mound of puree in the center of each of 4 warmed serving plates. Top with a piece of salmon. Spoon the citrus sauce all around the potatoes, top with some of the citrus salad, and garnish with the chervil.

WHERE TO BUY

Wild salmon: Monterey Fish Market, 510-525-5600, www.webseafood.com

Roasted Salmon (*continued*)

and to drink
$ 2003 Bourgogne
Chardonnay, "Signature,"
Maison Champy, France
$$ 2000 Ramey Chardonnay
Russian River, California

chef's notes To make the recipe's original artichoke puree, you'll need 4 artichokes and a lemon half. Bring a large saucepan of water to a boil. To prepare the artichokes, cut off the stems and the thorny tips of the leaves. Trim the bottom so that none of the hard green skin remains. As you work, rub the cut portions of the artichokes with the lemon to prevent discoloration. Place the trimmed artichokes in the boiling water and cook until tender when pierced with a knife, 20 to 30 minutes. Drain and cool the artichokes. When the artichokes have cooled, remove and discard the tough outer leaves, then scoop out the chokes with a teaspoon and slice the hearts. Combine the sliced hearts with the cream and continue with the recipe above.

la folie

2316 POLK STREET   SAN FRANCISCO, CA 94109

415-776-5577   WWW.LAFOLIE.COM

For invigorating French cuisine, look no farther than this Russian Hill restaurant, where chef Roland Passot dreams up memorably updated French classics. The restaurant's sleek setting, with its earth-tone walls, deep burgundy banquettes, and crisp white linens, sets the perfect tone for chef Passot's inventive cuisine. Try the sinfully rich foie gras soup with truffled day boat scallop ravioli or the Dungeness crab napoleon surrounded by a pool of apple gelée. Passot clearly has a talent for combining eclectic flavors and textures, as one bite of the warm pig feet, sweetbread, and lobster terrine perched atop a bacony lentil salad will attest. Choose from fantastic three-, four-, and five-course menus (five is best), but save room for the elaborate, oh-so-decadent desserts.

salmon with pureed onions
and merlot sauce

SERVES 4

Merlot Sauce

1½ tablespoons unsalted butter

1½ pounds (about 16) shallots, chopped

2 tablespoons cracked black pepper

1 bay leaf

½ bunch fresh thyme, or 2 teaspoons dried

8 cups merlot

8 cups beef broth

Coarse salt, to taste

Onions

1 tablespoon unsalted butter

2 onions, thinly sliced

1 teaspoon coarse salt

½ teaspoon freshly ground black pepper

Salmon

2 tablespoons olive oil

Four 5-ounce pieces salmon fillet

Coarse salt and freshly ground black pepper, to taste

1. To make the merlot sauce, in a large saucepan, melt the butter over medium heat. Add the shallots, cracked pepper, bay leaf, and thyme and cook, stirring frequently, until the shallots begin to soften, about 5 minutes.

2. Pour in the merlot, raise the heat to high, and bring to a boil. Reduce the heat and simmer until the liquid has been reduced to about 2 cups, 20 to 25 minutes. Add the broth and continue to simmer until the sauce thickens and the liquid is again reduced to 2 cups, 25 to 30 minutes.

3. Strain the sauce through a fine-mesh strainer and return it to the pan. Season to taste with salt. Set aside.

4. To make the onions, in a medium saucepan over low heat, melt the butter. Add the onions, salt, and pepper and cook, stirring occasionally, until the onions are very soft but not brown, about 15 minutes.

5. Transfer the onions to a food processor or blender and process until smooth. Return to the pot and set aside.

6. To make the salmon, heat the oil in a medium sauté pan over high heat. Season the fish with salt and pepper and cook, turning once, until lightly browned and cooked to the desired doneness, about 3 minutes per side for medium.

7. To serve, reheat the onion puree and merlot sauce if necessary. Divide the puree among 4 plates and top each with a piece of salmon. Spoon about ¼ cup of sauce around the plate and over the fish.

WHERE TO BUY

Wild salmon: Ferry Plaza Seafood, 415-274-2561, www.ferryplazaseafood.com

and to drink
$ 2005 Concha Y Toro Trio
Merlot, Chile
$$ 2004 Merryvale Reserve
Merlot, Washington

chef's notes When it comes to salmon, go wild. Whenever possible, choose wild salmon over farm-raised for your table. Wild salmon tastes better and is healthier for you and for the environment. Farmed salmon, just like commercially raised chickens, are kept in crowded pens where they are prone to disease. To control this, fish farms commonly use antibiotics and other chemicals. Farmed salmon can also escape their net cages and can endanger the health of the wild fish population. Plus, the natural diet of wild salmon makes them tastier than penned salmon.

jardinière

300 GROVE STREET   SAN FRANCISCO, CA 94102

415-861-5555   WWW.JARDINIERE.COM

Housed in a landmark Civic Center area building, Jardinière features chef and co-owner Traci Des Jardins's award-winning French-California cuisine in the elegant two-story interior designed by her partner, the restaurateur and designer Pat Kuleto. With its sweeping staircase, dramatic velvet aubergine drapes, and inverted champagne glass dome over the bar, Jardiniere manages to be both festive and intimate. The restaurant's menu, realized by chef de cuisine Robbie Lewis, reflects a strong commitment to sustainability, featuring ingredients and products purchased from farmers, artisanal cheesemakers, fishermen, and ranchers, including the exclusive use of grass-fed beef, naturally fed and raised pork and chicken, and organic vegetables. Try the warm bread salad with baby artichokes and marinated Crescenza cheese; duck confit salad with candied kumquats, medjool dates, and toasted pistachio; and Alaskan halibut with caramelized fennel, spring onions, and saffron-braised fingerling potatoes. Between its twenty-plus wines and champagnes by the glass, the late-night menu and the live jazz Sundays through Tuesdays, Jardiniere's bar is one happening spot.

This summer-fresh salad is an ideal balance of seasonal flavors. Ripe peaches can be substituted for the nectarines.

nectarine, prosciutto, and endive salad with honey-thyme vinaigrette

SERVES 6

7 ripe nectarines

2 cups cold water

½ cup sugar

⅓ cup extra-virgin olive oil

2 tablespoons lavender honey or regular honey

1 sprig thyme

3 tablespoons fresh Meyer lemon juice or regular lemon juice

1 tablespoon Dijon mustard

Coarse salt and freshly ground black pepper, to taste

6 heads Belgian endive, stem ends trimmed, heads separated into leaves

1 bunch arugula, stems discarded, leaves well rinsed

8 fresh mint leaves, thinly sliced

1 bunch fresh chives, minced

1 shallot, minced

½ pound sliced prosciutto

¼ cup chopped Marcona or toasted almonds

1. Slice the nectarines in half and remove the pits. Place the pits and 1 chopped nectarine into a small saucepan with the water and sugar. Bring to a boil over high heat, lower the heat, and simmer until the liquid is reduced by three quarters and you have a thick syrup, about 15 minutes. Strain the mixture, discard the solids, and set the syrup aside to cool.

2. Place the olive oil, honey, and thyme in a small saucepan over medium heat and bring to a simmer. Lower the heat and simmer for 5 minutes. Turn off the heat, cover the pan, and let the mixture steep for 15 minutes. Strain, discard the solids, and return the sauce to the pan.

3. In a large bowl, whisk together the nectarine syrup and the lemon juice and mustard. Whisk in the olive oil-and–honey mixture. Season to taste with salt and pepper.

4. Slice the remaining nectarines and add to the bowl with the Belgian endive leaves, arugula, half the mint, the chives, and the shallot. Toss with the vinaigrette and season with salt and pepper. Arrange the salad on 6 individual plates, drape slices of prosciutto over the salad, and garnish with the remaining mint and the chopped almonds.

chef's notes Meyer lemons are sweeter and less tart than ordinary lemons, although they can be hard to find. Check gourmet and specialty produce stores, or simply substitute traditional lemons.

Marcona almonds are large, naturally sweet almonds that are native to Spain.

WHERE TO BUY

Marcona almonds: La Tienda, 888-472-1022, www.tienda.com

Meyer lemons and organic produce: Pacific Organic Produce, 415-673-5555, www.pacorg.com

and to drink

$ 2002 Bassermann-Jordan Riesling Kabinett Deidesheimer Paradiesgarten, Pfalz, Germany

$$ 2002 Boxler Riesling Grand Cru Sommerberg, Alsace, France

kokkari estiatorio

200 JACKSON STREET   SAN FRANCISCO, CA 94111

415-981-0983   WWW.KOKKARI.COM

Named after a small fishing village on the island of Samos in the Aegean Sea, Kokkari elevates Greek cuisine to mythic heights. Settle in, and it's easy to imagine you're dining at the country estate of a wealthy Greek magnate. A massive roaring fireplace dominates one room, accented by comfortable armchairs, roughly hewn beams, and hand-wrought copper cooking vessels. Another large dining room is built around an open kitchen. That's where chef Erik Cosselmon's wide-ranging Mediterranean repertoire inspires the restaurant's Greek menu. Cosselmon, a CIA graduate who worked at Le Bernardin and Daniel before he headed west for Cetrella Bistro and Café in Half Moon Bay, infuses Kokkari's menu with a strong, ingredient-driven style. House specialties include starters like the platter of traditional Greek dips, eggplant and pepper puree, smoky roasted eggplant, and creamy taramosalata spiked with cured pink carp roe served with housemade pita hot off the grill. Fire-grilled anything is good here, including the king salmon with favas, potatoes, and porcini and the baby lamb chops with a lemon-oregano vinaigrette.

This recipe for roasted shrimp, fired on Kokkari's grill, can be cooked in the oven or on your grill at home. Use the best feta you can find. Chef Cosselmon presents the shrimp with their heads on—something the home cook doesn't need to worry about.

roasted shrimp
with dill and feta

SERVES 6

12 large shrimp

1 shallot, diced

1 clove garlic, minced

1 tablespoon dried oregano

2 tablespoons
extra-virgin olive oil

Coarse salt and freshly
ground black pepper,
to taste

4 ounces feta cheese,
crumbled

4 sprigs fresh dill, chopped

1. Peel the shrimp, but do not remove the shell from the tail sections. Working with one shrimp at a time, insert the tip of a knife or kitchen shears about three quarters of the way into the shrimp at the head end. Cut almost all the way through the flesh down the center of the shrimp's back to the tail. Use your hands to open the flesh of the shrimp until it lies flat. With your fingers or the tip of the knife, remove the dark vein running down the shrimp. Repeat with the remaining shrimp, then rinse them all under cold running water and pat dry.

2. Place the shrimp on a plate and sprinkle with the shallot, garlic, and oregano. Drizzle with 1 tablespoon of the olive oil. Refrigerate at least 30 minutes and up 2 hours.

3. Season the shrimp well with salt and pepper, place on a baking sheet, and cook under the broiler until the flesh becomes opaque, about 4 minutes (you can also grill the shrimp). Place on a warm serving platter and sprinkle with the feta, dill, and remaining tablespoon olive oil.

chef's notes If using frozen shrimp, it's easiest to butterfly them when the shrimp are still a little frosty.

and to drink
$ 2002 Dr. Unger, Grüner Veltliner, Classic, Kremstal, Austria
$$ 2003 Pascal Cotat, Sancerre, Les Monts Damnés, France

WHERE TO BUY
Imported feta: Cheese Plus, 415-921-2001, www.cheeseplus.com
Shrimp: Hawaiian King Shrimp, Honolulu Fish Co., 888-475-MAHI, www.honolulufish.com

masa's

648 BUSH STREET   SAN FRANCISCO, CA 94108

415-989-7154   WWW.MASASRESTAURANT.COM

Masa's is an urbane temple of classically New French and Californian cuisine influenced by northern California's abundance of ingredients, first-class purveyors, and artisans. And, according to uber-chef Thomas Keller, who worked with Masa's chef Gregory Short for seven years at French Laundry, Short is the "perfect steward to further Masa's reputation as one of the world's great restaurants." Masa's offers four-, six-, and nine-course tasting menus, along with a six-course vegetarian tasting menu. Each has much to recommend, like the chilled tomato soup with osetra caviar and lobster or the carnaroli risotto with squash blossoms and fava beans. The chilled foie gras is accompanied by peach and lavender honey jam, Gewürztraminer gelée, and perfectly toasted brioche. Desserts include warm pineapple beignets and chocolate and almond meringues with coconut milk sherbet. An exceptional wine list and gracious service earn high marks.

Chef Short uses porcini (also called cèpe) mushrooms in this deeply flavorful soup, but you can substitute portobello or oyster mushrooms without sacrificing much flavor.

cream of porcini
mushroom soup

SERVES 4

1 tablespoon unsalted butter

¼ cup sliced shallots

3 cups sliced fresh porcini,
portobello, oyster,
or white mushrooms

⅛ teaspoon curry powder

2 cups chicken broth

3 cups vegetable broth

1 cup heavy cream

Leaves from 1 sprig fresh
thyme, or ¼ teaspoon dried

Coarse salt and freshly
ground black pepper,
to taste

1 tablespoon
extra-virgin olive oil

1. In a large saucepan, melt the butter over medium heat. Add the shallots and cook, stirring, just until softened, about 2 minutes. Add the mushrooms and continue to cook, stirring frequently, until the mushrooms soften, 5 to 6 minutes. Add the curry powder and cook 1 more minute.

2. Add the chicken and vegetable broths, cream, and thyme to the mushroom mixture. Bring just to a boil, lower the heat, and simmer 30 minutes.

3. Strain the soup through a fine-mesh sieve, reserve the liquid, and place the solids in a blender, adding just enough of the liquid to make a puree. Return the puree to the pot and stir in as much liquid as needed until you have a creamy soup (you may want to add all the liquid).

4. Reheat the soup and season to taste with salt and pepper. Ladle into bowls and drizzle with olive oil before serving.

and to drink

$ 2003 Silverado Vineyards Chardonnay, Napa Valley, California

$$ 2002 White Burgundy Colin Deleger, Chassagne-Montrachet, France

chef's notes   Porcini, also known as cèpes and boletes, are distinguished by their stout stems and spongy surface (rather than gills) underneath their brown caps, which range in size from 1 to 10 inches in diameter. Grown in Washington and Oregon, or imported from France or Italy during the summer and fall, they are expensive but are generally considered to be the finest tasting of the wild mushrooms.

WHERE TO BUY

Porcini or cèpe mushrooms: Earthy Delight, 800-637-4709, www.earthy.com

town hall

342 HOWARD STREET   SAN FRANCISCO, CA 94105

415-908-3900   WWW.TOWNHALLSF.COM

With brothers Mitchell and Steven Rosenthal (also executive chefs at Wolfgang Puck's Postrio) helming the kitchen, Town Hall opened in late 2003 with quite a pedigree. Add in partner and noted maitre'd-about-town Doug Washington minding the front of the house, and it only gets better. Then there's the setting: a stand-alone warehouse in the South of Market neighborhood built in 1907 after the city's earthquake. The transformed bright and airy rustic space sets the perfect mood for the Rosenthals' regional American and New Orleans–inspired comfort food. Every flavor note rings true with entrées like the slow-roasted duck with toasted wild rice, pecans, and gingersnap gravy, and the peanut and Tasso ham–crusted pork chop with buttermilk smashed potatoes. Don't skip the warm biscuits with Smithfield ham and pepper jam—they're worth every calorie. For a very happy ending, finish with the roasted pear and sour cherry crisp, topped with a melting scoop of vanilla ice cream.

This crowd-pleasing main dish can be made a few days ahead of time and reheated in the oven right before the party starts.

smoked andouille sausage
jambalaya

SERVES 6

2 tablespoons olive oil

2 cups diced onions

2 cups ½-inch dice andouille sausage or kielbasa

1 cup diced celery

2 cups diced, seeded poblano peppers

1 tablespoon minced garlic

1 jalapeño, seeded and finely diced, or to taste

1 tablespoon tomato paste

1 cup canned, diced tomatoes, drained

1 bay leaf

1 teaspoon salt

½ teaspoon freshly ground black pepper

⅓ cup Paul Prudhomme's Seafood Magic® seasoning blend

3 cups chicken broth

2 cups basmati rice, rinsed

1. Preheat the oven to 350ºF.

2. In a large, heavy-bottomed pot, heat the oil over medium heat. Add the onions, reduce the heat to low, cover the pot with a lid or with aluminum foil, and cook, stirring occasionally, until the onions are golden brown, about 25 minutes.

3. Add the sausage and cook, uncovered, for 2 to 3 minutes on low. Then add the celery, poblano peppers, garlic, and jalapeño. Raise the heat to medium and cook, stirring constantly, until the vegetables are tender, about 5 minutes. Stir in the tomato paste, diced tomatoes, bay leaf, salt, and pepper and bring to a boil. Stir in the Seafood Magic and cook for 3 minutes more. Add the chicken broth and bring back to a boil.

4. Cover the pot with a lid or foil and place in the oven. Bake until heated through, 25 to 30 minutes.

5. Meanwhile, cook the rice by bringing 3 cups lightly salted water to a boil in a medium saucepan with a tightly fitting lid. Add the rice, stir once, cover, and simmer over low heat until the rice has absorbed all the water and is tender, about 18 minutes. Set aside, covered.

6. Remove and discard the bay leaf from the jambalaya. Stir in the rice and serve immediately.

WHERE TO BUY

Andouille: Jacob's World Famous Andouille & Sausage, 877-215-7589, www.cajunsausage.com

Chef Paul Prudhomme's Seafood Magic seasoning blend: Chef Paul Prudhomme, 800-457-2857, http://chefpaul.com

Smoked Andouille Sausage Jambalaya (*continued*)

and to drink

$ 2003 Argyle Willamette
Valley Pinot Noir, Washington
$$ 2003 Brewer Clifton
"Ashley's" Pinot Noir, California

chef's notes Andouille is a spicy, smoked Cajun sausage that's used in such New Orleans staples as gumbo and jambalaya. It's commonly found, both in pork and turkey varieties, in supermarket meat departments with other smoked products.

michael mina

335 POWELL STREET   SAN FRANCISCO, CA 94102

415-397-9222   WWW.MICHAELMINA.NET

Tucked into the Westin St. Francis Hotel on Union Square, the elegant restaurant Michael Mina offers an innovative menu with a distinct blend of California and Mediterranean ingredients. Mina, whose growing restaurant empire includes restaurants in Las Vegas, Atlantic City, Dana Point, San Jose, and soon, Mexico City, manages still to dazzle San Franciscans with his bold moves and smart use of ingredients. Diners can build their own three-course menu, with each course offering three preparations of a theme element. A veteran of Charlie Palmer's kitchen at the upscale Aureole in New York City, Mina creates signature dishes such as a crispy-skin quail with white asparagus and bacon-braised morel, lobster pot pie, and whole fried chicken for two. Tableside service is a specialty here, with everything from black mussel soufflé and caviar service to a classic root beer float prepared *à la minute.* A selection of 2,200 wines from all over the world is included in the vibrant cellar.

Beurre blanc, which means "white butter" in French, is a classic sauce that includes wine, vinegar, shallots, and cold butter. At Michael Mina, this delicious appetizer is garnished with lobster, warmed in the sauce. Feel free to dress up the dish at home if you're so inclined. Sea scallops are a fine substitute for the more expensive diver scallops (see Chef's Notes, page 269).

seared scallops
with tomato beurre blanc

SERVES 4

3 shallots, sliced

3 tablespoons tomato paste

1 cup red wine

2 tablespoons
red-wine vinegar

3 tablespoons heavy cream

½ pound (2 sticks) cold
unsalted butter,
cut into small chunks

Coarse salt and freshly
ground black pepper,
to taste

2 tablespoons olive oil

4 sea scallops

1 tablespoon
chopped chives

2 cherry tomatoes, halved

1. Place the shallots and tomato paste in a small saucepan and cook over medium heat, stirring constantly, until the tomato paste is lightly browned, about 2 minutes. Whisk in the wine and vinegar, bring to a boil, reduce the heat, and simmer until the liquid is reduced by two thirds, about 10 minutes.

2. Stir in the cream and simmer for 1 minute. Reduce the heat to low and slowly whisk in the cold butter, a chunk at a time. Strain through a fine-mesh sieve. Season with salt and pepper and keep warm.

3. Heat a small sauté pan over medium-high heat. Add the oil and heat until it just begins to smoke. Season the scallops well with salt and pepper and place in the pan. Reduce the heat to medium and cook until golden brown, about 1 minute. Turn and cook until the other side is golden brown, about 1 more minute. Remove from the pan and place on paper towels to drain.

4. Spoon 2 to 3 tablespoons of the tomato sauce onto each of 4 plates and top with a seared scallop. Garnish with the chives and half a cherry tomato.

WHERE TO BUY

Diver scallops: Ferry Plaza Seafood, 415-274-2561,
www.ferryplazaseafood.com

chef's notes Unlike bivalves such as oysters and mussels, scallops don't attach themselves to a permanent anchorage, but move through the water by opening and closing their shells. As a result, the muscle that controls the '"hinge"' of the shell is much larger than that of oysters or clams. And that's the delicious morsel we eat.

Chefs favor using diver scallops, which are exactly what the name implies—scallops that are collected from the ocean by divers hand-picking each one. Most scallops on the market are harvested by boats that drag heavy chain sweeps across the ocean floor, collecting plenty of grit and debris along the way. Diver scallops are a more ecologically friendly way of harvesting scallops. They're also more expensive.

the dining room at the ritz-carlton

600 STOCKTON STREET   SAN FRANCISCO, CA 94108

415-773-6168   WWW.RITZCARLTON.COM

Long a pinnacle of the city's gastronomic scene, the Dining Room at the Ritz is now home to chef Ron Siegel, a storied professional best known for being the first American to win the Japanese television show *Iron Chef* when he defeated chef Hiroyuki Sakai in the "lobster challenge." Siegel, last of Masa's, boasts quite a résumé: he's worked at Aqua, the French Laundry, and Charles Nob Hill and trained for a year under Daniel Boulud in New York. Against the Dining Room's opulent formal setting, Siegel prepares three- and nine-course menus that include the likes of snapper poached in lobster broth, port-glazed Tasmanian sea trout with porcini mushrooms, white corn pudding, roasted figs, and hot foie gras served with spicy pickled Bing cherries.

Chef Siegel pairs chicken breasts with lemon verbena leaves and morels when he makes this dish at the Ritz. We substituted lemon zest for the hard-to-find verbena leaves and wild mushrooms for the pricey morels. If you want to splurge, however, morels are absolutely divine.

crispy chicken with lemon peaches, asparagus, and mushrooms

SERVES 4

8 stalks asparagus

2 peaches, cut into 1-inch cubes

1 tablespoon grated fresh lemon zest

4 tablespoons (½ stick) unsalted butter

3 ounces morels or other wild mushrooms, sliced

Coarse salt and freshly ground black pepper, to taste

1 cup chicken broth

4 boneless, skin-on chicken breast halves

2 tablespoons olive oil

1. Preheat the oven to 300ºF.

2. Bring a medium pot of salted water to a boil. Add the asparagus and cook until just tender, about 3 minutes. Cool the asparagus in a bowl of ice water, drain, and pat dry. Set aside.

3. Place the peaches and zest on a lightly oiled sheet pan and bake until tender, 15 to 20 minutes. Set aside.

4. In a medium sauté pan over medium heat, melt 1 tablespoon of the butter. Add the mushrooms and cook, stirring, until the mushrooms are tender, about 5 minutes. Season with salt and pepper to taste.

5. In a small saucepan, bring the chicken broth to a boil over high heat. Lower the heat and simmer until reduced to ½ cup, about 10 minutes. Cut 2 tablespoons of the remaining butter into 4 chunks. Remove the reduced broth from the heat and whisk in the butter a chunk at a time. Keep warm.

6. Season the chicken with salt and pepper. In a large skillet over medium-high heat, cook the chicken, skin side down, until the skin is very browned and crisp. Turn and cook until the chicken is cooked through, 5 to 7 minutes more.

7. Melt the remaining tablespoon butter in a large sauté pan. Add the asparagus, mushrooms, and peaches and cook just until reheated. Divide among 4 serving plates and place a chicken breast on top of each. Spoon the reduced chicken broth onto each plate and serve.

and to drink

$ 2002 Stefan Gerhard, Hattenheimer Hassel, Kabinett, Rheingau, Germany

$$ 2002 Chablis, "La Moutonne," Grand Cru, Domaine Long Depaquit, France

chef's notes Morel mushrooms are revered for their rich, earthy flavor and wonderful, toothsome texture.

WHERE TO BUY

Morels: Earthy Delights, 800-367-4709, www.earthy.com

slanted door

1 FERRY BUILDING #3   SAN FRANCISCO, CA 94111

415-861-8032   WWW.SLANTEDDOOR.COM

The Slanted Door is a legendary Vietnamese restaurant so popular that the likes of Mick Jagger and former president Bill Clinton stop in whenever they're in town. Located in the renovated Ferry Building Marketplace with stunning views of San Francisco Bay, Slanted Door offers a Vietnamese-inspired fusion menu with special emphasis on produce, ecologically farmed meat, game, and poultry found at small farms around the Bay Area. Chef Charles Phan's flavorful food, the restaurant's clean lines, the Riesling-driven wine list, fresh squeezed juices, and hard-to-find Chinese teas all speak to a strong commitment to quality. Starters such as crispy spring rolls filled with minced shrimp, pork, and fresh green herbs and a spicy green papaya salad never disappoint. Try the clay-pot catfish, succulent lamb chops brushed with tamarind sauce, and the shaking beef, which is the recipe featured here.

Although chef Phan uses filet mignon in this dish, you can substitute sirloin or another cut of steak without sacrificing flavor.

shaking beef (bo luc lac)

Beef

2 tablespoons chopped garlic

2 tablespoons canola oil

1 teaspoon sugar

1 teaspoon coarse salt

½ teaspoon freshly ground black pepper

2 pounds filet mignon, trimmed of all visible fat and cut into 1-inch cubes

Vegetables and Sauce

¼ cup rice vinegar

1 tablespoon sugar

¼ cup rice wine (mirin) or sherry

2 tablespoons light soy sauce

1 tablespoon fish sauce

1½ teaspoons coarse salt

1 teaspoon freshly ground black pepper

Juice of 2 limes

8 tablespoons vegetable oil

3 scallions, cut into 1-inch pieces

½ small onion, thinly sliced

2 teaspoons unsalted butter, cut into 4 pieces

1 bunch watercress

and to drink

$ 2003 Bründlmayer Grüner Veltliner Kamptaler Terrassen, Austria

$$ 2003 Riesling, Nikolaihof Steiner Hund Reserve, Kremstal, Austria

1. To make the beef, combine the garlic, canola oil, sugar, salt, and pepper in a large nonreactive bowl. Add the filet mignon and refrigerate, covered, for 2 hours.

2. To make the vegetables and sauce, in a small bowl, combine the rice vinegar, sugar, rice wine, soy sauce, and fish sauce and set aside.

3. In another small bowl, combine the salt, pepper, and lime juice and set aside.

4. Heat a wok or large, heavy skillet over high heat. Add 2 tablespoons of the vegetable oil to the wok. When the oil smokes, add a quarter of the beef and leave undisturbed until browned on one side. Using a spatula, turn the meat and brown again, about 1 minute. Add a quarter of the scallions and onions to the wok and cook for 30 seconds more.

5. Add 3 tablespoons of the vinaigrette to the side of the wok and stir to release the beef. Add ½ teaspoon of the butter and continue to stir and shake the pan until the butter is melted. Remove from the wok and keep warm. Wipe out the wok and repeat three times with the remaining vegetable oil, beef, scallions, onions, and butter.

6. Divide the watercress among 4 plates. Spoon the hot beef over the watercress and serve with the reserved lime sauce on the side.

chef's notes Fish sauce, or *nam pla,* is a staple of Thai and Vietnamese cooking. Available in supermarkets and Asian grocery stores, fish sauce is to Thailand what salt is to the West and soy sauce is to China. A little goes a long way, which is fine, since nam pla has a long shelf life, lasting in the pantry for up to one year.

WHERE TO BUY

Mirin and fish sauce:

Asian Food Grocer, 888-482-2742, www.asianfoodgrocer.com

Casa Thai, 415-431-3789

index